BREAK-THROUGH RAPID READING

REVISED

PETER KUMP

PRENTICE HALL PRESS

Prentice Hall Press

A member of Penguin Putnam Inc.
375 Hudson Street
New York, New York 10014

www.penguinputnam.com

Library of Congress Cataloging-in-Publication Data

Kump, Peter
    Breakthrough rapid reading/by Peter Kump. —Rev.
      p. cm.
    Includes index.
    ISBN 0-13-793563-3. — ISBN 0-7352-0019-X (pbk.)
    1. Speed reading. I. Title.
  LB1050.54.K85   1998   98-30376
  428.'43—dc21   CIP

The author wishes to thank the following publishers for granting permission to reprint excerpts from copyrighted materials indicated below:

From *Plants Are Like People* by Jerry Baker. Reprinted by permission of Nash Publishing Corporation.

From *The Copper Kings of Montana* by Marian T. Place. Reprinted by permission of Random House, Inc.

From *You, Inc.* by Peter Weaver. Reprinted by permission of Doubleday & Company.

From *Harrison's Principles of Internal Medicine,* Revised Eighth Edition, by Wintrobe et al. Used by permission of McGraw-Hill Book Company.

From *The How and Why Wonder Book of Weather* by George Bonsall. Used by permission of Grosset & Dunlap, Inc.

From *Man and the Living World* by Karl Von Frisch. Reprinted by permission of Harcourt Brace Jovanovich, Inc.

From *Language in Thought and Action,* Third Edition, by S.I. Hayakawa. Reprinted by permission of Harcourt Brace Jovanovich, Inc.

This publication is designed to provide accurate and authoritative information in regard to the subject matter covered. It is sold with the understanding that the publisher is not engaged in rendering legal, accounting, or other professional service. If legal advice or other expert assistance is required, the services of a competent professional person should be sought.

—From a Declaration of Principles jointly adopted by a Committee of the American Bar Association and a Committee of Publishers and Associations.

Printed in the United States of America
10 9 8 7 6 5 4 3 2 1 (C)   20 19 18 17 16   *(P)*
ISBN 0-13-793563-3 (C)   0-7352-0019-X (P)

ATTENTION: CORPORATIONS AND SCHOOLS

Prentice Hall books are available at quantity discounts with bulk purchase for educational, business, or sales promotional use. For information, please write to: Penguin Putnam Inc., 375 Hudson Street, New York, New York 10014.

FOR EVELYN NIELSEN WOOD

through whose untiring efforts in the face of unimaginable obstacles was able to effect the "speed reading revolution" and introduce her exciting ideas to millions

AND FOR M. DOUGLAS WOOD

the man who always stood behind her and without whom it never would have been possible, at any stage of the long way

....

ACKNOWLEDGMENTS

....

Thanks first and foremost to all of my students from whom I've learned so much . . . to Thurston Smith, my teacher, who got me so very excited about the course . . . to Dr. Harry Wachs who gave me the first opportunity to teach rapid reading and develop my own techniques . . . to Pat Cafferata who gave the first sensible answers to many of my questions . . . to George Webster who hired me to open the Pittsburgh Reading Dynamics Institute . . . to Adele Rosenstein, my first "trainer" . . . to Karen Riedel who assisted me in developing new ideas and techniques . . . to Connie Fisher for her supportive advice . . . to the teachers of the Pittsburgh and New York Institutes who so ably put up with my experiments . . . to Chip Chapin who gave me many opportunities to expand . . . to Dan Theodocion who selected me to teach the White House Staff . . . to Lori Mammen, my able companion at the New York Institute . . . to Charles Durakis who gave me an opportunity to work much more closely with Evelyn Wood . . . to Martha White, Vicki Morgan, and Charlotte "Speaking" Taucz who endlessly typed so many of the books and manuals . . . to Georgie Reynolds who typed and assisted and continued on even after she took another job in despair . . . to Mary Gussman who collaborated with me on making the training films and writing one of the course manuals . . . to Verla Nielsen, who offered such good support in Salt Lake City . . . and to the many friends at Reading Dynamics including Judy Loughman, Marianne Hayes, Bob Boles, Pat Lynch, Hilda Takeyama, Bernie Kelly, Max Cohen, John Kilgo, Art Kramer, Lou Kohn, Doug Hall, Revetta Young, Lockwood Smith, Margaret Walsh, and many, many more including the hundreds of teachers I worked with and trained over the years.

Special thanks with work on this book goes to Jo Guttadauro who has assisted me for many different years in many different projects, to David Ross for his invaluable counsel, to my parents who made Schloss Matzen available, where most of this book was peacefully written, also to Denny Modiglian, Arthur Abelman, Margaret Paull, and Janet Cohn. Illustrations are by Carlos Madrid.

What Breakthrough Rapid Reading Means to You

Learn to Read More Than 3 Times Faster with Better Understanding, More Retention and Improved Recall—at Home—in Only 6 Short Weeks

It's not difficult to jog a mile in eight minutes, yet the world's fastest miler can barely do it in half that time.

If you watch a champion swim a 100-meter race you can easily see that he can't swim twice as fast as you can—if you can swim even reasonably well.

Yet there are people who can read three, five, even ten times faster than you can. In fact, as long as there have been books printed, there have been a few people—a very select, small percentage—who could read at incredible rates, going through books at a breakneck pace.

Maybe you've heard that John F. Kennedy was one of these rapid readers. Theodore Roosevelt used to read a book a day, *before breakfast,* while he occupied the White House. Oliver Wendell Holmes could glance at pages while walking to the Supreme Court and then answer questions about the material in great detail. These are just some of the better-known rapid readers. There have also been many ordinary citizens who can breeze through books and magazines as well.

The Rapid Reading Breakthroughs

It wasn't until the 1940's when the first major breakthrough in rapid reading was made. A Salt Lake City school teacher discovered how to turn average readers into super-fast readers. Since then, thousands of people have successfully learned to at least triple their reading speeds and improve their comprehension skills. But this could only be taught in a classroom, and the students had to pay hundreds of dollars for this instruction.

But now, for the first time ever, all of these revolutionary techniques are available to you in this brand-new self-teaching format of easy-to-follow drills and exercises. It has taken four years of careful development, research and testing to arrive at these self-teaching methods which now make it possible for you to learn them at home, in your spare time. You can just imagine what this will mean. Every conceivable subject that has been written about and the whole world of knowledge will lie at your fingertips. And you can do this in just a few short weeks.

Undoubtedly you are aware that you are almost buried, literally, under over one million words, every day of your life. Magazines and newspapers. Study materials. Business correspondence. Reports. Books you want to read—*when you get time.* You are practically drowning in an ocean of print. That's because publishing increases yearly and more has been printed in the last ten years than in all of the centuries of printing prior to that time. And it increases daily. But with these new methods you will discover how you can become one of the world's fastest readers in this sea of words.

SOME OF THE BREAKTHROUGHS YOU'LL LEARN

You will discover how to read both smarter and better. Smarter means that you will read as fast as you can think in any material. You will know when to speed up and when to slow down. You will learn all the "tricks" of good readers. You will absorb the information at a rate you never believed possible. And the side effects are tremendous. As an example:

You will find out how to remember what you have read. Concentration will become second nature in reading. You will begin to think more clearly, and to organize your daily reading. This will give you much more free time for your outside interests. You will quickly become more interesting to your friends, your family, even to yourself, as you pore over more and more materials.

When you follow the tested and proven method in this book, you will find your mind growing closer to its potential than you ever believed possible. Most important, there are few "practice" reading passages. You immediately begin to apply the techniques in the materials that you need to read.

Get started today, and by the end of the week you should be at least 30 percent faster—which means absorbing 40 pages in the time it used to take you to read 30. Without machines or gimmicks of any kind, you will learn to use your own built-in reading pacer. Then you will start using the breakthrough drills which have enabled hundreds of thousands to double and triple their reading rates in just a few short days.

You will discover writers' secrets that unveil the writing patterns which will help you to go even faster. You will begin cracking through the most difficult, abstract writing. And you will also discover the many different ways of reading—yes, there are more than the *one* you already know.

Even your attitude can affect your reading rate, and you will discover what you can do about it. Four chapters are devoted to study reading, how to study better and faster with all of the latest methods that help many students to get top grades in as little as one-half the time that others spend. Learning to read the newspaper "instantaneously" will allow you to read much more than just one a day, or two magazines a week. The fascinating possibilities—and realities—of reading a book a day are also included. And there's much, much more.

How I Became a Rapid Reader

Let me tell you how I began reading fast. In 1966, I was very worried about my reading assignments in graduate school. Then I saw a television commercial showing a young man running his finger down a page and reading thousands of words per minute. I immediately called to reserve what turned out to be the last seat in a Saturday morning class of an Evelyn Wood Reading Dynamics course. Within just a few weeks this exciting course had helped me to read over five times faster. Keeping up with my reading in school turned out to be incredibly easy. In fact, it was so easy to keep up with my studies that I had the time to hold down a full-time job (with the Reading Dynamics organization which I had been invited to join) while also going full-time to graduate school. I even had time left over!

In 1967 I met Evelyn Wood, a wonderful and dedicated woman who has spent her life trying to help others to enrich their lives through reading. And it was from her that I learned that mind organization starts with the ability to absorb printed material rapidly. Within a few short years, I had not only taught this amazing skill to the President's staff at the White House, but I also had become the National Director of Education for Evelyn Wood Reading Dynamics—at Evelyn Wood's personal request.

After leaving the Reading Dynamics organization, I determined to find a way for people to teach themselves these techniques and thus make them available to the hundreds of thousands who need them so badly but can't afford the expensive classroom instruction. *Breakthrough Rapid Reading* represents an entirely new self-teaching format, with drills and exercises especially for someone who is working alone. The drills allow you to work both according to your own rate of progress and also according to the amount of time that you have to practice. You will find all of the theories and techniques which are taught in the best rapid reading courses, as well as new ones which I have discovered and developed in the course of my own work—to be found nowhere else.

For the very first time, the long-guarded secrets of rapid reading are available to everyone. Anyone can take this book and discover the principles and skills essential for becoming an efficient and fast reader. And this book can even be used by graduates of rapid reading courses to continue developing and refining their skills—or to review areas in which they need more work.

Having successfully taught thousands of people of all educational backgrounds to read faster and better, I am convinced that there is no better way for anyone to improve his or her reading ability. With this book, you can not only learn these breakthroughs yourself, but you can do it in an astonishingly brief span of time.

The breakthroughs of rapid reading are now in your hands. You are about to change your reading—and, by doing that, your life itself.

Peter Kump

CONTENTS

SAVE TIME BY STARTING TODAY

People often say that they need a course in rapid reading but they don't have time to take it because of the great amount of reading they already have to do. From the morning newspaper, to combing through endless e-mails, many of us are drowning in information. If too much reading is keeping you from becoming a rapid reader, then maybe you should reconsider. Although initial practice may entail extra time the first or second week, within two weeks you should be reading fast enough to practice not only rapid reading but to read or study your required materials as well. So if you don't have the time to do both, then now is the time to learn this time-saving skill.

Learning the skills of efficient reading is relatively simple. Just read one chapter of this book at a time, doing the short exercises before going on to the next chapter. This will average about twenty minutes per session, often less time than that. After the first six lessons, you will find a special section of drills. These are to be done daily while you are completing the next six lessons. The time you spend on the drills can be varied according to how fast you wish to improve your skills. There are six groups of six lessons, each with its own set of drills.

The first week will go very quickly. You'll learn a few things about fast reading, then you'll test your present ability, and you'll learn how to immediately begin improving your reading rate. By the end of this week you'll be reading at least 10 percent faster, perhaps much more. Of course as you learn to read faster, you'll go faster through this book as well.

RAPID READING IS A SKILL

Rapid reading is not a difficult skill to learn. Most of the learning we do as adults is considered conceptual learning that is quite different from developing a skill. Conceptual learning is mainly a process of developing an *understanding* of the subject and can often be done through listening or reading. This is primarily intellectual. In developing a skill, there is also an understanding, but this understanding must be coupled with the *practice* of what you are learning. Sometimes you must practice without an intellectual understanding because that comes only when you can *do* it.

There is another difference between learning conceptual subjects and developing a skill. Learning conceptual subjects can sometimes be done very rapidly, especially for adults. But learning a skill, certainly a complex one such as reading, is rarely something that can be acquired immediately. You must master each aspect of the skill before going on to the next. Reading through this book in one evening and just understanding it will not suffice.

SUCCESSFUL SKILL LEARNING

In learning new skills, it is generally best to practice a little bit every day. If you try to learn it all at once you may wind up understanding *how* it is done but not be able to do it very well. To get the most out of this book and to progress most rapidly I suggest that you plan to finish one chapter at a time, ideally one chapter a day.

It is often difficult to get started learning a new skill. One tends to put it off until later in the day, especially when you're first learning it. A definite time each day is imperative. Mornings are usually best because things have a way of getting put off in the evenings. Before you begin to learn rapid reading decide how much time you can devote to it each day. If you make it a part of your daily routine, then you will find yourself progressing very quickly.

A SENIOR "STUDENT" MAKES IT

Arthur, one of my older students, was a recently retired senior partner of one of Wall Street's most respected brokerage firms. A Yale graduate, this determined individual had decided upon retirement he would take up his education and personal development with the same planning and vigor he had given to his career. He felt that a good reading course would be an excellent beginning and he plunged in with the vitality and optimism of a person one-third his age.

There's quite some truth to the saying about teaching old dogs new tricks, and trying to learn new reading habits after over sixty years of one technique is not easy. But after a slower than average start, Arthur came through reading more than three times faster with better comprehension. But his own statement that he was now able to get much more reading in, and was using the valuable learning techniques to great advantage, was far more important to me than any statistics. And when he finished, he didn't even feel that it was as difficult as he had anticipated.

One word of caution: Do not read through the book planning to come back and do the exercises later because many of the exercises will lose their effect if you know what to expect in advance. Master each concept and drill before moving on to the next one. If you do this you most assuredly will improve your reading skills.

A GOOD READER IS A FLEXIBLE READER

Learning to read faster and more efficiently will not simply speed up your rate. You will be learning to read in a completely new way. When people ask me how fast I read I am not able to answer with a single words per minute rate. It's comparable to asking a driver how fast he can drive a car. He might answer that it depends on the condition of the car, the condition of the roads, the weather, the traffic, and his familiarity with the route. It would also depend on how compelling it is to get to his destination.

Like this driver, the efficient reader varies his or her rate according to the difficulty of the material, the organization of the reading matter, their familiarity with the subject, and their purpose in reading it. So instead of reading everything the same way, starting at the beginning and going word-by-word straight through to the end, you will learn many different ways to read, and how to adapt each one to meet your specific purpose in reading the material.

WHAT YOU CAN EXPECT TO LEARN

In the most difficult type of reading, technical or study reading, the average student should be able to cut one-third to one-half the time from his or her studying and know the material better. Professionals or businesspersons should be able to read reports, e-mail, regular mail and professional journals from two to four times faster than they do now. When you are just reading for your own pleasure, you should be able to reach rates of five to ten times faster in most novels and easy reading material.

You will not just learn to read faster, but also how to read much better. This includes how to get better comprehension when you read, how to remember what you read, how to determine your purpose for reading different types of material, and how to concentrate better. Reading is a tremendously complex skill and there are many new things to find out about it. Whatever your reading needs, if you apply yourself to the lessons of this book, you will begin to improve immediately, and, within six weeks, become not only a fast reader, but an efficient one as well.

Sherri Weisman was a very gifted student who became a very fast reader in a matter of weeks. One day in English class her high school teacher gave the students the last 15 minutes to read a chapter in a book that the entire class had been assigned to read. Sherri finished in minutes and had begun something else when her teacher noticed that she wasn't reading the book. When called upon to explain she replied that she had finished. But her teacher refused to believe her and ordered her to the front of the class to tell what the chapter was about. Sherri complied but the teacher was still incredulous. Obviously, according to the teacher, Sherri had read it before class.

HOW TO GET STARTED

The first thing you should do is test yourself and evaluate your reading abilities. This means establishing your beginning reading rate and how much you can retain of what you've read. This will be the topic of the next chapter. First there is a short exercise to complete.

After you have done that, there are a few materials to assemble.

This first exercise will prepare you for other exercises in the course—and it will take only five minutes at the most. You will need to use your progress profile for the exercise (you'll be using it for many of the exercises and drills in this book) and you will find it at the end of the book.

EXERCISE NO. 1

Materials: *Progress profile at the end of this book. Pen or pencil (Or, if you prefer, use the word processing program on your personal computer. Create a file specifically for this purpose.)*

First Part: *If you had only six months to live and could read any ten books during that time, what would they be? List as many as you can on the progress profile in three minutes. They need not be books you feel you should read, but rather books you really want to read.*

Second Part: Taking no more than two minutes, list any topic or subject that you would like to learn more about if you had the time.

Once you have completed this first exercise, you should gather the few materials which you will need for the next chapter. I have found over the years that if students practiced in their own reading materials—materials relevant to them—it becomes much easier to alleviate personal reading problems and progress much faster in the course. You will find all the materials you need in your home or office or certainly no further than the bookstore, newsstand or online sources. The materials are simply books that you might normally read, magazines and newspapers that you subscribe to or read, or printouts from selected online articles. Collect them now and you will then be ready to test yourself tomorrow.

Materials You Will Need for the First Week

1.   A pencil or pen.
2.   A timing device. Any one of the following will do: a watch or clock *with a sweep second hand;* a stop watch; a tape recorder; or any timer that will time a *one-minute period.* If you prefer, you can use the clock on your computer. Many feature both digital and the regular clock face screens.
3.   A book for testing yourself. This should be a book that you haven't read, preferably on a general subject or perhaps a biography. Try to avoid novels and how-to-do-it books; magazines are not usually satisfactory for testing since most articles are not long enough.

4. Another book of your choice. This may be any book that you might ordinarily read for pleasure. It should not be too difficult and it is permissible to use a book you've read before.
5. Paper, 8 1/2 × 11 sheets. (Or open a file on your computer to track your speed reading progress.)

While you are assembling the above items, you should also look for the books you listed in Exercise No. 1. While the exercise assumes that you would have six *months* to read these books, there's a good chance that you'll be able to read them during the next six *weeks*. If you don't have these books, then plan to pick them up at your local library, nearest bookstore or order them online. You won't need them all at once, but when you do need them, they should be available.

As soon as you have the materials for this week then you are ready to begin the next chapter. If you have already done this, pick a regular daily time to do the chapters, and then plan to begin at that time tomorrow.

2

TEST YOUR READING RATE TO SEE WHERE YOU STAND

Most people feel that they read too slowly—but they have no idea of how fast they really read. Now you will find out how to test your own reading rate, and also how to measure how much you retained of what you read. It tends to be a more accurate self-test if you use the type of material that you regularly read: e.g., nonfiction, texts, business reports, fiction, etc.

If you would like to have a broader picture of your reading skills, then you should plan to test yourself in more than one book. In this case, the second book should be a contrast to the first: if the first book is nonfiction, which is preferred, then a novel or biography would be a good second choice. If you test yourself in several books, you may find a variation in your abilities. That's because most people are more knowledgeable in one field than in another, and your reading rate will usually reflect this fact.

TIMING YOURSELF

To test yourself, you will be reading for three minutes, and you must know when the time is up. It is not difficult to time yourself. If you use a stop watch, simply start the watch when it is time to begin, then glance over at it from time to time until the three minutes are up.

If you use a tape recorder, record a three-minute time period in the following manner:

Record onto the tape: *"Ready? Begin reading"*

Then leave a three-minute silence.

Next record onto the tape: *"Stop, please"*

If you use a watch or clock with a sweep second hand, simply place the watch or clock where you can see it easily. Wait until the second hand is at the "12," then begin your reading. Glance over at it from time to time until the reading time is up. Don't worry if you run slightly over or under the correct amount of time. A few seconds will not make a great difference, and soon you will find it quite easy to do. You might also have a friend time you, but this will not be practical more than a few times.

Better still, if you have a PC, use the timer on one of your computer programs.

TESTING YOURSELF

Once you have your test book, pen or pencil, and a timing device, then you are ready to begin. When you are reading to test yourself, try to read as you would normally read material of this nature. Do not lightly skim a textbook as though it were a novel, nor read a novel as though you were studying it for a very comprehensive test.

To test yourself, simply follow the steps below:

Beginning Reading Evaluation

Directions: *Read through the four steps carefully. When you understand everything, come back to the first step and begin.*

1. Select a section of your testing book that is about ten pages long and that you have not read.
2. Read as far as you can in the material for three minutes. Use your timing device.
3. At the end of the three minutes, make a pencil or pen mark where you stopped reading, then close the book.
4. Prepare a separate sheet for evaluating your reading retention by numbering from 1–20 down the left. Write down everything you can remember from the reading on this sheet *without looking back at the reading selection.* If you've created a file on your computer, do the same in your word processing program. You may take up to six minutes; use your timing device. (If using the tape recorder at the end of the three-minute period, prior to the testing, record a six-minute period.)

Now complete your reading evaluation according to the steps above before reading on.

COMPUTING YOUR READING RATE

Getting a words per minute reading rate is really quite easy if you just follow these four steps:

First, you must find the average number of words per line in your book. To do this count the number of words in any three full lines and divide the sum by three. For example, if there are 33 words in three full lines, the average would be 11 words per line, WPL. But if there were only 31 or 32 words, you should put the count at ten WPL because it is more accurate to round down in determining your reading rate.

Second, count the number of lines that you have read during the time allotted for reading. You will undoubtedly come across some partial lines. In this case count two halves as one line; a single word or two on a line you may simply omit, and if the line is only a word or two short, then count it as a full line.

Third, multiply the number of lines that you have read by the average number of words per line. This will give you the total number of words that you have read.

Fourth, divide the answer in the third step, just above, by the number of minutes used for the reading, in this case three, to find your words per minute rate. The answer will be your reading rate or WPM.

To Find Your Reading Rate

1. First find the average number of words per line:
(a) __11__ WPL
2. Count the total number of lines read:
(b) __40.5__
3. Multiply "a" by "b" for total amount you read:
(c) __445.5__
4. Divide "c" by the number of minutes you read:
__148__ WPM

In the first class of my courses, I ask everyone to bring an easy book and read for a minute at their very highest rate. It's exceedingly rare for anyone to go over 400 words per minute even though they have no responsibility to the material, no test, report, etc. Obviously they are pushing as hard as they can which is easy to see from the pained expressions on their faces. Within a few lessons this same rate is usually representative of their lowest, study-reading rate, and by the end of the course when we repeat this same "test" everyone is amazed—not so much at how far they've come but that their former top rate now seems so very slow.

EVALUATING YOUR RETENTION

To obtain a beginning evaluation of your retention, count the total number of items listed that you were able to remember on the "Beginning Reading Evaluation." This figure will give you an idea of how much you can remember from the material. In this very informal type of evaluation you have an excellent way of watching your progress. At any point that you wish to find out how well you are doing, you may simply repeat this same test *using the same book but a different passage.*

This test does not attempt to evaluate your comprehension, which is very difficult to do accurately. Most tests of comprehension measure what the test writer wishes to measure, not necessarily what is important to you. Many tests do not even measure what they are intended to measure very well.

To evaluate your comprehension, the easiest and best thing to do is simply to read through the material again and note every idea or detail that you feel should be understood *and retained.* Then check your own paper to see if you remembered as much as you feel you should have. Rate yourself as either adequate (good) or needing improvement. Don't be discouraged if you forget a great deal; most people do in the beginning and no one can be expected to remember everything. Your ability to recall the information completely from memory, as you have attempted to do here, is the hardest test of retention.

KEEPING YOUR PROGRESS PROFILE

When you have computed your reading rate and evaluated your retention, record the figures on the progress profile for the appropriate chapter and test. If you continue to record all of your rates and scores, you will have a good picture of your progress as you develop your skills. (See worksheets at the end of the book.)

EVALUATING YOUR PRESENT SKILLS

It is always interesting to have an idea of how one's reading relates to others, especially when beginning a rapid reading course. A chart such as the one on page 11 cannot possibly take everything into consideration or be held as very authoritative, but it can give you a good general evaluation.

BE SURE YOU'RE READY TO BEGIN

If you found that your reading rate was under 120 words per minute, you may not be ready to begin this course. Nothing in this book can harm you, but if you are not ready for a rapid reading course it could be somewhat frustrating. There are many possible reasons why you might not be ready for this course.

If you are an adult and your reading rate is less than 120 words per minute, you may be testing yourself with a book that is too difficult. In such a situation, test yourself again in easier material.

If you are under fifteen, you might try reading regularly any books or materials that you enjoy, for 30 minutes or more every day, and then retest yourself in one or two months to see if you are ready to begin.

If you are reading in a second language and your rate is 150 words per minute or less, you may need to do a lot more reading in the language you wish to read faster, in order to build a larger vocabulary. If you decide to proceed with this course, then take it very slowly with lots of extra practice and reading.

Anne Marie was a very quiet student who began with a double handicap; she was not only a slow reader, but English was her second language. When you're working in a second language it's often quite difficult to get beyond doubling your reading rate. Anne Marie also had rather low comprehension and poor retention or recall. She was a

IF YOUR READING RATE IS:	AND YOUR RETENTION IS:
Under 120 words per minute: You are a below average reader.	*Adequate or Needs Improvement:* You probably should consult a reading specialist through a local university, school, or reading clinic. If you are under fifteen, you may be able to benefit from this book. A fuller explanation follows this chart.
120–180 words per minute: Your reading rate is below average unless you are under sixteen.	*Adequate:* One of your biggest problems may be that you do not read enough. Plan to spend at least thirty minutes extra each day reading in books or magazines which you enjoy. *Needs Improvement:* In addition to needing extra daily reading time, you should plan to spend at least one hour per day drilling, emphasizing comprehension drills.
180–240 words per minute: You are an average reader.	*Adequate:* You should benefit a great deal by following this book carefully. *Needs Improvement:* You should work hard with comprehension and retention drills. Extra reading time on a regular daily basis would be of great value; use materials you enjoy.
240–350 words per minute: You are reading on an average college level.	*Adequate:* With regular practice you should see a quick and large improvement. *Needs Improvement:* You tend to be careless in your reading, probably a result of poor habits. Careful attention to comprehension exercises should help to remedy this.
350–500 words per minute: You are an above average reader.	*Adequate:* You should improve quickly. Some initial exercises may appear easy, but do them carefully to insure a good foundation. *Needs Improvement: You do not have good control of your reading. You need to learn when to slow down. Pay special attention to organizing techniques which you may have an impulse to gloss over.*
Over 500 words per minute: You are a superior reader.	*Adequate:* Some of the beginning techniques may slow you down. Be patient and the improvement will soon follow. *Needs Improvement:* You may have to pay special attention to slowing down and learning how to be careful when it is necessary. As there will be plenty of time to speed up, do not fear a rate decrease initially. Pay special attention to learning how to adjust rate to purpose.

good student who attended all the sessions and did most of the home practice. I kept expecting her not to appear, as sometimes happens with students who don't do their practicing (and subsequently feel very guilty) or who experience difficulty at first. But Anne Marie was more determined than I could see.

At the second to the last session she raised her hand and said she wanted to thank me because though she was just up to 600 words per minute (no modest achievement since she had started at under 200) she had gained immeasurably from the study reading techniques. She said she was finding that not only had she cut her study reading time significantly, but also she knew the material much better and was already getting better test scores at school. Most important to her, she related that never had she felt so confident before. *It is most important to understand that to be ready to take a rapid reading course you must be able to already read easily.* If you have *any* question about this, a simple test is to read aloud from a newspaper to someone. If you stumble or have trouble with as many as one out of ten words, then it would be better to seek help from a specialist.

Let's assume you are ready to begin. You've found your beginning reading rate, already learned how to compute your rate in words per minute, and have a good idea of how well you retain what you read. So now start to improve on it.

A FEW WORDS ABOUT YOUR EYES

Few people have regular eye examinations. If you experience any visual difficulty or eye strain while reading for more than a few minutes at a time, or if you have not had an eye examination in the last year or two, it would be advisable to do so as soon as possible. This should provide maximum visual efficiency and assure minimum physiological stress.

In one set of classes which I taught at the Pennsylvania Vision Institute in Pittsburgh, as an experiment, all participants were given a visual examination. Over thirty percent of the class needed some attention. Lenses were advised, at least for reading, if they did not already have them. If they already wore lenses, often an adjustment of the prescription or vision training was suggested. I was very surprised as I had never expected such results.

If you would like to see a doctor about your eyes but don't know one, consult the local optometric or ophthalmological society or the yellow pages of your phone book or online and call one of these specialists for an appointment. Or consult with your Health Maintenance Organization, or HMO, if you are a member. Most HMOs cover members' vision care.

The various professions dealing with the eyes can be confusing. Here's a key to help you thread your way through.

OCULIST: An outdated and infrequently used word which usually means an Ophthalmologist.

OPTICIAN: A specialist who makes or sells corrective lenses but is not licensed to prescribe them.

OPHTHALMOLOGIST: A physician who specializes in surgery and diseases of the eye. He may prescribe lenses as well as vision training.

OPTOMETRIST: A professional specially trained to examine, measure and treat visual defects by means of corrective lenses and other methods such as vision training. While he or she does not operate, in some states they can use drugs for diagnostic as well as therapeutic purposes.

3

START USING YOUR BUILT-IN READING ACCELERATOR

It may surprise you to learn that you already possess the greatest reading accelerator that has yet been discovered: your hand. Hundreds of thousands of dollars have been spent on fancy machines to help speed up reading rates, and even computer software, but none of them has ever begun to equal the human hand.

WHAT YOUR EYES DO WHEN YOU READ

Before you learn how to read with your hand, you should know why you read slowly. And first you must know something about how your eyes work when you read. The eyes are constantly moving around in little jerky movements. In order to see something, it is necessary for them to stop and fixate on an object for a brief moment in order to register an impression. It's somewhat like taking a picture with a camera.

We have all been taught to read one word at a time, which means a rate of about 240 words per minute. This is because your eyes need a quarter of a second to fixate on an object. Therefore, if you read one word at a time, as you were taught to do, you read one word every quarter of a second. With a little easy arithmetic, that comes to four words per second or a rate of 240 words per minute.

REGRESSIONS SLOW YOUR RATE CONSIDERABLY

More than likely, you read *fewer* than 240 words per minute. The average reader makes many regressions, going back and looking at words, 10 to 11 times for every 100 words read. This means that the average reading rate is about 215 words per minute.

There are two kinds of regression, conscious and unconscious. You may sometimes feel that you did not understand something particularly well, so you decide to go back and reread it. This is a conscious regression and there is nothing particularly wrong with it. It is not the most efficient way to get the best comprehension, but it is certainly one way.

Unconscious regressions exist because poor habits were formed when you first learned to read. They occur when the eyes, unconsciously, go back and look at words. You will learn how to eliminate this habit shortly and immediately increase your reading rate because of it. Even if you are reading faster than 240 words per minute, you probably make some regressions. Learning to eliminate them is the first step in learning to read faster.

WHAT YOU SHOULD KNOW ABOUT READING CONDITIONS

There are two things you should know about reading conditions: what lighting you should have and the best position, or posture, for reading.

Did your mother ever say to you, "There's not enough light there, you'll ruin your eyes!" when you were absorbed in reading something? It's possible that your mother was mistaken because Americans tend to overlight on the whole. You should have lighting that is neither too bright nor too dim; either one can be a strain on your eyes.

The best lighting for reading is diffused lighting, or lighting that comes from several sources and does not create a glare on the page. If you can read the material without any strain, then there is probably enough light. Too much or too little light can cause a strain. A good test is to put your hand about a foot above your reading material. If there is a strong, sharp shadow then the light is too bright. It is preferable to have almost no shadow at all. Small high-intensity lamps are not advisable.

READING POSITIONS

Many people will not like to find out that the best position for reading is sitting up in a chair with your back firmly against the back of it. Slouching, lying down, and other alternative reading positions are simply not the best way to read.

Sometimes correcting your posture is uncomfortable at first, but if you are truly interested in efficiency, then you would do well to make this a permanent habit.

FIGURE 1. MOST EFFICIENT READING POSTURE

A book is best set at a 45 degree angle to your eyes, as in Figure 1. Set like this, your eyes do not have to readjust their angle of vision constantly. This results in less work for them and therefore makes it less tiring for you. It will make it easier if you take a book or binder two to three inches thick and place it under the book that you are reading. This usually achieves the 45 degree angle that is most comfortable.

There is always a student who asks about reading in bed. I usually answer that by pointing out that if you want to learn to read fast, you're interested in efficiency. You can read in bed, of course, but that's not the place to be concerned about your rate. I personally read slowly when I'm in bed because it usually puts me to sleep.

HOW TO USE YOUR HAND IN READING

To use your hand to increase your reading rate, begin by pointing your index finger as in Figure 2. Then run the tip of your finger along each line of print just underneath the words you are reading. As your finger moves along, read above it. When your finger comes to the end of the line, *lift* it up about half an inch and bring it *quickly* back to the following line and begin the whole process again.

Although this may at first seem a bit awkward, you will quickly get used to it. And almost as soon as you begin using your hand when you read, you will start increasing your rate. That's because it helps you to eliminate unconscious regressions. In fact, doing this alone helps the average person speed up from **10%** to **20%**. But it will take some practice to achieve that. Here are some exercises to help you begin.

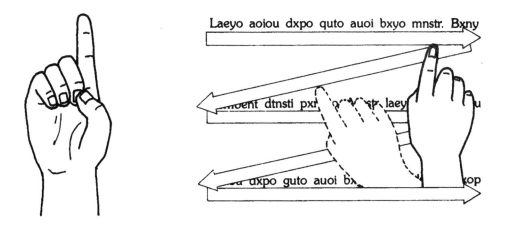

FIGURE 2. USING THE INDEX FINGER AS A READING PACER

EXERCISE NO. 2

Materials: *This book.*

Purpose: *Learn to do the first hand movement smoothly and automatically.*

1. Practice doing the first hand movement (underlining with your index finger) for several minutes on the passage of nonsense material that follows this exercise.
2. With your index finger extended, move your hand under each line in about one second. Count "one" *out loud* as you move under each line.
3. Lift your finger at the end of the line and quickly return it. Continue on all of the lines, counting "one" each time.
4. When you finish the section begin it again, continuing until the movement is smooth and automatic, never jerky. You should not have to think of what you are doing; just be looking at the nonsense words.

PRACTICE PASSAGE OF NONSENSE MATERIAL

XXXXXX XXX XXXXX XXXX XXXXXX XXX XXXX XXX XXXXXX XXXX XX
BB BBBB BBBBBB BBB BBBB BBB BBBBBB BBBB BBBBBB BBB BBBBBB
XXXXXX XXX XXXXX XXXX XXXXXX XXX XXXX XXX XXXXXX XXXX XX
BB BBBB BBBBBB BBB BBBB BBB BBBBBB BBBB BBBBBB BBB BBBBBB
XXXXXX XXX XXXXX XXXX XXXXXX XXX XXXX XXX XXXXXX XXXX XX
BB BBBB BBBBBB BBB BBBB BBB BBBBBB BBBB BBBBBB BBB BBBBBB
XXXXXX XXX XXXXX XXXX XXXXXX XXX XXXX XXX XXXXXX XXXX XX
BB BBBB BBBBBB BBB BBBB BBB BBBBBB BBBB BBBBBB BBB BBBBBB
XXXXXX XXX XXXXX XXXX XXXXXX XXX XXXX XXX XXXXXX XXXX XX
BB BBBB BBBBBB BBB BBBB BBB BBBBBB BBBB BBBBBB BBB BBBBBB
XXXXXX XXX XXXXX XXXX XXXXXX XXX XXXX XXX XXXXXX XXXX XX
BB BBBB BBBBBB BBB BBBB BBB BBBBBB BBBB BBBBBB BBB BBBBBB
XXXXXX XXX XXXXX XXXX XXXXXX XXX XXXX XXX XXXXXX XXXX XX
BB BBBB BBBBBB BBB BBBB BBB BBBBBB BBBB BBBBBB BBB BBBBBB

When you have spent a few minutes on Exercise No. 2, then you should be ready to begin using your hand to read. This is a very important step because from this moment *on you should use your hand for all of your reading,* especially while you are learning this skill. It is vital to your success that the use of your hand becomes second nature to you while you are reading.

Using your hand to pace your reading can truly be described as miraculous. Recently I had a young student, a sixth grader named Daisy. Because her younger sister was born in the same year they were both in the same grade. Daisy had been informed directly and indirectly that she was one of the slowest readers in her class. Even her younger sister read faster. Daisy told me that once while reading in the library the librarian asked her what she was doing behind the book. When I tested her reading I found that she was just slightly below average which should not have caused any great concern, but it stood out because she was in a very good school with lots of excellent students. And she therefore felt very badly about her reading; so we went to work.

By the end of one session, Daisy was reading well above her grade level, probably as fast as anyone in her class, which would only be an educated guess. I wish you could have seen the change in her; she had obviously been trying for years to read faster, and now she found it so simple. I'm certain that she'll never forget to use her "secret" method—her hand as a pacer—whenever she wants to speed up.

EXERCISE NO. 3

Materials: *Any easy book, not your testing book.*
Timing device. (A watch or the clock on your PC will do.)

Purpose: *Learn to begin eliminating regressions through using the hand as a pacer.*

1. Open your book to any place you wish to begin reading. For three minutes practice running your finger under the lines of *one* page, counting "one," to yourself, as you go under each line in one second. Use your timing device to make certain you practice this for three minutes.
2. In material that you haven't read, but in the same book, use your hand and read for another three minutes. Mark your beginning and ending points.
3. Compute your reading rate for the three-minute reading.
   To do this, follow the steps below:

   a. Find the average number of words per line (the total number of words in three full lines divided by three).
   b. Count the total number of lines read.

    c.   To find the total number of words that you read, multiply "a" by "b."

    d.   Divide "c" by 3 (3 minutes) to find the words per minute.

4.   When you have your words per minute rate, record it on your progress profile.

5.   Repeat steps "2" through "4," reading a new passage and computing the reading rates.

When you finish, compare your reading rate with the beginning rate that you recorded when you first tested yourself. Are you going faster yet? Many people are, but it takes some people a little longer to get used to the hand as a pacer. In fact, a few people will go more slowly when they start using their hand, but that is nothing to worry about. If your rate has not improved yet, don't worry; it will improve soon enough. The important thing is to get used to using your hand.

In these exercises, you have learned how to use your hand to pace your reading. You are developing the coordination of your eyes with your hand: your eye is learning to follow your hand which is pacing it. It may take you several days before this is easy and comfortable, or before you won't have to think about what you are doing.

Try to read as much as you can, using your hand, before you begin the next chapter. Ronald Vivio, a teacher who used to work with me, when emphasizing the importance of reading *everything* with the hand as a pacer, would tell his students that there were to be no exceptions: when driving and approaching a stop sign, they must read it with their hand; when they went to a foreign movie, he would expect to see their hands also raised, moving along under the subtitles! Nowadays you can even add your computer screen to that list – if you can keep it clean, however. And these are not such far-fetched ideas. The student who takes the use of his hand seriously is well on his way to becoming a good and efficient reader.

····················· 4 ·····················

ELIMINATE REGRESSIONS AND SPEED AHEAD

···

There are many famous people who could read extremely fast. It was said that England's Samuel Johnson could read almost as fast as he could look at the pages. While in the White House, President Theodore Roosevelt used to read a book every day before breakfast, and he occasionally read three a day. John F. Kennedy was well known for being able to read 1,200 words per minute. These are just a very few of the famous *naturally* fast readers, and there must be thousands of less well-known ones as well.

There was a naturally fast reader, Jeanne Leone, in one of the first classes I ever taught. Incredibly her rate shot up to well over 5,000 words per minute in the second class, while the rest of the class was reading around 400 or 500 words per minute. In talking to her, I found out that she was used to reading a book a day, in about an hour, while waiting for her husband to come home from work. She didn't think that she was unusual, and most naturally fast readers I've encountered feel the same way.

Perhaps you've been aware that some other students can read and retain information better than you can. A friend of mine back in the tenth grade could read an assigned chapter in our English class in about a third the time that it took me. She also could remember more about it than I could. Today, she holds down a part-time job, is a wife and mother of three children, and she still reads as many as six books a week. Obviously, if she were reading the way you and I had been taught, she couldn't read that many books.

HOW PEOPLE READ FAST

When you first learned to read, you probably saw a group of letters individually. You looked at each one, "L," then "O," then the next "O," and finally "K." If you can recall from an earlier chapter, it takes only a quarter of a second for the eyes to focus on one object, so you can easily find out a beginning reader's rate. If he or she spends one quarter of a second on each letter, then it would take them one second to read a four-letter word. Assuming that in beginning reading books the words average four letters each, the beginning reader reads 60 words per minute, or one word a second.

The next step in reading is when the reader begins to recognize whole groups of letters at one time. You are probably able to do this with your own name first. With long words, you might have to look at both halves. As you begin to be able to recognize more and more whole words, your rate jumps from 60 words per minute to about 175, usually in the sixth grade when most reading instruction ends. Your rate slowly continues to improve the more you read, usually getting up to around 240 words per minute.

THE NEXT BIG STEP

The only way to read faster than 240 words per minute is to be looking at more than one word at a time. If you see two words per eye fixation, then you can read 480 words per minute. A rate of more than two words per fixation will allow you to read even faster. You've already made the first step when you've learned to respond to whole words instead of individual letters. Learning to respond to groups of words is merely a matter of practicing repeatedly and doing the correct drills.

ELIMINATING REGRESSIONS

If you've been using your hand to read, then you've been experiencing reading with fewer regressions. You've also been developing a coordination of your eye movements with your hand movements. You should now be ready for some more work on eliminating regressions and starting to see more than one word at a time. This consists of an exercise in rereading a passage several times. When you drill by rereading, you help to eliminate regressions more quickly, since the mind can relax and not worry about missing something: you've already read it, so you can learn to speed up very easily. When you know that you're not missing anything, you can begin to train your eyes to look at the words only once.

EXERCISE NO. 4

Materials: *Any easy book.*
      Timing device. (A watch or the clock on your PC will do.)

Purpose: *Learn to go faster by eliminating regressions through rereading.*

1. Open your book to any place you wish to start. Using your hand, read as far as you can for three minutes.
   Make a "1" where you finish reading.
2. Go back to the beginning and reread the same section in three minutes. Try to go a bit faster and try to pass the first mark, "1." Make a new mark, "2," *if you read further ahead.*

3. Go back and reread the same section in three minutes, going a bit faster. You've seen everything before so you should be able to move more quickly. At the end of the three minutes, make a new mark, "3," *if you read further ahead.*

4. Read the passage once more, again trying to go faster, in three minutes. Make a new mark, "4," *if you read further ahead.*

5. Finally, read in new material (from "4" if you wish) for three minutes. Remember to always use your hand. When you finish reading, make a new mark, "5."

6. Compute your reading rate for the last three-minute reading, from "4" to "5." To do this, go through the following steps:

   a. Find the average number of words per line.
   b. Count the total number of lines read.
   c. Multiply "a" by "b" to find the total number of words that you read.
   d. Divide "c" by 3 to find the words per minute rate.

7. When you have computed your rate, record it on your progress profile.

ALWAYS USE YOUR HAND

It constantly puzzles me that there is usually one student who tries to learn this skill without using his or her hand. Perhaps they've decided it's a nuisance, or perhaps they're just lazy and doesn't want to be bothered. Occasionally, I suspect they think that they can do it better without their hands. If this is the case, then I can't understand why they paid to study with me.

In my opinion, trying to learn to read faster without using your hand is like trying to write faster without a computer. Certainly you can learn to write much faster without a computer, but with one—after learning how to use it—it's *so* much easier. The great part about using the hand to help you read faster is that you always have it with you.

When I was National Director of Education for Evelyn Wood Reading Dynamics, there were many different studies in my files on the use of the hand as a pacer. There is so much evidence that shows how helpful the hand is, how superior to any "non-hand" method, that I hope I can convince you. I always tell my students to think about how lucky they are. They are not only born with their "reading pacer" but if they happen to wear one out, they even have another.

I hope that you aren't having any trouble using your hand. Most people become used to it within a few days. If you use it for all of your daily reading while you are completing this course, then you will undoubtedly find it quite difficult to read without it.

Before you begin the next lesson, try to get a good hour of reading with using your hand. It can be a magazine or book, the newspaper, a print-out from the internet, or whatever you wish, but just do it with your hand.

GETTING AHEAD

Some of my students ask what they can do to get further ahead than they would with just the exercises. The best thing you can do with most skills is to practice daily, but also continue to practice beyond the time suggested. One word of warning—occasionally you can get frustrated if you don't improve more in the second hour than you did in the first hour; that could be a bad experience for you. But at this point, extra practice can be of value. If you have extra time and you would like to start getting ahead before the next lesson, here's what to do:

1. In any book you wish to read, do Exercise 4 from this chapter.
2. Immediately after doing the exercise, continue reading in your book, using your hand, and going as fast as you can for ten minutes.
3. Repeat Exercise 4 again, in new material.
4. As soon as you have completed the exercise, read on as fast as you can for ten minutes. If you have the time, it is profitable to repeat this for an hour and a half. If you do this, you may be quite surprised to see your reading rate begin to climb. Eliminating regressions is just the beginning, and soon you'll start becoming aware of just how quickly you can begin to read much faster.

There are many reasons why these techniques succeed so often and so quickly. First, the method is a very natural one, being derived from the observation of naturally fast readers rather than from a theoretical basis. Second, when a person fails at first in reading, it is often not because they can't do it, but only that their instrument, the body and the brain, is not ready to learn it. Then if they have another opportunity to learn when they're ready, it can be surprisingly easy to do.

Joan, a mature young woman in one of my "children's classes," was a high school junior who had a great deal of courage to register and attend a class which included third graders. I'm sure she soon found how wise she was to join this class. Within a few brief sessions, and without even completing the assigned home drills, she was reading above her grade level. When she began she had been on a sixth grade reading level. Once she saw how quickly she was progressing she started doing more of the practicing and of course started progressing even faster. She finished as one of the most successful students in the course, but I'm sure that just being able to keep up, and even get ahead in school, was the best reward for her.

5

BUILD YOUR READING RATE THROUGH DRILLING

Besides making regressions, another reason you read slowly is that you subvocalize the words you are reading. This is something that we still do not know a great deal about, but it is basically the tendency to say a word to yourself, in your mind's ear, as you read it. It is not real sound, but the memory of the sound of the word.

Since we were taught to read out loud, almost everyone subvocalizes. After the teacher knew that we understood the symbols by saying them, she told us to read to ourselves, and that's when subvocalization begins.

The trick of the naturally fast readers is really quite easy to understand. Most people comprehend the words they read both through *seeing* the words as well as by *saying* the words, silently, to themselves. Natural speed readers have somehow developed the ability to just see and understand, so they can go as fast as they can *look* at the words. Everyone does this when looking at photographs or illustrations. But for the rest of us, when we're reading, we're going only as fast as we can speak the words to ourselves.

THE THREE STAGES OF SUBVOCALIZING

Subvocalizing can go through several stages. At first, young readers may actually move their lips as they read, but without emitting any sound. This is not difficult to control. If you do this, either hold a pencil between your teeth as you read, or else practice making a sound, like a tea kettle, sort of a whistle, as you read until the habit is broken. It generally takes only a few days to correct this.

In the next stage, readers no longer move their lips, but their voice box, or for a man, his Adam's apple still moves as though they were speaking. This may be stopped with biofeedback training, but it really is no problem.

The last stage is saying the words to yourself, silently, in your mind's ear, without any physical movement. Whether or not you are aware of this, it is most likely that you do it.

It is not yet practical to teach a person not to subvocalize, although some teachers claim to be able to do this. I have found that if a person becomes concerned with subvocalizing, they usually finish a reading with little comprehension except a very good awareness of whether they were subvocalizing. In learning to read rapidly you will learn to go faster than you can subvocalize all of the words, although you will proba-bly always subvocalize some of them.

PROPER PRACTICE IS THE KEY

In most skills, you develop gradually, improving bit by bit. That's why most teachers teach the skills in the same way—one step at a time. However, in rapid reading you must do just the opposite. In order to drill properly, you don't advance as fast as you can read. In fact, you don't just go as fast as you possibly can, you *practice* by going much faster than you can. Understanding how to drill properly is the objective of this chapter. It is most important that you understand this well, because your ability to practice *properly* is the key to your success.

HOW TO LEARN TO DISCERN INFORMATION MORE RAPIDLY

At this moment, your ears can take in exactly the same sounds that the ears of a blind person do. Yet a blind person can *discern more information* from these same sounds than you can. Where you might hear only footsteps, a blind person would make a character assessment, just as you do when you *look* someone over. In order to teach yourself to discern more information from the sounds that you can already hear, you would prob-ably have to wear a blindfold for a month or two. Then your hearing would become much more acute.

In order to learn to read faster, you have to do almost the same thing. At this mo-ment your eyes, looking at a page of print, see exactly what my eyes see. Yet most likely I can "read" those words much more quickly than you can. To phrase it differently, I discern more information from the same words in less time. If you looked at the words in as short a period of time as I do, then you would not perceive as much information.

In order to train yourself to be able to discern information more quickly, you must put "blinders" on, only in this case it will be "earplugs" instead. Not real earplugs, of course, because you are not hearing real sounds. When you read you are only recalling the sounds of the words to yourself in your mind's ear. *The secret to good drilling is to go faster than you can say all of the words to yourself; yet you must still be seeing all of the words.*

The following exercise will help you to learn to practice properly. You will need to set your timing device for decreasing intervals. You'll be starting with a three-minute reading, then reducing the time to two minutes, and then to one minute. The easiest timing device for this particular drill is a tape recorder. You should merely record onto it, *"Ready? Begin,"* and then a three-minute silence before saying, *"Stop, please."* Next leave a few seconds before saying, *"Ready? Begin,"* after which you would leave a two-minute silence, and so on. Like all the drills, this one can be done with any clock or watch with a sweep second hand or using a timing device or clock on your computer.

EXERCISE NO. 5

Materials: *Any easy book of your choice*

Timing device, preferably a tape recorder

Purpose: *Learn how to* practice *seeing more than one word at a time by learning to make your mark*

1. Read in new material for three minutes, using your hand.
    Make a mark where you finished reading.
    Optional: Compute your reading rate.
2. Re-read the same section in three minutes. If you finish before the time is up, go back to the starting point and begin again.
3. Practice read the same section in two minutes; be sure to make the mark. At this point, you may not be able to read every word, but that doesn't matter. Just keep your finger moving fast enough to get to the end by the time your two minutes are up and let your eyes try to follow your finger.
4. Practice read the section in one minute. Remember that you must always reach the goal in the set amount of time.

NOTE: By making the goal in one minute, you are going three times as fast as you were able to read. This is called *practicing* or *practice reading.*

5. Read in new material for one minute from the end of the section you have been practicing. Make a mark where you stoppped reading and compute your rate as follows:
    a. Find the average number of words per line.
    b. Count the total number of lines read.
    c. Multiply "a" times "b" for your words per minute. (As this was a one-minute read, it is not necessary to divide "c" by another number.)
6. When you have your reading rate, record it on your progress profile.

If you were relaxed and made the mark easily each time, you may think that you are doing something wrong because it seems so easy. Well, it is easy. But if you're not able to make the mark, then the reason is that you are still trying to "read," and now you must learn to go faster than you can read, which is what "practice" is.

You will always be "reading" at the first and last steps of the drills and exercises, but almost never in the middle parts. In the middle steps you are always practicing, not reading, and the most important thing is to reach your goal with your hand. If you haven't seen all of the words, no matter. If you've had to skip words or jump entire lines, it's unimportant. Making the mark is what's important. Anyone can do it easily; you just have to move your hand fast enough.

There is always a student who tells me that he or she can't move their hand any faster. Usually I ask them to put their hand in the air and rapidly shake it back and forth. Then I tell them to do the same thing under the lines of print, while keeping their eyes open just to see whatever they can see. With a little patience, I've never had a student who couldn't reach the mark.

Learning to practice properly is vital to any skill. The old adage, practice makes perfect, only holds true when the practice is proper. The last exercise is so important that you should repeat it at least one more time. This time do it with a slight variation, but faster!

EXERCISE NO. 6

Materials: *Same as Exercise No. 5*

Purpose: *Same as Exercise No. 5*

1. Read as far and as fast as you can for one minute. Mark where you stop reading.
2. Practice read the same section in 45 seconds. Make the mark. If you get there early, return and begin reading again.
3. Practice read the same section in 35 seconds.
4. Practice read the same section in 25 seconds. Make the mark and try to do it in the proper amount of time, as going too fast can also become a problem.
5. Read in new material for one minute. Mark the point where you stop reading. Compute your rate and enter it on your progress profile.

Usually, you notice a gain in your reading rate after a series of practices. As soon as you start drilling properly, always reaching your mark with ease, then you start developing your ability to respond to more than one word at a time. When this happens, your rate just naturally, and fairly rapidly, begins to go up.

GETTING AHEAD

If you have extra time, try to find some more time to read, always using your hand of course, before going on to the next lesson. You can always repeat the last drill in this chapter and then do 30 minutes of reading. Remember, the more you use your hand, pushing yourself to go as fast as you can understand, the better you will do, faster.

6

ASK THIS SIMPLE QUESTION AND START GETTING BETTER COMPREHENSION

Developing good reading comprehension or understanding really means developing good thinking. No one can teach you how to improve your thinking overnight, but there are steps you can take which will help you to improve much faster than you might imagine.

The word comprehension implies so much that almost no two reading experts have the same definition for it. For the purposes of this book, reading comprehension will mean *understanding or knowing what you are reading while you are reading it*. If you can't remember it on a test at a later time, this may only mean that you cannot *recall* the information. Recall is also very important, but we'll deal with it in other chapters. The true test of reading comprehension is an open book test. Only then can it be found whether or not you understand the material you are reading.

WHEN YOU CAN'T UNDERSTAND

If you cannot understand a passage, there are generally two reasons why this happens. Perhaps you do not have the vocabulary. You might be reading a medical textbook or a book on a computer programming language and too many of the words simply have no meaning for you. This would obviously result in very poor comprehension. In some cases, it might almost be like reading a foreign language. The best solution to this problem is to begin reading in the easiest books on the subject and work your way up in the subject as you develop more knowledge and vocabulary. If you must read such a difficult book, perhaps you will have to go along just looking up, maybe even memorizing, all of the new and difficult words.

However, it's also possible that the passage was not written very well, or that it was written rather obtusely. Some writers seem to go out of their way to write long and confusing sentences. Unfortunately, some people pick up the impression that long sentences with difficult words mean better writing. Sometimes the material is just very badly organized. If you face any of these problems in your reading, there are techniques which you will learn in this book to cut through the confusion and to learn to understand it more easily.

PARAGRAPHS HOLD THE FIRST
KEY TO COMPREHENSION

The purpose of having paragraphs in writing is simply to organize a group of sentences into a unit. Therefore all of the sentences in a paragraph *should* relate to one subject. Since a rapid reading course, and this book, presume that you can already read and understand most of what comes across your desk, we will not deal with vocabulary. We will start working with the paragraph as the first unit of thought.

The first step in developing your comprehension is to practice finding out what the subject of a paragraph is. Most of the time you understand this without even thinking about it. But it is important to practice doing it so that you will be able to do it when you have to deal with very difficult passages. Try this simple exercise and see how fast you can do it:

EXERCISE NO. 7

Materials: *This book*
  Paper, pencil

Purpose: *Learn to identify what a paragraph is about.*

1. One at a time, read each sentence or paragraph below as quickly as possible, *with your hand*, and find what it is about.
2. On your paper letter from "A" to "F." After reading a sentence or paragraph *once*, look away, and on your paper write down what the paragraph is about in as few words as possible.

CAUTION: It is important to read each passage only once! Try to avoid looking back.

  A   Most of the trees are green.
  B.   Many birds fly south in the winter.
  C.   John washed the dishes; his wife asked him to do it.
  D.   Bill loved to play soccer. He hoped to play professionally some day.
  E.   Holland's best known philosopher was Spinoza. He was a Jew.
  F.   Masi was a charming young woman with short dark hair. Her unusual name was a nickname. Her parents were of Japanese extraction.

Probably you did not have any trouble with the simple passages in Exercise 7. Did you notice that the subject of each passage was always in the first sentence? This is usually the case in all writing. In fact, in almost 95 percent of all paragraphs, the topic is presented in the first sentence. This is also why this sentence is often referred to as the topic sentence.

Now there is another exercise, using all of these principles and taking them one step further. In the following passages the paragraphs are longer. Once again you are simply to find out what they're talking about. In fact *that's all you are to do,* and as quickly as possible. Since in almost every case the topic is in the first sentence, read the first sentence carefully trying to find what this passage is going to be about. If you find it, you've obviously met the purpose that I have given you. But there is always a chance, even though it is a slight one (probably less than five percent), that the real topic is given somewhere else in the passage. So you should continue reading in order *to see if everything relates to the topic* you've already found. But of course now you should be able to go much more quickly.

EXERCISE NO. 8

Materials: *This book*
Paper, pencil

Purpose: *Find what each paragraph is about* as quickly as you can, *reading it only once and with your hand*

1. On your paper letter from "G" to "M."
2. Read each paragraph as quickly as you can, only for the purpose of finding what it is about, one time. Cover it with your hand after reading it, so that you can't look back at it.
3. Looking away, write down the word or words of what it is about on your paper.

   G. All the animals on the farm were quite contented. The cows were all grazing happily, the horses were running around their pasture, and the chickens were scratching everywhere looking for things to eat.

   H. One of Bavaria's last kings was Ludwig II. He was thought to be insane and was ultimately deposed. He built several castles which almost bankrupted the royal treasury. Today, these castles are among the chief tourist attractions of Bavaria.

   I. All but one of the children at the school went out to play basketball. One boy stayed behind. He was handicapped and couldn't play ball. Sometimes the children made fun of him.

   J. Granddad was a very stern old man. He rarely visited, but Rachel disliked him anyway. Even though he was her grandfather, she thought he was too strict. His rigid ways often upset her father as well.

K.   *In and around the pond are many different animals, insects and fish. One of these begins life swimming like a fish but becomes an animal that likes to eat insects. He's often thought of as lazily sitting on a lily pad.*

L.   *Diane went to the mall. Corinne and Brenda were already there. Sarah didn't want to go, but finally she did. When they all met they were having a good time at the Thai restaurant.*

M.   *John went out to milk the cows. Mother was already baking bread. Father was harvesting the tomatoes. When his brother returned there would be work for him to do as well. Life on a farm was not easy.*

Answers:
A: Trees B: birds C: John D: Bill E: Spinoza F: Masi G: farm animals H: Ludwig I: handicapped boy J: granddad K: frog L: mall M: farm life

---

You might have found many of these passages quite simple. But did you have any difficulty with paragraph I? The topic is only indirectly referred to in the first sentence. Perhaps for paragraph K you didn't deduce that it was about a frog. It's not very common for the topic of a paragraph not to be spelled out. But since it is always a possibility, I thought that you should become aware of it. Also, paragraph M is difficult because the topic sentence is the last sentence, again something that you will not generally encounter.

COMPREHENSION VERSUS SPEED

Occasionally, when working on comprehension, it is easy to forget your reading speed. And that is all right. In this method of rapid reading, you develop your speed with a certain degree of independence from your comprehension. In other words, you'll be working on both separately. Later on you'll begin to work with both of them together. Comprehension will always govern speed, except when practicing, because obviously reading without understanding is not reading at all.

When you are developing the skill of fast recognition of words we will not be concerned with comprehension, as has been explained when practice reading was discussed. Similarly, when you are working on comprehension exercises speed must not be your first concern. However, when a specific purpose is defined in a reading, such as *only find what the passage is about,* you should certainly go no more slowly than it takes you to do this. If you've discovered what it is about, don't continue to read and analyze every other part of the passage with the same concern. Quickly breeze through it, merely checking to see if everything relates to what you've chosen as the paragraph's topic. You should be able to do this fairly quickly with a little practice.

GETTING AHEAD

If you wish to begin doing more work on your comprehension, it's quite easy to do so. Pick up any book, take a piece of paper and a pencil, and see how many paragraphs you can find the topics of in a five-minute period. You should be able to do about five per minute with a little practice. Simply select a random paragraph, read it as quickly as possible once through to try to find what it's about. Looking away, jot down on your paper what it's about. Then skip to another paragraph that doesn't immediately follow. It's more challenging this way. Continue seeing how many you can do. Your ability to quickly identify what a passage is about will help you a great deal in the future steps to develop good reading comprehension.

Practice Drills for Week 2

Today you should spend as much time as you have working on the drills which follow, without reading an additional chapter. Then tomorrow continue with Chapter Seven followed by a repetition of these drills. In the following days, read the following chapters, after which you should repeat as many of these drills as you have time to do. The amount of time that you spend drilling will relate directly to how fast you will be able to read when you complete this book. Assuming that you have begun this course of study as an average reader (reading around 200 words per minute), and that you practice as instructed, then the following chart will give you an indication of what you can expect to achieve:

IF YOU DRILL EACH DAY FOR:	IN SIX WEEKS YOU SHOULD BE ABLE TO READ* APPROXIMATELY:
20 Minutes	400 to 800 words per minute or double a rate of 300 WPM or less
40 Minutes	600 to 1200 WPM
60 Minutes	800 to 1500 WPM
90 Minutes	1200 to 2000 WPM
120 Minutes	over 2000 WPM
(Over 90 minutes should be divided in two sessions)	

*As reading rate will vary with the type of material, your purpose, and other factors, this will indicate a high rate in fairly easy material.

   It is best to start your practice by completing a chapter, and then begin doing the drills from this section. Do the drills in the order presented. If you practice only 20 minutes a day, do just the first drill each day. If you practice 40 minutes a day, begin with the first drill, and then do the second, etc.

   Some drills may be repeated, either immediately or after finishing the subsequent drills. This is always indicated on the drill. If you have not successfully met the objective of the drill, it is a good idea to repeat the drill until you do so. The objectives are not difficult. If you are not meeting them, then perhaps you are expecting too much of yourself. You might be setting a higher standard than what is expected of you, such as expecting to understand more of the material than the reading purpose states.

   Each drill is presented in both a diagram form and with a written explanation. Most of the drills have been thoroughly explained in a previous chapter; the rest are similar to them. At first you may find it easier to use the written explanation of the drill. When you are repeating the drill, the diagram will most likely become quicker to follow.

   To use the diagrams, you may need to know that (1) the first vertical line always indicates the point in the book where you begin reading, (2) the arrows indicate the amount of material that you are reading or how far, and (3) the diagrams are to be read or followed *downward;* in other words you first drill according to instructions on the highest arrow, next you drill according to instructions on the next arrow, and so on.

Materials you will need for this week's drills

1. *A timing device.* You will need to be timing one-, two-, and three-minute intervals.
2. *Pen or pencil.*
3. *Paper.* Preferably use unlined large sheets, 8 1/2 x 11 inches, which is typewriter size paper.
4. *One or two books.* General books of fiction, biography or nonfiction that are not too difficult.
5. *One or more books* from the list on your progress profile.

DRILL NO. 1

Materials: Basic List   Purpose: Begin eliminating regressions
Estimated Time: 15 Minutes   Objective: Read a line or two further with each re-reading

---

THIS DRILL MAY BE REPEATED UNTIL READING 400 WPM AT WHICH POINT BEGIN WITH DRILL NO. 2

DIAGRAM:

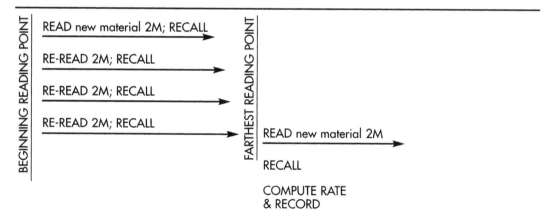

EXPLANATION:

---

1. Read in new material for two minutes.
   Mark where you stop reading with a "2."
   Start a written summary, put down in as few words as possible what the material is about *without looking back at the passage.*
   Optional: Compute your beginning reading rate for the day.
2. Re-read the same material in two minutes trying to go farther.
   Make a new mark "3," if you read farther ahead.
   Add to the written summary without looking back at the passage.

3. Re-read the same material in two minutes, try to go farther.
   Make a new mark "4," if you read farther ahead.
   Add to the written summary.

4. Re-read the same material in two minutes, try to go even farther.
   Make a new mark "5," if you read farther ahead.
   Add to the written summary.

5. Read new material from the "5," as fast as you can for two minutes.
   Mark where you stop reading with an "X."
   Add to the written summary or begin a new one.
   Compute your reading rate from "5" to "X" and record it on your progress profile.

CAUTION: Always use your hand to pace your reading.

DRILL NO. 2

Materials: Basic List   Purpose: Increase your rate with comprehension
Estimated Time: 15 Minutes   Objective: Always make the mark

THIS DRILL MAY BE REPEATED

DIAGRAM:

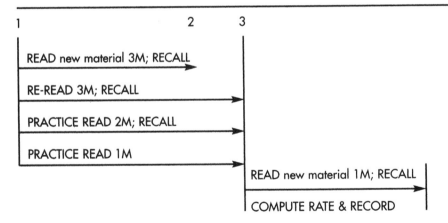

EXPLANATION:

1. Read in new material for three minutes.
   Mark where you stop with a "2."
   Start a written summary and recall briefly.

2. Re-read the same material for three minutes. Try to go farther.
   If you went farther, mark with a "3."
   Add to the written summary briefly, if you can.

3. Practice read the longest section read in two minutes.
   If you can add anything to the written summary, do so. Do not slow down in order to remember—you must make the mark.

4. Practice read the entire section in one minute. Make the mark. *Go directly to the next step without recalling.*

CAUTION: **If you have not made the mark in the set time, continue to practice read the entire section in one-minute periods until you can do so. Remember, this is not reading and it is not necessary to see every word or even to cover every line, but** *try* **to.**

5. Read in new material for one minute.
   Mark where you stop with an "X."
   Add to the written summary briefly, if you can.
   Compute your reading rate from "3" to "X" and record it on your progress profile.

DRILL NO. 3

Materials: Any book from the list of ten books you prepared.
Purpose: Practice new technique in a normal reading situation
Estimated Time: 15 Minutes   Objective: Set a time goal and keep it

---

THIS DRILL MAY BE REPEATED

DIAGRAM:

Find Highest Reading Rate × 10 =   words
Set up _____ word section
DIVIDE in 5 equal parts

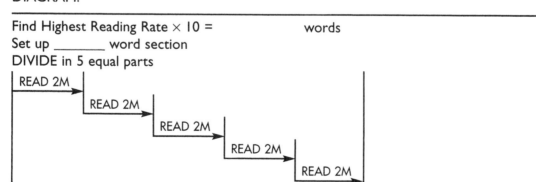

COMPUTE & RECORD any 2M section

EXPLANATION:

1. Find your highest reading rate from Drills No. 1, 2 or 3.
   Multiply this rate by "10."
   In one of the books from your reading list compiled in Exercise 1, set up a section of words equal to the length that you have just determined.
   Divide the entire section into five equal parts.
2. Using your hand as a pacer, read the first part in two minutes.
3. Read the second part in two minutes.
4. Continue, reading each part in two minutes or less.
5. Compute the reading rate of any section and record it on your progress profile.

DRILL NO. 4

Materials: Basic   List Estimated Time: 5 minutes
Purpose: Develop awareness of the paragraph as a thought unit
Objective: See how quickly you can find what a paragraph is about

DO THIS DRILL ONCE PER PRACTICE SESSION

DIAGRAM:

Select any random paragraph
READ as quickly as you can

RECALL, without looking back what it is about
RECORD number completed

EXPLANATION:

1. Select a random paragraph from a book.
   Using your hand, read it as quickly as you can find what it's about.
2. On a piece of paper write down in as few words as possible what the paragraph is about. *Do not look back at the paragraph.*
3. Select another paragraph at random in the book, and continue this drill.
   Try to increase the number of paragraphs you are able to do in five minutes.
   Always remember to read only to find what it's about.
   Record the number completed in five minutes on your progress profile.

7

DON'T READ JUST FOR ITS OWN SAKE

When your reading instruction was completed in the sixth grade, you were left with three misconceptions which have influenced your reading ever since. Your teacher didn't purposely mislead you; most likely there were no teachers or books available to teach you anything more. It was therefore implied that you knew how to read and that what you had been taught was all that you needed to know.

THE FIRST MISCONCEPTION

The first misconception is that you should read everything the same way, word by word. Whether you are reading the newspaper, a novel, a hard copy printout from the internet, or a physics textbook, it was implied that you should start at the beginning and go once through, from the beginning to the end. This is a waste of your time and it is possibly the worst habit that you have to break in your development as an efficient reader.

THE SECOND MISCONCEPTION

The second misconception concerns comprehension. It was implied, again because you were taught nothing else, that if you read material using this once-through approach you should be able to understand it. Of course you now know that many times you have not been able to understand a passage even though you read it as you had been taught. Yet what techniques were you given to use when a passage was difficult? Probably none.

THE THIRD MISCONCEPTION

It was finally implied that if you read a passage once through you should not only understand it but you should also be able to remember what was important. Yet how many times were you given tests on passages which you had read once through and found that you didn't remember as much as you should have? Perhaps your teacher told you to "study" harder next time. But what did that mean other than to read it once through once more?

ONCE THROUGH IS NOT ENOUGH

We have all been taught to read everything the same word-by-word method regardless of what we were reading. Too often this results in reading for its own sake, or for the sake of the word-by-word progress that we have been taught. This next short exercise will help you to appreciate why this old method doesn't work very well.

EXERCISE NO. 9

Materials: *Any easy book*
Timing device
Pencil or pen
Paper
(Or use your favorite word processing program)

1. Open the book to any section that you haven't read. Read for one minute for very good comprehension, go as slowly as you wish, but be certain to use your hand. Mark where you stop reading at the end of the minute. On the paper, without looking back at the book, write down as much as you can remember about what you have read. Just phrases or words are enough; you don't need to write complete sentences. If you prefer, you can also jot down the information using a word processing program.

2. Re-read the same section trying to get more information or a better understanding of the material, again in one minute. On the paper or on your computer, without looking back at the book, write down anything more that you can now remember.

3. Re-read the same section again for one minute. Look for anything more that you may have missed or forgotten. Without looking back at the book, see if you can add anything more to your notes.

The exercise is really quite easy. Do you see what you were finding out about your reading ability? Undoubtedly you got more out of the passage with each re-reading unless the passage was something like "Mary Had a Little Lamb" and you already had it all but memorized. After the three readings, is there anything more in the passage that you think you might find if you read it again? Possibly there is. I hope that you will never again feel that you "got everything" going once through material.

The answer to the problem of not being able to get everything on one reading is to develop a whole new approach to reading. In fact, this whole book is an alternative to the once through method of reading. A reading method should serve whatever purpose you have for reading the material. That sounds very obvious but most of us go through the motions of an outmoded reading process which pays no attention to the purpose and does not question it.

Basically, you must learn how to define your purpose for any given reading, and then use the techniques which will most efficiently enable you to meet that purpose. Here is an example of how easy reading can be when you are working with a very specific purpose:

EXERCISE NO. 10

Materials: *Timing device*

1. In ten seconds or less, find how many times the word "cat" appears in the following passage: (Be sure to use your finger!)

THE CAT

The cat sat on the window sill in the warm sunshine. Though apparently asleep, he had one eye always on the little blue and white bird in the brass cage. As the bird chirped its cheerful song the cat kept watching and waiting for its opportunity. Possibly the cat thought that the bird could get out of the cage and he was just waiting for the little door to open. Whatever was going on in the cat's mind, there apparently was no doubt whatsoever that it would catch the bird sooner or later. Watching the cat was a great lesson in patience.

Whether or not you got the correct answer in the exercise is not really important. What is important is that with a specific purpose you are able to read the material much more efficiently, more quickly and succeed at "getting" what you need. Probably you were able to find out that the word "cat" appears five times (not counting the title).

GET SPECIFIC WITH YOUR PURPOSE

It is not always easy to state a purpose as specifically as I did for you in the last exercise. You might be reading a chapter in a business textbook because your instructor asked you to study it. Or you could be reading a novel for "kicks," or perhaps a work of literature which needs to be read carefully. These are purposes for reading, but they are examples of poorly defined purposes. They won't help you very much with your reading. The more specific a purpose is, the easier it is to do the reading.

Some students always insist that they must get everything out of a reading. They are really telling me why they "must" go slowly. Perhaps they haven't been practicing enough and are trying to excuse their lack of progress. But having to get everything is the best reason for being able to define your reading purpose. That's because you have only two choices: you can either read something many times in order to be assured that you got it all, or else you can define your purpose and use techniques which will assure that you have met it and gotten what you need.

KNOW YOUR PURPOSE AND YOU WON'T HAVE TO WORK SO HARD

I once had a student who was very compulsive about her reading. She felt that she had to absorb everything she read. She was spending an amazing number of hours each day studying – as many as 15 – trying to know everything that was assigned. When I mentioned that no teacher would ever expect their students to know all that had been assigned to be read, she looked at me dubiously.

The next week in class her hand shot up. She announced to the class that I had indeed been correct in saying that teachers didn't expect their students to know everything that was assigned. She had called her brother, a teacher at a university in New York State. Reportedly, he had asked several of his colleagues and they had all agreed with my statement, "You don't expect a student to know everything you assign."

This awareness does not necessarily solve the problem of getting a purpose. If teachers don't expect you to know everything they assign, how are you to know what they do expect you to learn? This is an ability that you will develop both with experience and while studying this course.

USE THESE QUESTIONS TO START SETTING YOUR PURPOSE

Reading everything many times would not be worthwhile, and it would also take a tremendous amount of your time. Therefore, you are left with the alternative of learning to set a specific reading purpose. There are two questions that you can ask yourself which will help you to set a purpose in your reading.

First: In an overall scheme of things, how worthwhile is the material that I am reading? Once that question is answered, then try to narrow your purpose down:

Second: What do I want or need to remember, as specifically as possible, from this material that I am about to read?

Answering the first question makes the second question easier. For example, you are reading a newspaper. You select an article. But how important is it? Is it an article about a car accident that will be forgotten in a few weeks? Or is it an article about new technology that can help make life easier for millions? Or is it an article about style or fashion that will be outdated in a few weeks anyhow? Asking this simple question—how important is what I am reading to me in the long run?—allows you to evaluate how worthwhile the material is.

This can be applied to anything. If you are reading a textbook, does it have lasting value to you or is it part of a required course—one in which you have little interest? Are you reading the sports page of the newspaper just to find out some scores, or are you a Ph.D. candidate studying artificial intelligence?

With the first question answered, then you can deal with the second. I'll use the same examples and follow them through: The news article about an accident, what do you want to know and remember? If you have any friends involved? Do you just wish to know how it happened, or are you reading it because you have some time to pass waiting for a bus? Do you want to remember the victims' names? It takes only seconds to decide these things, but the answers will determine how fast or slow you should read the material, and how carefully.

With the news article on the new technology or style and fashion, do you wish to just find out the main points? Do you wish to be able to recall the the key points? In dealing with the textbook, do you need to know a great deal of information and detail to pass a thorough test, or do you just need a few ideas to take a brief quiz? Maybe you just need to know where to be able to find certain information when you need it, or do you have to memorize certain procedures? Maybe you just have to discuss the main points of a few chapters in a seminar.

SET A PURPOSE FOR EVERYTHING YOU READ

Start setting a purpose for every question you do, even if you are just reading the back of a cereal box as you eat your breakfast. In most cases it takes only a second to do, but it's a very important habit to develop. If you can begin doing it right way, as best you can, you will help yourself a great deal.

Once you have answered the two questions about any reading you are about to do, then you are ready to start applying the techniques you have to meet your defined purpose. At this point, it would mean reading faster or slower, or perhaps reading something more than once. This is just the beginning of a whole group of techniques that you will soon learn and be able to use.

In the coming week's drills, a reading purpose will be given for each reading drill. Except for the comprehension drills, the purposes will usually be very minimal at first. Practice reading implies a limited purpose; it means a very fast speed. And you can't "memorize" or "get everything" when the purpose is to develop speed. Some students immediately tell me that they never read for such slight purposes as I assign them in the speed drills. I explain that if you wish to read better and faster, then you must do a lot of fast practice with a minimal purpose. After you can go very fast with a minimal purpose, then you can begin increasing the responsibility of your reading purpose.

Don't waste your time by practicing what you can already do, reading slowly. Push your rates as high as you possibly can in all of your practice. Limit your purpose, i.e., when reading for this course barely follow the plot line and get into the excellent habit of deciding a purpose for everything else you read outside the course. Now turn back to the Practice Drills and do as many as you can to complete this day's work.

8

BECOME ONE OF THE WORLD'S FASTER READERS!

Would it surprise you if I told you that you may already be among the world's fastest readers? If you were among the top one percent, would you consider yourself pretty good? Well, perhaps you are, and, if not, you soon will be. That's because less than one percent of Americans can read faster than 400 words per minute. Unbelievable? It's true. Very likely you've already experienced reading, or at least practicing, that fast. And soon you'll find it a very comfortable rate.

Being able to read faster is based on your ability to simply see a word and understand it. You can do this because you do not need to hear a word in order to understand what it means. When you look at a picture you do not "tell" yourself what it is about. Rather, you just look at it and understand. When you look at a clock you do not have to read all of the numbers on the clock's face in order to tell the time. No, you see all of the numbers at once. You don't think about where the hour and minute hands are pointing.

As we discussed in an earlier chapter, in learning to read rapidly you will learn to go faster than you can subvocalize all the words. *But you will probably always subvocalize some of them.* You may wonder why the subject of sub-vocalizing is brought up at all if we can't solve it. Whether or not I discuss it, you will more than likely become aware of it. As you start to move faster, you may feel that you aren't "reading" all of the words. Perhaps you may even feel that you are not "seeing" some of them. This will be your first awareness of a lack of vocalization, something you must get used to eventually.

THE "SECRET" OF SPEED READING

Once a student in a class raised her hand and excitedly told me that she had figured out the secret of rapid reading. Naturally, I wanted to know what it was so that I could share it with my other students. She told me that the secret was not to read all of the words, especially the little words such as "a," "of," "the," and so forth. I had to agree with her, but only partially. I asked her how she knew which words not to read. She wasn't sure about that. Of course she had to *see* the words and know what they were before deciding not to "read" them.

For the first time this student was simply understanding a word visually without sounding it out to herself. This is a very exciting thing when it happens. We are all capable of it, and it does indeed increase our reading rate. But you don't have *to try* to do it. If you use your hand to pace your reading—if you do the drills—then this will start to happen almost automatically. And as soon as you begin to move faster than two or three hundred words per minute, you will be vocalizing less. This means you will not be "reading" the little words any more.

A NEW DRILL CAN INCREASE YOUR RATE EVEN MORE

Now that you have been practicing the basic technique, you can begin to push a lot harder and develop a much faster rate. Here is a new drill with a slightly different concept than the ones with which you have been working. Just because it is different—or "new"—doesn't mean it is more difficult. As long as you understand the concept of practice reading—as long as you can do it and make your mark—then you won't have any difficulty with these drills.

EXERCISE NO. 11 (THE EXTENSION DRILL)

Materials: *An easy book*
            Timing device
            Pencil

1. Read for one minute in new material, marking with a pencil the beginning and ending points "1" and "2."
   Optional: Compute your rate.

2. Re-read the same section for one minute, trying to go further.
   If you read further ahead, mark the new ending point "3."

3. Re-read the same section again in one minute; try to go further still.
   If you read further ahead, mark the new ending point "4."

4. Count the number of lines between point "2" and point "4."
   Write the number "5" *ahead of point "4"* however many lines you counted between points "2" and "4," *but no less than 5 lines.*

5. Practice read from point "1" to point "5" in one minute.
   You must make the mark!

6. Set up a point "6" the same number of lines ahead of point "5" that point "5" is ahead of point "4."
   Practice read from point "1" to point "6" in one minute.

7. From point "6" read for one minute, using your finger, as fast as you can understand the material.

    Mark your ending point with an "X."

    Compute your reading rate (point "6" to "X") and enter it on your progress profile.

Did you realize the difference between this drill and your previous ones? Before, you always read the same passage. Trying to go a little further, you re-read the same passage over, going a bit faster each time. But in this drill, you must cover new material that you haven't seen before. That makes it harder, but it will also have great results. For the first time you are learning to go much faster in unfamiliar material. You may not be able to understand all of it, but that will come with practice. Try to stay relaxed when you do the drilling, and make your mark with ease.

PUSH UP EVEN WHEN YOU'RE "READING"

In all of these drills, you are asked to "read" at the beginning and at the end of the drill. That, of course, is the time to read at your own rate, but even then you should always be pushing just as much as you can. The more time spent "reading" faster means better *comfort* with the skill and more comprehension. Some students insist on returning to their old rates whenever I say "read," because that is the only rate at which they feel comfortable. But they are only postponing the inevitable. In fact, they are just insisting on using their practice time to read slowly.

When it is time to reach the goal mark, then reaching it is the only thing that matters. Whether or not you understood very much is not important in those parts of the drills. Just remember, you are basically getting practice "seeing" more than one word at a time. Sometimes you may not even feel that you are seeing all of the words, but that is all right. Just make the mark! You're also avoiding a lot of vocalization; you have no time to "say" all the words.

Below is another version of the extension drill—the drill that you just did. But this version should make you go even faster. Do the best you can with it, but most importantly, just relax and try to enjoy it. Getting tense about the drill will not help you at all.

EXERCISE NO. 12

Materials: *Any easy book*
Timing device
Pencil

1. Read in new material, using your hand, for one minute.
   Mark your beginning and ending points "1" and "2."

2. Re-read the same section in one minute, trying to go further.
   Mark your new ending point "3."

3. Re-read the same section again in one minute, going a bit further.
   Mark the new ending point "4."

4. Make a new point "5" *one-half page* beyond point "4."
   Practice read from point "1" to point "5" in one minute.

5. Make a new point "6" one-half page beyond point "5."
   Practice read from point "1" to point "6" in one minute. Make the mark!

6. From point "4" read as fast as you can for one minute.
   Mark your new final ending point with an "X."
   Compute your ending rate (point "4" to "X") and enter it on your progress profile.

Were you able to keep up and make the mark? Once again, remember when you are practice reading you are not really reading, you are getting practice seeing the print. You do this as long as your hand can make the mark. If you doubt it, then try shaking your hand back and forth in the air as rapidly as you can. I've clocked hands going up to 4000 words per minute. You'll see that you can do it—that it is really easy to always make your mark. If you had any trouble, repeat this drill until you can do it easily.

IT CAN BE EASY TO REACH YOUR GOAL

You are most fortunate if you are using a tape recorder because you can help yourself even more than you already have. If you tape the drills, you'll find it very easy to do them. You can also add this aid: during the parts of the drills where you must reach your goal, on the tape record when there is twenty seconds left, then when there is ten seconds left. In this way, when you hear the twenty second warning, you can quickly estimate how much farther you have to go and if you have to speed up or not. The same effect can achieved with certain computer programs that allow you to record your voice and play it back.

If I were drilling you in a classroom and you taped me, it would go something like this:

Prepare to read for good comprehension in new material. Ready? Begin.
(1 minute of silence)
Stop, please! Write the number "2" where you stopped reading and go back to the beginning to re-read the section again. Ready? Begin.

(1 minute of silence)

Stop, please! Write the number "3" where you stopped reading and go back to the beginning to re-read the section again. Ready? Begin.

(1 minute of silence)

Stop, please! Write the number "4" where you stopped reading and write the number "5" one-half page beyond the number "4." Then go back to the beginning and wait to begin practice reading.

(10 seconds of silence)

Ready? Now practice read from the beginning to point "5." Begin.

(40 seconds of silence)

You have twenty seconds left to make your goal.

(10 seconds of silence)

Ten seconds left, make the mark!

(10 seconds of silence)

Stop, please! Now write the number "6" one-half page beyond the number "5." Then go back to the beginning and wait to begin practice reading.

(10 seconds of silence)

Ready? Now practice read from the beginning to point "6." Ready? Begin.

(40 seconds of silence)

Twenty seconds left, make your mark!

(10 seconds of silence)

Ten seconds left, make the mark or pass it!

(10 seconds of silence)

Stop, please! Now go back to point "4" to read as fast as you can for comprehension. Are you ready? Begin reading.

(1 minute of silence)

Stop, please! Make an "X" mark where you stopped reading; then compute your rate.

If you do not have a tape recorder or a taping program on your PC, then perhaps you have a friend who will time you. If not, you are probably becoming quite adept with a watch or clock. When I was learning rapid reading, I had only my watch with a sweep second hand. By merely keeping it close to my book, I developed the ability to glance over as I was reading, and then speed up if I wasn't close to my mark. Even if you had no timing device, you could still learn this skill. It would not be quite as precise, because the computations are more accurate in judging improvement. But just following the basic principles will help you improve.

At this point you should be quite warmed up and ready for some more drills. Turn back to the Practice Drills for Week 2 and do your drilling for the day. You should be hitting greater speeds as a result of your excellent warm-up.

9

USE THE MAGIC LINE TO DEVELOP BETTER READING RECALL

Comprehending information and the ability to retain it, implying the ability to call it forth, are closely related. There are two main ways in which they differ. Comprehension occurs while you are reading a passage. Recalling the information happens later, often quite a bit later. Although they are both based on thinking, there is a major difference in time.

The ability to understand a certain amount of material is one thing—but being able to recall it is quite another. In fact, recalling material is very hard to do, since you are recalling it from memory with no cues to aid you. While the mind is a "computer" of sorts, it can't recall everything. Being able to decide whether a statement is true or false, by contrast, is an example of being able to *recognize* the correct information. That is much easier than having to recall it.

THE "ACID" TEST OF COMPREHENSION

Recall might be called the hardest test of comprehension. That is one of the reasons we use it so much in developing reading comprehension. Because the two are so closely related, often working on one automatically includes working on the other.

The first step in developing your reading retention and recall is to develop a habit of immediately recalling the information that you have just read. This is quite easy to do and when you combine it with the comprehension question ("what's it about?"), you will start developing these skills together, almost effortlessly.

THE MAGIC LINE

The magic line mentioned in this chapter's title has magical properties only when you use it. It is actually only a simple diagonal line on which to write the word or phrase describing what a passage is about. We begin with diagonal lines and ultimately work into visual patterns which become devices for remembering information. This makes it much easier to remember than when the information is just written out, as in a regular prose passage, or perhaps an outline. This "device" is called a recall pattern.

Here is how to use a recall pattern: when you are reading a passage, draw a diagonal line on a piece of blank paper. As soon as you have completed your reading, using the diagonal line, write down what the passage is about. *Do not look back at the passage.* Always write as little as possible on the diagonal line. A few words will suffice. Perhaps one word is enough. If you were to begin a recall pattern for the nursery rhyme "Humpty Dumpty," Figure 3 shows what it would be like.

However, this is the simple part, since you have already been practicing how to find out what a passage is about. Next, you would add details to your diagonal line, *on branches running alternately upwards*, as a tree grows. Figure 4 shows how a recall pattern is developed for "Humpty Dumpty." It reads from bottom to top. In this type of *immediate recalling* of the information merely stop at the end of a reading and try to remember anything that you can. You don't have to organize it. That will all come later. At the moment, just see how much you can write down without looking back at the passage. This is a skill which will develop quickly, and, the more you do this, the more you will be able to remember whenever you do it. In this way, you will start to develop your reading memory. How to retain it will come with future lessons. The next drill is designed to develop your immediate recall ability. It also helps to develop your comprehension.

FIGURE 3. HOW TO BEGIN A RECALL PATTERN

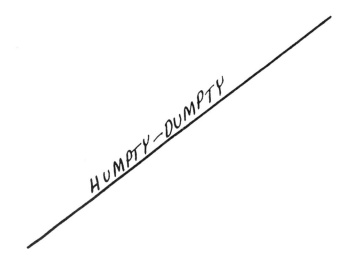

FIGURE 4. A MORE DEVELOPED RECALL PATTERN

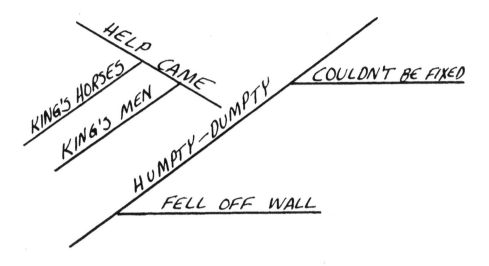

EXERCISE NO. 13

Materials: *Pencil or pen*
Paper

1. After reading a paragraph below, cover it with your hand.
2. On a separate piece of paper, draw a diagonal line and write what the passage was about in as few words as possible. On branch lines, *working alternately* from bottom to top, write as many other things as you can remember. Figure 5 provides you with an example.

There are many squirrels living in the woods.
They like to eat nuts.
Some of them are quite tame.

A. The Manhattan skyline is a very impressive sight. It has one of the largest collections of tall buildings anywhere in the world.
B. San Francisco is considered by many people to be the most beautiful city in the United States. It is surrounded by water on three sides and is built on seven hills, as is Rome. Most of the buildings are relatively new, because the earthquake and subsequent fire of 1906 destroyed much of the city.

FIGURE 5.

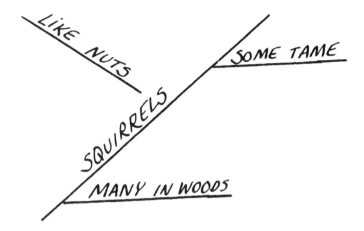

C. New Orleans is one of the most popular cities in the United States for tourists. The French and Spanish architecture of the French Quarter is most appealing. The city also features some of the best food in America. Some people travel to New Orleans just to eat.

D. Seattle is considered one of America's most up-and-coming cities. Located in America's beautiful Pacific Northwest, it has become a magnet for high tech companies. It is also home to a major airplane manufacturer and is located near Vancouver, another hot tourist spot.

E. Miami is fast becoming America's gateway to Latin America. Home to millions of Cuban-Americans and others from throughout Latin America, the city has a distinct Latino flavor. It is also a popular tourist and business destination for those visiting the US from South America.

___

One of the most important things to remember is to never look back at the passage when you are practicing recall. Think of recall as a sort of muscle: the more you exercise it, the faster and stronger it grows. If you look back at your reading passage, then you are practicing how to copy material, not recalling it. You must decide which you want to learn.

COMPREHENSION VERSUS SPEED

While learning to read rapidly, it is important to understand that you must develop your reading rate with a certain detachment from your comprehension. You learn to work on each skill separately. Once both have been developed to a certain point, then you will find that you can bring them together—being able to read much faster and comprehend better at the same time. Try not to let one get confused with the other. When working on comprehension and recall, forget about trying to read fast. But do remember what your purpose is, and go as fast as you can comfortably meet that purpose.

Here is an exercise to let you practice comprehension and recall while keeping in mind a simple purpose. If you keep your purpose in mind, you should be able to go fairly quickly and meet it.

EXERCISE NO. 14

Materials: *Any easy book*
Pencil or pen
Paper

1. On a piece of paper, number from one through five on one side and from six through ten on the other. Space the numbers out so that each one has plenty of room.
2. Opening your book to new material, select the longest paragraph on the first page. Read it as quickly as you can *for the sole purpose of finding out what it's about.*
3. Without looking back at the page, make a diagonal line after the number one on your paper, then write *in as few words as possible what the reading passage was mainly about. If you can remember anything more, put that down on branches working alternatively from the bottom up.*

CAUTION: **If you are remembering much more than just what the passage is about, you may be going too slowly. Read the passage as fast as you can just to meet your purpose.**

4. Repeat steps 2 and 3 on nine more pages, taking the longest paragraph on each of the pages.

There is always "one" person in just about every class who becomes an example of what not to do. Of course there is never *only* "one" person who makes all the mistakes, and just about everyone makes some of them. Regarding recall, there is usually someone who resists using the recall pattern, insisting on writing everything out in longhand. It is usually this person who stresses that he wants to learn how to improve his memory.

Using recall patterns is not the only way to improve your reading recall, but it is an effective way that has been proven with thousands of students. Before trying to find a better way to recall, it would probably be wise to learn to do it well. Try it a number of ways, then find your own method. But to half-learn something is a waste of your time. As in using your hand to read faster, if you're serious about wishing to improve your retention, then immediately begin using these simple patterns. They will develop into one of the best techniques you could ever imagine.

GETTING AHEAD

Eventually you'll be using the recall pattern in two ways: one for comprehension drills with paragraphs, the other for reading exercises and drills. Whatever the purpose, when you've finished reading the passage, draw a diagonal line. Recall what the passage is about. If you remember more details, put them on the branches.

Just remember, always put down as few words as you can (just enough so that *you* can remember) and never look back at the reading passage. Now do your practice drills for the day—and add some recall patterns to them.

TURN TO PAGE 34 FOR THE PRACTICE DRILLS TO COMPLETE TODAY'S WORK.

10

STRETCH YOUR RATE HIGHER WITH A DIFFERENT DRILL

If you've been doing the regular daily drilling, then your reading rate is undoubtedly beginning to get faster. The use of your hand to pace your reading has probably become second nature. By the end of this week, you will be ready for some new drills. This chapter is about those drills.

So far, we have been working solely with linear reading. Linear reading is the type of reading that you were taught to do in school. It is reading line by line, following normal word order. Linear reading comprises most of the reading we do and is the foundation for all difficult reading, including most study reading.

THE RANGE OF EFFICIENT LINEAR READING

The highest rate that you can achieve with linear reading is about 1,200 words per minute. And that's pretty fast. I put "about" because it depends on several factors. Depending on these factors, including the difficulty of the material and how much previous knowledge you have, a good linear reading rate should be able to range from 500 to 1,200 words per minute.

It is quite possible that you have already experienced reading within this range. Maybe you have gone even faster, above 1,200 words per minute. If you are going faster than 1,200, don't push yourself any further during the following week. Let this be a time for consolidation. Later on, there will be plenty of time to practice high rates of reading. If you have not yet reached 500 words per minute, don't let it worry you. At this point, most people haven't reached 500 words per minute. We all progress at very different degrees and many students don't achieve quality readings at 500 words per minute for several weeks. You are constantly working to develop each aspect of your reading range.

YOUR READING RATE WILL VARY

Do not expect to achieve a certain rate, let's say 500 words per minute, and then be able to read everything at that rate. Nor should you expect to see your rate improve every day. As you develop your linear reading skills, you will find your reading rate fluctuating within the peak range by as much as 500 words per minute, or between 500 and 1,000 words per minute. It could vary, depending on certain factors, such as how you feel on a certain day, how difficult the book is, and how much reading you've been doing (the more you read, the faster you generally go, just like typing). Variation is a good sign of progress. Since we've been taught to read everything at the same rate, one word at a time, beginning to break away from this habit is a positive sign of your development as an efficient reader.

THE DOUBLE/TRIPLE DRILL

This new drill is truly astounding; the results it gets when done properly make you see how miraculous speed reading can be. The drill has a slightly different concept than previous drills you've been doing. Although it is different, don't think that it is any more difficult. As long as you understand the concept of drilling (making your mark), then you'll have no difficulty mastering this new drill.

In this drill you first re-read a passage two times, then you practice read twice the amount that you have read. Next you practice read three times the amount that you could read, after which you do a final reading for comprehension. Once you have done the drill two or three times, then you should find it quite easy. And the results it produces more than justify any difficulty you may have in learning it.

EXERCISE NO. 15
(THE DOUBLE/TRIPLE DRILL)

Materials: *An easy book*
          Timing device
          Pencil or pen

1. Put a "1" where you will start reading.
    Read in new material for one minute, using your hand.
    Put a "2" where you finished reading.
    Optional: Compute your reading rate.
2. Re-read the same passage, try to go faster and farther, in one minute.
    Make a new mark, a "3," if you read further ahead.
    Determine *approximately* how much you have read, i.e., 1 1/4 pages, 2 1/8 pages, etc., from point "1" to point "3."
3. Mark a *new* passage from point "3" onwards and ending with "4," that is approximately the same amount as from point "1" to point "3."
    Practice read from point "1" to "4" in one minute.

CAUTION: You are now practice reading twice the amount that you read with the third reading. To do this you must move through each half of the total material in thirty seconds. If you are using a tape recorder or a recording device on your computer, put a "warning" on the tape or program when 30 seconds are up so that you will know that you must be to the "3"—and if you're not, you must move faster.

4. Mark another new passage from point "4" onwards and ending with "5" that is approximately the same as from "3" to "4."
   Practice read from point "1" to "5" in one minute.

CAUTION: You are now practice reading three times the amount that you originally read. Now you must be moving through each third of the material in 20 seconds. If you are using a tape recorder or other device, put a "warning" on the tape when twenty seconds are up and when forty seconds are up so that you will know that you should be at the "4" and the "5" respectively.

5. From the "5," read as fast as you can for one minute.
   Make a new mark "X" where you stopped reading.
   Compute your reading rate, from "5" to "X," and record it on your progress profile.

In this drill you must cover a lot of *new* material. That makes it somewhat more difficult at first, but it produces much better results. For the first time, you are learning to go much faster in unfamiliar material. You may not be able to understand all of it, but that will come. Try to remain relaxed when you do the drilling and have to make the mark. Remember, it is just practice reading.

READING VERSUS PRACTICE READING

In all of the drills, you are asked to "read" at the beginning and the end of the drill. This is the time to read at your own rate, but even then you should always be pushing just as much as you can. Some students seem to slow down whenever we say "read." Apparently, they want to practice going slowly, stopping to listen to each word as they go. Remember, you want to learn to go faster. At first, when you go faster, the comprehension will not be as good as it was. But this is largely a matter of habit. If you slow yourself down so that it feels the way it used to, all you are doing is practicing what you can already do. The more you practice going faster, the sooner it will become comfortable for you.

It may help you to remember what your purpose is. In all of the drilling so far, your only reading purpose has been to be able to understand the story *as you are reading it*. Once you have built up your reading rate, then we will start to work with more serious purposes. If you are following my directions, then you should learn this quickly. If you are doing it another way, then it will probably take you much longer to learn it.

You may have to exhaust your way until you discover that it doesn't help, then come back and do it my way. The choice is yours.

Remember that the premise of learning rapid reading is to separate comprehension from rate development. You must do this yourself when you are practicing—and if you keep the reading purpose in mind, it may be easier for you.

ARE YOU MAKING THE MARK?

In this drill, you are going as fast as you will for at least another week. So if you weren't able to make the mark, you'll have plenty of opportunity to learn to do so. But always remember that when you are practice reading, you are not really reading: you are primarily getting practice just seeing the words. Don't think that you can't "see" all of the words. Of course you can. Turn a book upside down and look at a whole page of print. You can see all of it. You may not be able to discern each word, but you can see them. Sometimes people confuse seeing with understanding. It's not the same thing at all. You can see words in a foreign language but that doesn't mean you can understand them. When you are practice reading, it should be the same thing: simply relax, move your hand very quickly, and just look at the words as though you are going over words in another language. *See* them all—you don't need to understand each one.

HOW TO MOVE YOUR HAND FASTER

We've already discussed the movement of your hand. Sometimes there are students who say that they can't move their hands fast enough. If you have trouble with that, then try to move your hand from the wrist down, not your whole arm. Moving the whole arm can tire you very quickly. It's simply like waving your hand and saying good-bye to someone. Do that, then see how fast you can shake your hand back and forth. Pretty fast I suspect. I've clocked "average" hands going 4,000 words a minute. If you are working in a linear reading range, under 1,200 words a minute, then practice reading means going three times as fast, or 3,600 words a minute. If it becomes necessary, take two or three lines at a time in order to make your mark. But try to have a moment for all the lines because the more movement the better.

This chapter is really a full one. Learning to do this drill is a major accomplishment. Once you can do it, all of the other drills will be relatively easy. If you have the time, go back and do this drill again. And do not go on to another chapter until you feel that you can do the drill, always making the mark.

TURN TO PAGE 34 FOR THE PRACTICE DRILLS TO COMPLETE TODAY'S WORK.

11

KNOW WRITERS' TECHNIQUES AND HELP YOURSELF

If you know how writers write, especially how they organize their writing, then you can cut through to the gist of the material *when that fits your purpose.* In fact, when you have a definite, well-defined purpose and you know how to go about finding where the writer has put what you need, you can save yourself a lot of time. Often this can save you over half your reading time, sometimes even more.

Luckily, there are some common ways writers organize their material. Almost everything you read will fall into one of three basic organization patterns. There is the news article format, the nonfiction form, and the most difficult, oddly, is fiction. In this chapter we'll discuss the last two.

THE BASIC FORM OF NONFICTION

A newspaper feature story, most editorials, essays, and other *expository* writing such as general information books and textbooks, employ a simple pattern. The expository form usually has three basic parts: an introduction, a development, and a conclusion. It's that simple. And the conclusion is often the most important part.

An efficient reader, limited by time, would first look at the beginning and ending sections in a work of nonfiction. He does this because he knows that the most important parts of the material are usually contained in those sections. The middle part will be the least important. It often goes like this: the author either states his or her main point in the beginning, tells you where they're going, or perhaps poses a question. Next, they develop their points, giving you the reasoning behind their ideas. Finally, you're led to the conclusion.

In a textbook or any material which is much longer than an article, you will usually find this basic pattern repeating itself within the overall pattern. For example, the author of a whole book would use the introduction, or the first chapter, to present the main idea or thesis. This chapter would be written using the same formula: first, the presentation of the main point; a development; and then a conclusion. The subsequent chapters, all having their own main point, and organized accordingly, would be parts of the development of the whole book's main idea. And the final chapter, afterword, or epilogue, would usually serve as a device for drawing together the author's main ideas.

Do the following exercises and find out for yourself how this works.

EXERCISE NO. 16

Materials: *A book of nonfiction, a text, a news story downloaded from the internet, or a magazine with long articles (not short stories). It's your choice.*
Pencil or pen (or your PC if you prefer)
Paper

Purpose: *Practice discovering the organization pattern of non-fiction*

1. Select any short chapter or article to read. *Make certain that it is not fiction.*

2. Read the first two to four paragraphs (enough to tell you what this will be about), then skip to the end and read the last two to four paragraphs (there should be concluding statements summing things up).
    Make a recall pattern without referring back to the passage. Try to put down what the passage is about, its main point and whatever else you remember, using just key words or phrases.

3. Read the whole chapter or article from the beginning. Without referring back to the first recall pattern, write down your recall on the other side of the paper or on a new screen.

Compare the amount of information you got from reading the chapter with what you got from reading just the beginning and ending paragraphs. Take into consideration the different amounts of time spent.

Undoubtedly, you got more from reading the whole passage than from just reading the beginning and ending paragraphs. If you hadn't, the writer's editor certainly would have cut all of those middle passages. Just how much more of importance there was is impossible to generalize for different books. Sometimes the middle parts are relatively unimportant illustrations and examples; other times they are careful point-by-point developments of difficult ideas.

But if you just had a limited amount of time, or *if your purpose were only to know the main idea,* would you have spent your time better reading the whole passage—as far as your time would permit—or reading the beginning and ending paragraphs? Perhaps it has already occurred to you that the well-trained reader would also speed up in the less important passages and slow down where the more difficult ideas are. This is something that you can begin doing as well.

Just as it is important to begin the habit of deciding a reading purpose before you read anything, it is also important to take a few seconds to determine the organization of the material so that you can begin developing a plan on how you will attack it. In other words, you are learning to decide what you want from the material, and the quickest way to get it.

THE FORMS OF FICTION

The organization forms of fiction are the more difficult. Some people think that fiction is the easiest, and in a way that is true. Almost everybody can relate to it, because it is based on common human experience. Everyone can't relate to expository writing. "Life of the Monkeys on Gibraltar" may not interest you, and you may know very little about monkeys. But everyone is familiar with the basic human emotions, so even characters in foreign lands with different customs and manners can still be quite engaging.

In spite of fiction's deceptively simple appearance, its structure and organization are often difficult. Whereas expository writing is a form of communication of information, fiction is an art form. And it is a part of most artists' technique to conceal the structure. The basic purpose of fiction is not to inform you or instruct you, but rather to involve you. To complicate things further, there are probably as many organizational patterns as there are authors.

The simplest and best proposal I have ever heard comes from the wife of the late Walter Pitkin, author of many best-selling books including the well-known *Life Begins at Forty* and one of the first books on rapid reading. Katharine and Walter were wonderful and close friends of my family. Katharine had worked for years with Walter, on his books helping him to put them together. She gave this advice to me when I was about 14 and struggling to write a short story for English class. "A short story is simply a tale of one character who gets into a jam and proceeds to get out of it." That simple idea helped me get out of my jam, finishing that story. When I began teaching rapid reading many years later, its wisdom became even more apparent to me.

The basic structure of most fiction is simply that we are initially presented with one or more characters trying to do something. Then the story usually gets complicated, like getting into a jam, after which it is resolved. You'll find this pattern repeating itself not only in short stories, but also in novels. Within a chapter you will find this pattern, or possibly the pattern will overlap with others, one character involved with his jam and another in hers.

With careful application, the awareness of various forms of writing will immediately help you to become more efficient. Do not despair, however, if when first using this new knowledge you slow down a bit. Sometimes that happens when learning a new technique, even one that will eventually allow you to go much faster.

In a few chapters, when you start using higher reading speeds, applying different purposes to different reading situations, and learning various other techniques, you will find your efficiency in reading growing like the proverbial snowball.

TURN TO PAGE 34 FOR THE PRACTICE DRILLS TO COMPLETE TODAY'S WORK.

1 2

Don't Let Turning Pages Slow You Down

While you've been doing the drills, you may have wished for an easier way to use your hand to reach your goal. There are ways to do it, and now is the time to learn some of them. In this chapter, you will learn a new hand movement and a new way of turning pages. Both will enable you to do even faster drilling. That, of course, means higher reading rates ultimately because the faster you drill, the faster you will soon be able to read.

"Dusting"

The first hand movement you were given was an underlining movement. The second one is quite different, It is called "dusting" because it is somewhat like dusting the lines of print on the page. Here is how to do it:

> Place your whole hand just under the top line of print on a page; your middle finger should be in about the center of the line. Your hand should be relaxed and there should be spaces between your fingers. Now begin brushing your fingers from side to side, from one margin to the other, as though you were erasing the print, very quickly. As you are dusting, slowly begin pulling your hand down the page.

The first use of dusting will be when you are doing the practice reading on the Double/Triple Drill. In other words, it is for practice reading and not for your reading. To see how well it works, hold your hand outstretched in front of any object, such as a pencil. Begin dusting as quickly as you can over the object. When you do it quickly, you can see right "through" your fingers and see the object quite distinctly. If you do it slowly, then it is very hard to see the object. Figure 6 illustrates what it looks like when you are using it to drill.

Be certain to practice doing this hand movement in your own book before using it in the next exercise. Open to any page and follow the instructions below. Remember, though, you're not reading.

FIGURE 6. THE DUSTING HAND MOVEMENT

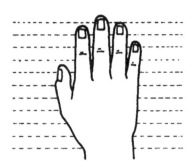

Starting position of the hand

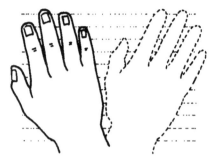

View of the hand dusting

1.   Place your hand palm down, relaxed with your fingers slightly spread, underneath the top line of print.

2.   Begin dusting the line, moving your whole hand just from the wrist (not the whole arm), moving from the left margin very quickly to the right margin and back again. Be sure to keep your hand moving back and forth. Keep the action continuous and avoid any jerkiness.

3.   As your hand is dusting, slowly draw your arm down the page so that you have "dusted" the whole page. Cover the whole page in ten seconds or less. You may wish to count "one—and, two—and, three—and . . ." up to ten, until you can do it easily. After practicing a few pages, you should be ready to use this hand movement in a Double/Triple Drill.

EXERCISE NO. 17

Materials: *An easy book*
        Pencil or pen
        Timing device

1.   Put a "1" where you will start reading.
      Read for one minute, using your hand.
      Make a mark, "2," where you stop reading.
      Optional: Compute your reading rate.

2.   Re-read the same passage, in one minute, try to go faster and farther.
      Make a new mark, "3," where you stopped reading.

3. Determine approximately how much you have read between points "1" and "3"; set up a new section after point "3" and ending at point "4."
    Practice read from point "1" to "point "4" in one minute, using dusting. Be careful not to go too fast!
    Try to pace your practice reading to the amount of time given.

4. Set up another section approximately equal to the amount of material between points "3" and "4," ending in point "5."
    Practice read from point "1" to point "5" in one minute, using dusting.

5. From point "5" read as fast as you can for one minute.
    Use the underlining hand movement.
    Make a new mark "X" where you stopped reading.
    Compute your reading rate, from "5" to "X," and record it on your progress profile.

Did you find it much easier to reach your goal? Perhaps you are wondering why this wasn't introduced when the Double/Triple Drill was first given. The reason is simple: until you have experienced trying to get comprehension when doubling and tripling, and thus understand the concept of correct drilling, you are not ready for this. In other words, when you are practice reading you must first of all reach the mark in the set amount of time, and whether or not you understand anything is not important. BUT, you must, at the same time, be trying to get something out of the material. So when you use dusting you must still be trying to get something out of the passage. It merely allows you to make your mark much more easily.

THE GLORIOUS SAGA OF THE WINDSHIELD WIPER

This hand motion has had many variations and some of the names will give you a good idea of a few: the windshield wiper, the broom, brushing, and so on. My most unusual experience with hand motions was while teaching in Pittsburgh when an assistant teacher called me from my office quickly, to observe a certain well-known student during a drill session. He was well known to us because he was rather unusual: a good student who worked hard, achieved good results, but who interpreted our instructions very literally on occasion. In this instance he was busy executing "the windshield wiper" over his book: with his thumb anchored to the end of his eyebrow closest to his ear, his hand was flapping up and down as a windshield wiper. And then as he began the next page he would switch hands and eyes as well. To get him to do the hand motion on the page required coming up with a new name for it; thus I decided upon "dusting," and it worked.

SOLVING A NONREADING PROBLEM

At this time, you may be having some difficulty turning the pages of your book. If you have been using paperback books, you may find that it is hard to get the pages to lie flat. If you are using hardcover books, you may find that you have to stop to turn the page right in the middle of the drill—thus losing valuable time. There are solutions to both of these problems, and this is the time to learn them.

First, you must know how to "relax" a book because if it is stiff and new it won't lie flat when you want it to. And as you've probably discovered, it must lay reasonably flat for ease of page turning and hand movements. The solution is simple; just follow the directions with the illustrations in Figure 7.

Place the spine of the book on a flat surface. Hold the book with both hands, vertically to the surface. (Figure 7A)

Open just the front and back covers and run your thumbs up and down the pages as close to the binding as you can. (Figure 7B)

Take a few pages from the front, and a few pages from the back, and again run your thumbs up and down the binding. Continue this, a few pages at a time, till you reach the center. (Figure 7C)

When finished, ruffle all of the pages several times to make them more supple. (Figure 7D) A few words of caution when you are "relaxing" a book. Be careful not to open it up in the very center and start to run your thumbs up and down the binding. This may well crack the binding of the book, especially with paperbacks which are usually glued together and need very careful handling. Always work from the outside in.

FIGURE 7. FOUR STEPS TO "RELAXING" A BOOK

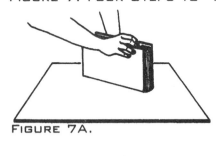

FIGURE 7A.

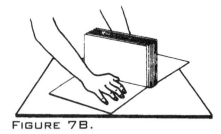

FIGURE 7B.

FIGURE 7C.

FIGURE 7D.

And even being careful, some paperback books are bound with such an eye for profit (and so little glue) that it is impossible to "relax" them without cracking the binding.

TURNING PAGES THE FAST WAY

In Chapter Three, you learned that the best position for a book is at a 45 degree angle to the table on which it is resting. To achieve this, it is easiest to set a two or three inch thick book behind and under the book you are reading, as in Figure 8.

Once this is done, the easiest way to turn pages is with the hand that you are not using to pace your reading. Right-handers would use their left hand, and left-handers their right. At first, this may seem awkward, but it will become quite easy with a little practice. And don't think that it's not worth the trouble to learn. If you expect to move up into the higher reading rates, it is absolutely vital for the practicing. So, it is best to learn this now and make it a comfortable habit. Then, when you are ready to move on, you will have to concentrate only on the reading skills, not on purely mechanical skills.

To turn pages in this new manner, follow the instructions with the illustrations in Figure 9.

Right-handers grasp the book with the left hand holding the center binding; the arm should be curled up around the book.

While the right hand is pacing down the left page, the left hand is picking up the corner of the right page in preparation for turning it.

As the right hand nears the bottom of the right page, the left hand begins to turn the page.

Without stopping, the left hand turns the page and the right hand returns to the left side to begin pacing on the new (left side) page. In this type of page turning, the left-hander obviously has the advantage. He or she can turn with their right hand as they pace with their left, probably the way they used to do. The left-hander should do all of the hand movements in reverse. With the page turning, you may (only if you are left handed) turn the pages either from the bottom or from the top, whichever you find easier.

FIGURE 8. THE BEST POSITION FOR A BOOK

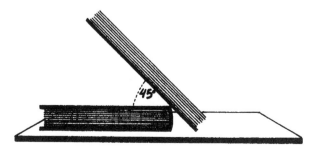

FIGURE 9. RAPID PAGE TURNING

FIGURE 9A.

FIGURE 9B.

FIGURE 9C.

FIGURE 9D.

To practice page turning, it is easiest to do it as part of a drill. Here is a page-turning drill which you can do with the dusting hand movement, thus getting practice with both of them.

EXERCISE NO. 18

Materials: *Any book*

1. Relax the book in order to make certain that the pages will lie flat.
    Start from the outside and work in toward the center; then ruffle the pages.
2. Propping the book up on another book in order to achieve a 45° angle, hold the book open with your left hand (for right-handers) and place your right pacing hand on the left page.
3. Dust down the left page in about ten seconds.
    Count to ten as you go, aloud or silently.
    The left hand should be preparing to turn the page by picking it up a bit.
4. Dust down the right page in about ten seconds.
    As you near the bottom, turn the page with your left hand.
    Your right hand should come back to the "new" left page and immediately begin dusting down that page.
5. Continue doing this for several pages until you can do it fairly easily.

Once you've mastered these mechanical skills, which should take only a few days of practice, you'll be ready to move ahead.

GETTING AHEAD

If you wish to become really adept with these mechanical skills and fully prepared for the drilling that lies ahead, then practice the page turning and dusting with this variation: after mastering Exercise No. 18 at ten seconds per page, do it at eight seconds per page, then six seconds per page, finally working down to two seconds per page. When you can do this easily, turning pages without missing a beat, then you've mastered these easy mechanical skills.

TURN TO PAGE 34 FOR THE PRACTICE DRILLS TO COMPLETE TODAY'S WORK.

Practice Drills for Week 3

As soon as you have completed Chapters One through Twelve, having spent a good six days doing the first set of Practice Drills, then you should begin doing this next set. First spend an entire session doing this new section of drills. Then on the subsequent days read a new chapter each day, beginning with Chapter Thirteen, and follow it by repeating these drills, or at least as many as you can do.

Always do the drills in order, preferably after having finished the day's chapter. As before, if you practice only twenty minutes a day, do just the first drill. If you practice forty minutes a day, then do the first and second drills, etc.

If you practice more than an hour a day, it may be wise to break up the practicing. For instance, a very highly motivated student who wishes to achieve very high rates and who also has two or more hours a day for practice, should spend two different sessions practicing. About one and a half hours is the maximum time that you should practice for any single practice period.

Materials You Will Need for This Week's Drills

A timing device.
Pen or pencil.
Paper. Preferably unlined $8\frac{1}{2} \times 11$ inches.
One or two books from your list.

DRILL NO. 5

Materials: Basic List   Purpose: Double your reading rate
Estimated Time: 20 Minutes   Objective: Make the mark with ease

---

THIS DRILL MAY BE REPEATED THREE TIMES PER SESSION

Diagram:

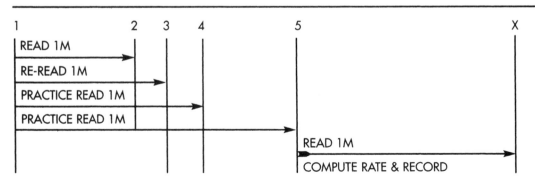

Explanation:

---

1. Make a mark, "1," where you will begin, reading.
   Read for one minute, using your hand.
   Mark where you stop reading with a "2."
   Optional: Compute your reading rate.

Reading Purpose: Understanding the story as you're reading it. You do not need to remember anything to meet this purpose. See how fast you can meet your purpose.

2. Re-read the same passage, go faster and farther, for one minute.
   Mark the new ending point with a "3."
3. Mark a new passage from "3" to a new point, "4," that is approximately equal to the amount from "1" to "3." Practice read from "1" to "4" in one minute.
4. Mark a new passage from "4" to a new point, "5," that is approximately equal to the amount from "3" to "4." Practice read from "1" to "5" in one minute.

CAUTION: Repeat step 4 until you can make the mark when practice reading before going on to step 5.

5. From "5" read as fast as you can for one minute. Make a mark, "X," where you stop reading. Compute your reading rate, from "5" to "X," and record it on your progress profile.

DRILL NO. 6

Materials: Basic List
Estimated Time: 25 Minutes

Purpose: Double your reading rate
Objective: Make the mark with ease

NOTE: THIS IS A VARIATION OF DRILL NO. 5 WITH AN EMPHASIS ON COMPRE-HENSION AND RECALL

Diagram:

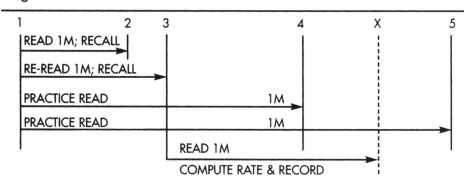

Explanation:

---

1. Make a mark, "1," where you will begin reading.
   Read from the "1" as far as you can for one minute. Mark where you stop with a "2."
   Begin a recall pattern; start with what it's about on a diagonal line.

2. Re-read the same passage, go faster and farther. Mark the new ending point with a "3."
   Add to your recall.

3. Mark a new passage from "3" to a new point, "4," that is approximately equal to the amount from "1" to "3."
   Practice read from "1" to "4" in one minute.

4. Mark a new passage from "4" to a new point, "5," that is approximately equal to the amount from "3" to "4."
   Practice read from "1" to "5" in one minute.

5. Go back to "3" and read as fast as you can for one minute. Make an "X" mark where you stop reading. Add to your recall or begin a new one for no more than one minute. Compute your reading rate, "3" to "X," and record it on your progress profile.

DRILL NO. 7

Materials: Basic List

Estimated Time: 10 minutes

Purpose: Learn to quickly identify what a paragraph is about

Objective: See how many paragraphs you can do in 5 minutes

1. Select a new passage of material from one of your books. Use paragraphs of four to ten lines, if possible.

2. Using your hand, read a paragraph as quickly as you can, keeping your reading purpose in mind.

Reading Purpose: Only to find what the paragraph is about.

3. Without looking back at the paragraph, draw a short diagonal line on a piece of paper. You should be able to fit at least six on one side of a sheet of paper. Write on the diagonal line what you recall from the paragraph. This should be only a word or a very short phrase.

4. If you remember anything else, write other details on branch lines, putting them on alternate sides from the bottom up.

CAUTION: Remember, to recall details is NOT your Reading Purpose, only to know what it's about.

5. Record on your progress profile how many paragraphs you were able to do in five minutes. You should be able to do more each day if you do the exercise in the same book or in books of similar difficulty.

DRILL NO. 8

Materials: Basic List	Purpose: Experience applying new techniques in daily reading
Estimated Time: 10 minutes	Objective: Sustain a higher reading rate than your beginning rate

---

THIS DRILL MAY BE REPEATED BUT IT IS BEST TO DO IT AFTER DRILL 5 OR 6

Diagram:

---

1 -- ABOUT 10 PAGE SECTION -- 2

PRACTICE READ 10 sec/page: Use "DUSTING" ⟶

PRACTICE READ 5 sec/page: Use "DUSTING" ⟶

READ: Use "UNDERLINING" & Observe Purpose ⟶

Explanation:

---

1. Select a section or chapter of about ten pages from one of the books on your list. Be prepared to time how long you will be reading.
2. Practice read the entire section using the dusting hand movement at about ten seconds per page (you may count to yourself, "One, two, . . . ," if it will help). Take no more than one-and-a-half minutes for ten pages.
3. Practice read the entire section at about five seconds per page. Take no more than one minute for ten pages.
4. Noting your time, read the entire section as fast as you can, keeping in mind your reading purpose.

READING PURPOSE: Awareness of basic story line only. If you're getting more than this, go faster.

5. Compute your rate; then record it on your progress profile. To compute your rate: First, find the total number of words read (take average number of words per line, multiply times number of lines read). Second, divide the number of minutes into the number of words read. EXAMPLE: Pages read: $9\frac{1}{2}$ Words per line: 8 Lines read: 212 Total number of words read: $8 \times 212 = 1696$ Time used for reading: $3\frac{1}{2}$ minutes To find words per minute: $1696 \div 3.5 = 484$ WPM

13

Make Difficult Reading Easy

Generally—while reading—you don't have to worry about whether or not you can understand the passage. However, there are exceptions. If you are a student, you might be assigned a very difficult piece of material. You might understand each word in a paragraph, but you might not understand the meaning of the paragraph. This may be due to the fact that the author's writing is too abstract.

How Abstract the Writing Is Affects Your Understanding

When we're reading, it is more difficult, and takes more time, to read abstract writing than concrete or specific writing. This is because when you come across an abstraction, you must often stop and form a model, a specific example, in your mind in order to understand it. For instance, if I mentioned "the theory of relativity," in order to understand that phrase, you must review in your mind just what that theory is (if you know it at all). But if I said "two apples and two apples are four apples," you would have no trouble knowing what I mean.

Similarly, if a writer was discussing a "colored beverage container," you must figure out what he means. "Colored" is not specific; it can mean many different colors. "Beverage" can also mean many things, as can "container," which might mean a glass, a pitcher, or a milk can. But if the writer simply wrote about a "red coffee mug" you would instantly know what he meant.

Much difficulty in reading comprehension comes when an author is writing on an abstract level. Luckily, there are ways of tackling these reading problems. It was only recently discovered that everybody writes and speaks in a certain pattern. When you understand how all writers write, you can usually analyze difficult writing and find the meaning. This can help greatly in developing better reading comprehension.

How People Write and Speak

When people write or speak, they do so in "paragraphs," or groupings of sentences around a single thought. They usually start by telling you about what they're going to write, and then just tell you more about it. It helps to know when the subject or topic is first introduced that it may be on an "abstract" level. This is often the point when understanding may be difficult.

As writers or speakers continue their "paragraph," they will become more specific and concrete, and thus become easier to understand. That's because the rest of the "paragraph" either gives examples or explanations about the first part. Usually, the examples or explanations become more and more specific and easy to understand. In working with difficult passages, if you cannot understand one part, you can usually understand another part. If you learn how to grasp the relationship of one part to another, it makes understanding difficult passages much simpler.

LEVELS OF GENERALITY

Since a sentence is more or less abstract, general or specific, we can give it a "grade" which tells us just how abstract it is. Developing this awareness is the key to cutting through difficult passages. Fortunately, it is quite easy to do.

Perhaps 95 percent of the time the topic sentence, the first sentence of any paragraph, is given a grade of "1," which means that it is on the most general level. Any sentence which becomes more specific (easier to understand) receives a higher grade or number. This is easy to determine because a sentence can do only two things. It can tell you more about the topic sentence, or it can tell you more about the sentence immediately preceding it.

Usually only three patterns exist, and they are easy to identify. Here is one of them:

A blue coat was left in the check room. Its sleeve was torn. No one knew whose it was.

In this case, the first sentence tells us what the paragraph is about, and therefore receives a grade of "1." It is the most general sentence. The second sentence, "Its sleeve was torn," tells us *more* about the "blue coat." Since it has become more specific, we'll give it a grade of "2." The third sentence does the same thing. "It" refers back to the topic sentence, but does *not* tell us anything more about the sleeve. Therefore it also gets a "2." This is how you would diagram the paragraph:

Level "1"	A blue coat was left in the check room.	
Level "2"	Its sleeve was torn.	No one knew whose it was.

The second pattern is as easy to identify as the first one. In the second pattern, each sentence tells you more about the sentence just before it. Changing the above paragraph a bit makes it easy to see:

A blue coat was left in the check room. Its sleeve was torn. Apparently it had been done with a knife.

Again the first sentence receives a grade of "1," as it is still the most general (and the topic) sentence. The second sentence is still doing the same thing as in the first pattern, telling us more about the first one. It therefore still receives a grade of "2." The new third sentence is doing something different. Unlike the first paragraph, it is *not* referring directly back to the topic sentence. It is telling you more about the sentence just before it. Since it is becoming more specific, we give it a grade of "3." Here is how to diagram it.

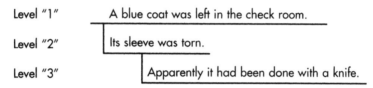

Level "1"   A blue coat was left in the check room.

Level "2"   Its sleeve was torn.

Level "3"   Apparently it had been done with a knife.

Quite simply, all a sentence can do is tell you more about the one just before it, or refer back to another, usually the topic sentence. Of course, you can have a variation of the two basic patterns, or a cross between the two, which will give you a third type of pattern:

A blue coat was left in the check room. Its sleeve was torn. Apparently it had been done with a knife. No one knew whose it was.

In this case everything starts out exactly as in the second example:

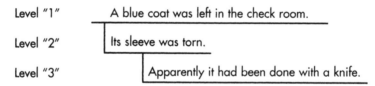

Level "1"   A blue coat was left in the check room.

Level "2"   Its sleeve was torn.

Level "3"   Apparently it had been done with a knife.

The last sentence is tricky. "No one knew whose it was" does *not* tell you anything more about the sentence just before it, but refers back to the topic sentence. Therefore it moves back up to a grade of "2."

If you can understand these simple patterns, then you know the secret of how writers write and how speakers speak. People begin with a *general* sentence, and then move downward, telling you *more specifically* about the subject. Sometimes they move back up, and then down again.

THE "TESTING" QUESTION

To find out whether a sentence refers back to any other sentence, simply ask yourself *what* in the sentence refers back to *something* in the other one. If you have any doubt (possibly it could refer to something in either of two sentences), ask which of the two sentences it is talking *more* about. Sometimes the two sentences use the same word.

Often a pronoun ("its") in one refers back to a noun ("coat") in the prior one. A synonym (word that means the same thing) or phrase might refer back to a single word. So, it can sometimes be hard, but there is always some word or phrase that refers back to another word or phrase to give you a clue. Now see how many you can identify.

EXERCISE NO. 19

Materials: *Paper*
Pen or pencil

1. In the paragraphs below find whether the third sentence is a level "2" or level "3" (tells you more about the first sentence or the second one). Diagram it on your paper.

    Example
    Mary Jones lives in Bethesda, Maryland. She enjoys playing sports. She loves rollerblading best of all.

    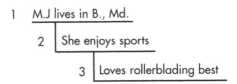

    A.   Tom Moody is a very unhappy student. He failed his marketing test. He hadn't studied for it.
    B.   Frank North lives in New York City. He enjoys surfing the internet. He is also a good student.
    C.   Polly Rankin comes from Cleveland, Ohio. She is a good student. She is also a member of many clubs.
    D.   Ronald Bricke loves to design. He designs the interiors of homes and offices. Sometimes he designs fabrics and wallpapers.
    E.   Lori Mammen lives in Florida. She used to live in Toronto, Canada. Now she prefers the warmer climate of Florida to that of Toronto.
    F.   Simone Beck is an inventive cook. She manages to balance her career and home life and still comes up with great meals. Her husband says she should try catering.
    G.   Sarah Bridges is bright student with dreams of attending an Ivy League school. She is on the honors list and is active in many extra-curricular organizations. She was voted "most likely to succeed."
    H.   Doug Wood has one of the sunniest dispositions of anyone I know. Even when he is sick, he seems to have a joke for everyone. Also there is always a smile on his face.

I.   Verla Nielsen is a wonderful teacher. One of her great qualities is patience. She can teach both adults and young people equally well.

J.   Anne is a very good athlete. Soccer is one of her favorite sports. She is happiest playing defense.

If you aren't sure of the answers to some of these, check the end of the chapter. But first see if you can do it by yourself. All you must do is find whether the third sentence tells *more* about the first one or the second one. And there is always word or a phrase which refers back to another *one in the sentence it connects with*.

If you've gotten pretty good with the three-sentence paragraphs, then it's time to try some examples with four sentences. In this case, the first sentence is the topic sentence and tells you what the paragraph is about. The second sentence, in all the paragraphs below, drops to a second level telling you something more about the first. The third sentence can tell you more about either the first or the second, and therefore it can be a level "2" or "3." The fourth sentence, depending on the one before it, could be a level "2," "3" or "4." Good luck!

EXERCISE NO. 20

Materials: *Paper*
Pen or pencil

1.   In the paragraphs below find whether the third sentence is a level "2" or a level "3" and diagram it on your paper.

2.   Then find whether the fourth sentence is a level "2" (telling more about the first one), a level "3" (telling more about the second one), or a level "4" (telling more about the third one) and add it to your diagram.

<u>Example</u>
Mary Jones lives in Bethesda, Maryland. She enjoys playing sports. She is also a good student. Math is her favorite subject.

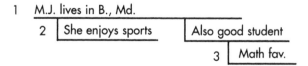

A.   John Franklyn lives in Tempe, Arizona. He enjoys playing sports. He is captain of the rugby team. But it is not his favorite sport.

B.   Alan Bell lives in New York City. He loves the country almost as much as the city. Vermont is his favorite country area. He loves to ski in Vermont.

    C.   Bonnie Raston lives in Los Angeles. She loves school. Business administration is her favorite subject. She also loves sports.

    D.   Mark Temple lives in Tiburon, California. His home is high on a hill. He is a good athlete and a good student. He used to play in Little League.

    E.   Steve Hudner lives in Tempe, Arizona. He enjoys playing sports. He is captain of the basketball team. Squash is his favorite sport.

It may take a little time to master the ability to quickly find whether a sentence is dropping or going up. But it is well worth learning, because once you can do this you'll find that you can analyze almost any difficult passage. Then, when you can't understand part of a passage, usually the most general part, you simply move down to where it becomes more specific. There's always a "concrete" part that you'll be able to understand. Once you can understand one part, then that should help you to understand the harder parts. Difficult reading can become easy once you know the techniques. In fact, you might think of it as a kind of intellectual sport, which it really is.

Before you begin your practice drilling for the day, if you want to see explanations of the various passages, here they are.

KEY TO EXERCISE 19: First the levels are given for all the sentences of each paragraph, then what word or phrase relates back to which in the other sentence.
A: "1"/"2"/"3" ("it" tells more about the "marketing test")
B: "1"/"2"/"2" ("good student" tells more about "Frank," nothing more about "surfing the internet")
C: "1"/"2"/"2" ("member of clubs" tells more about "Polly," nothing about "student")
D: "1"/"2"/"2" ("fabrics . . . wallpapers" tells more about "Ronald," not about "interiors")
E: "1"/"2"/"2" ("prefers . . . climate" tells more about "Lori," *not as much* about "Toronto")
F: "1"/"2"/"3" ("Balance" tells more about "Simone" not about "cook.")
G: "1"/"2"/"2" ("lives" tells more about "Sarah," nothing about "honors list")
H: "1"/"2"/"2" ("smile" tells more about "Doug," not about "sick" or "joke")
I: "1"/"2"/"2" ("teach . . . well" tells more about "Verla," nothing about "patience")
J: "1"/"2"/"3" ("Defense" refers back to "soccer" *more* than to "athlete")

KEY TO EXERCISE 20: First the levels are given for all the sentences of each paragraph, then the words which relate to the third and fourth sentences.
A: "1"/"2"/"3"/"4" ("rugby team" refers back to "sports," "it is not . . ." to "rugby")
B: "1"/"2"/"3"/"4" ("country area" refers to "country," "Vermont" to "Vermont")

C: "1"/"2"/"3"/"2" ("favorite subject" refers to "school," "loves sports" refers back to Bonnie because it doesn't tell us more about "Business Adninistration" or "school")

D: "1"/"2"/"2"/"3" ("good athlete and student" refer to "Mark" because they tells us nothing about "home," "Little League" tells more about "athlete")

E: "1"/"2"/"3"/"3" ("basketball team" refers to "sports," "squash" also refers back to "sports" since it tells us nothing more about "basketball")

TURN TO PAGE 72 FOR THE PRACTICE DRILLS TO COMPLETE TODAY'S WORK.

14

HOW PEOPLE READ REALLY FAST

The attempt to speed up our reading is a recent phenomenon. It came about because of the tremendous increase in the amount of printed and electronic material being published, and because, in our modern world, there are more and more demands on our time. Longer novels were once preferred because people had quiet evenings at home without television, the internet, radio, e-mail, movies, CDs, cell phones, laptops or even cars. Those "quieter" days are gone forever.

Early attempts to increase reading rates involved the use of various machines, such as a device called the tachistoscope and various reading pacers. They would usually produce good results while the students were using them, but the reading speeds tended to fall down when the machines were taken away.

EVELYN WOOD'S REMARKABLE AND SIMPLE DISCOVERY

More than fifty years ago, Evelyn Wood, then a counselor and reading teacher in a junior high school just outside Salt Lake City, began doing research on rapid reading. She was aware that some people could read much faster than was then believed possible. At that time, learning theories couldn't account for anyone being able to read much faster than 400 words per minute. But a friend and teacher of hers, Dr. Lowell Lees of the University of Utah, was astonishingly fast. When she tested him, he read over 6,000 words per minute with excellent comprehension. It was not surprising that he had a reputation as a "walking encyclopedia."

She sought out others, and eventually found over 100 persons who could read faster than 1,500 words per minute. She selected that rate as a minimum and studied these people in order to determine what they were doing, how they were doing it, and how they had learned to do it. She found out what they were doing, but not how they had learned to do it. Many of them were not aware that they were reading "differently." They just did it.

Her next step was to try to teach herself to read fast. She told me that it was a very difficult and frustrating process. She used to practice summers while she and her husband were at their cabin up in one of the canyons just outside of Salt Lake City. Once, while practicing in the book *Green Mansions*, she became so angry at her inability to read fast that she threw the book across a little creek. After picking the book up and while dusting the dirt off its pages, she realized that the movement of her hand was causing her to see and read more than one word at a time. Thus, she discovered the use of the hand as a pacer for her reading.

THE DIFFERENCES BETWEEN SLOW AND FAST READERS

The difference between these naturally fast readers and others that we can observe is the difference in the eye movements. As you know, in order for the eyes to see, they make tiny stops during which they register an impression, like a picture. The average reader's eyes are somewhat like a cursor moving across a screen: they jump from word to word and at the end of the line of print they return quickly to the left margin to start over again. A diagram of these eye movements looks like this:

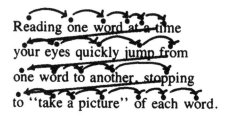

When Evelyn Wood examined the faster readers' eyes, she found a different movement. Their eyes made fewer stops, indicating that they were seeing more than one word at a time. In fact, anyone reading faster than 240 words per minute is doing this. Such eye movements might look like this:

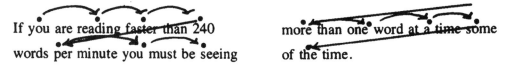

But with the very fast readers two more remarkable things were happening. Instead of moving along a line, their eyes tended to move downward on a diagonal line, such as this:

The eye movements of faster readers
tend to be downward rather than along
a line, indicating a diagonal pattern.

But even more astonishing, they also made stops on the return sweep rather than just returning to the left margin as the eyes of most readers would. It would therefore appear that they were reading backwards some of the time. Whatever they were doing, the eye movement pattern would look like this:

The astonishing thing about the eye
movements of naturally rapid readers
is that they are generally downward,
in a diagonal zig-zag pattern, and
they make stops both going from
left-to-right as well as from right-
to-left.

There's nothing mysterious about this pattern. Actually, it's completely natural. You look at a photograph or drawing in the same way. Your eyes sweep all over it. They don't look at just one point, nor do they go from detail to detail the way you were taught to read. In fact, that would be rather silly. Imagine looking at a photograph of a brick wall and having to look at each brick, from left to right, starting at the top and working your way down.

HOW TO SEE EYE MOVEMENTS

You may be wondering how to see eye movements. It's not really difficult, and it is rather interesting. Ask someone to read something while sitting at a table; have him or her read slowly at first. If you sit or crouch directly opposite them, watch their eyes, and soon you'll be able to see the little jerky stops the eyes make as they stop to "see" words. The sudden return sweep to begin the next line is also easy to see.

Eye movements can even be observed under difficult conditions. Sometimes a person has "heavy" eyelids, and it is difficult to see the eyes themselves. But a careful observer can even see the movements "through" the eyelids. It is also sometimes possible to observe the movements from a person's side. With a little experience, you'll see how easy it is.

HOW MUCH CAN THE EYES SEE?

We often assume that we can see only one word, maybe two, at a time. But this is not the case. The eyes see in a circle, not in a "line," and they can see pretty clearly an area about the size of a half dollar. So, whether you are aware of it or not, you are always seeing more than one word at a time. In fact, it is impossible to see just one word at a time. See for yourself. Look at the word "Bob" in the center of the paragraph below. See if it's possible to see only "Bob":

> Far along the riverbank there was a small shack. At least it looked like a shack. I could see a small column of smoke coming from what appeared to be a chimney. Bob could also see the smoke. We were both a little anxious as the Ranger told us that no one had been in this part of the forest for many months.

You probably quickly realized that you could not see only "Bob," but also the words on both sides of "Bob," the words above and below—and maybe even more. When you look at a picture, your eyes are using all of their seeing ability: your eyes are moving around taking it all in. But when you have been reading, you have been going word by word, saying each word to yourself, *pretending* as though you did not see the other words. But now you know that you *can* see more than one word at a time.

WHY YOU CAN'T UNDERSTAND LOTS OF WORDS AT A TIME

You must be wondering why you can't understand all of these words if you can see them. Maybe it has occurred to you that it must be rather difficult to try to understand words when they are out of order, one being on top of the other and so forth. Basically, you can't understand the other words because you have been trained to understand a word by seeing it and saying it to yourself. Now you must learn how to comprehend groups of words. Don't get frightened, though. It's not as hard as you might think (though it does take practice). In fact, you've already started doing it in a small way.

When you first started to read you probably looked at each individual letter. But then you started seeing groups of letters together, possibly first syllables, or parts of words, then whole words. Now when you look at a word, for example "difficult," you do not look at each letter. You see all of the letters as a whole. And you are not conscious of "reading" the letters from left to right or from right to left—you just look at the *meaning* of the word. This is very much the way it "feels" to read groups of words at a time.

TAKING THE FIRST STEP

The first step is a new hand movement. It's not very difficult, but it must be done very quickly. The purpose is to practice *seeing* groups of words at a time—not reading them—because that's the first step in learning to read really quickly.

The new hand movement is called "circling" because that's what you do: make lots of small circles as you move across a passage of print. Using your index finger, follow the pattern shown in Figure 10, coming across one line, then dropping down three or more lines and circling very quickly as your finger comes back from right-to-left.

FIGURE 10. THE CIRCLING HAND MOVEMENT

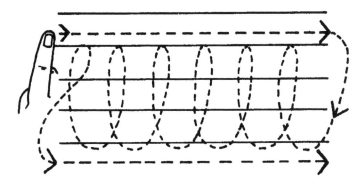

It is very important to do the circling very quickly. When you do it quickly the fast movement attracts your eye and you see "through" your fingers and are able to look at all of the words in the circles of three or more lines that you're circling.

You are not expected to be reading these words. If you do the circling slowly, you will block the words and not accomplish anything. At first you should count as you go (one-and, two-and, three-and, one-and, etc.) and take no longer than three seconds maximum to underline and come back doing the circling. Use the exercise below to practice so that you'll be ready to take the next step tomorrow. Before you go on, as tempting as it may be, be sure you've done your practice drilling for today.

EXERCISE NO. 21

Materials: *Any book*

1. Start at the beginning of any chapter.
   Practice circling by underlining the first line of a paragraph with your index finger; then drop down three or more lines and make quick circles coming back from right to left, drop down one line and begin again.
2. Make certain that you are seeing all of the words (*not* reading!): a simple test is simply to be aware that all of the words you've seen are English words or whatever language you're reading in.
3. Practice this for five minutes or until you find the hand movement easy and comfortable. You may repeat the same chapter as often as you wish.

TURN TO PAGE 72 FOR THE PRACTICE DRILLS TO COMPLETE TODAY'S WORK.

15

LEARN TO READ AS FAST AS YOU THINK

There are a great many people who can read at rates of several thousand words per minute and get good comprehension. There are also many who read quite slowly and have unacceptable comprehension. And there are fast readers with poor comprehension. Or slow readers with excellent comprehension.

Although you can probably find some reading "expert" who says that you can't read faster than such-and-such rate (I've read, or heard it argued, that it is "impossible" to read faster than 400 words per minute, though many "experts" admit rates up to around 1,200 words per minute), most teachers of efficient reading would agree that you can easily learn to read from two to three times faster than you do now. And instances of persons reading from five to ten times faster than they began are also very common.

Disagreement over how fast people can read seems to revolve around a definition of the word "reading." For our purposes, I define "reading" as looking at printed words and getting enough meaning from them to satisfy your purpose. Finding a name in a phone book would be reading, as would going through a novel or studying a textbook. The purposes vary (and so should the rates), what you understand and comprehend will vary, but that's as it should be.

"Experts" who feel that it is impossible to read over 400 words per minute think that "reading" is reading about one word at a time and vocalizing it to yourself. If you are to agree with their definition, you must accept their rate limitation. Then if you want to breeze through novels at rates in excess of 1,000 words per minute, you'll have to sacrifice looking at one or two words at a time and saying each word to yourself.

Anyone who wants to read everything at the same rate, for the same purpose (to "get" everything), deserves what he gets—unread books; inability to concentrate; mind wandering while reading; the feeling of not being able to keep up with things; never enough time.

"READING" AT HIGH RATES FEELS DIFFERENT

When you're reading at high rates, the feeling is very different. Perhaps you've experienced it a bit already. There's a lot less vocalizing (we can never eliminate it completely, remember?), so at first it feels very different. To some people it feels "empty," others at first feel very insecure with it. It takes a lot of practice to develop a feeling of comfort and security, but that's true in learning most skills.

You have probably experienced the "emptiness" when doing the Double/Triple Drill. We'll review what's happening, and it will help you to appreciate what you're doing. When you first learned to read, your teacher had you read out loud so that he or she knew that you were understanding the words. Then she told you to read to yourself. While "reading to yourself," you get comprehension in the following manner: a visual "signal" is sent to the brain because of the words you see, but also an audio "signal" is sent up because you are *recalling the sound of each word in your mind's ear.* Figure 11 is a crude picture of what this might look like.

When reading one word at a time you understand it by sending both a visual and an auditory message to the brain because you recall the sound of the word as you see it.

When reading more than one word at a time you must get meaning mainly from just seeing them because you are going too fast to say all of the words to yourself.

When you are practice reading, doing the "doubling" and the "tripling," you are going faster than you can say all of the words to yourself. Therefore, you are sort of

FIGURE 11. HOW THE MIND GETS COMPREHENSION WHEN READING

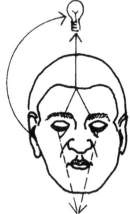

When reading one word at a time you understand it by sending both a visual and an auditory message to the brain because you *recall* the sound of the word as you see it.

When reading more than one word at a time you must get meaning mainly from just seeing them because you are going too fast to say all of the words to yourself.

exercising the visual signal to the brain. The brain is being "told" that it is just going to be able to see the words, not hear them as well. And it seems to accept this. Then when you complete the drill with a final reading for comprehension, you probably find your reading rate shooting way up (this usually happens only if you make your mark when practice reading on the "double" and "triple"). If you are one of the few lucky ones, perhaps your rate went way up, and your comprehension was fine. Some people find it even better than before. But the majority find their comprehension a little less than before, perhaps a bit shaky, or maybe they knew what they were reading *while* they were reading it, but as soon as they stopped, they couldn't remember anything.

The reason should be obvious. If your rate jumped way up, maybe 50 or 100 words per minute faster, or even more, you are certainly subvocalizing fewer words. So, you should expect the comprehension not to be as good. But the more you practice going at the higher rate, the sooner you and your brain will get used to it. Pretty soon, it will begin to feel comfortable, and you'll be remembering what you read. Now you should be able to understand why the doubling and the tripling are the most important parts of the drill. And if for the final reading you're making yourself slow down in order to be certain that you're understanding everything, you're not helping yourself one bit. You're just practicing slowness, which you can already do. You decide which way you want to spend your time practicing.

HOW TO GET COMPREHENSION AT HIGHER RATES

Since beginning to practice the circling hand movement, you must be wondering how you will ever understand when you're looking at so many words at one time. Not only that, but you're probably wondering how you can understand by going first one way, and then another (backwards) across the page. The answer that you probably don't want to read is that it comes largely with practice. But understanding what it's based on can help you to achieve it more easily.

When you first learned to read, most likely you were looking at each individual letter. Probably your own name was the first word that you could look at as a whole and grasp the meaning. But then you slowly started looking at almost every word as a whole rather than at the parts. Today, if you look at a word, as we already discussed, you are no longer consciously aware of the individual letters. You are only aware of the word as a whole and its meaning. Yet, if a word had an obvious mistake, such as birthqday, you would spot the wrong letter immediately. You are not looking at the letters forwards or backwards, but as a whole. Yet meaning comes to you, and mistakes are obvious. This is what visual reading will be like: seeing and getting meaning from groups of words at a time.

MEANING ISN'T CARRIED BY ALL THE WORDS

One of the reasons that you can read lots of words at a time is that the meaning of a passage is really carried by a minority of the words. It has been observed that there are over 600,000 words in the English language, yet fewer than 400 structure words (words which tie sentences and phrases together *but which carry no meaning*) are used about 65 percent of the time.

A study done at Brown University on the frequency of use of words was very interesting. Of a body of printed material totaling over 134,000 words, 122 words appeared most frequently. Only 20 of these were "content" or words carrying meaning, and 102 were structure words. The word "the" appeared 20,172 times and the word "of" appeared 10,427 times. It should be easy to understand why it is possible to learn to respond to many words together, as a unit, when so many of them carry no meaning and are so repetitious.

YOU CAN READ OUT-OF-EXPECTANCY ORDER

All attempts to increase reading rate prior to Evelyn Wood, at least that I am aware of, tried to get readers to read more than one word at a time along a line. Some courses still try to get students to respond to increasingly lengthy groups of words along a line. But Evelyn Wood found the naturally fast readers looking at groups of words, groups that included words above and below any given word on a line, as well as the words to either side of it. She discovered that people can read *out-of-word order.*

But how can you respond to words when they're not in sequence? Without question, this is the most difficult thing to understand without experiencing it. I will give you a simple explanation, and then we'll get into experiencing it. It is somewhat like looking at a picture. When you look at a picture, you actually focus on one part at a time, and your mind holds the rest together for you. When you look at a group of words, you will see all of them, focus in on some of them, then others, looking for meaning and ideas rather than individual words.

To experience reading out-of-word order *and comprehending* will take your cooperation. Beginning on page 96—*don't peek or you'll spoil the experience*—is a series of "paragraphs" which you are to "read" using the circling hand movement. There are at least five lines to each "paragraph," so you should simply underline from left-to-right the first line, drop down and circle from right-to-left the last four lines. Then quickly look up. This is most important or else you will continue looking at the passage and read it the old way.

You will also need something to cover up the "paragraphs" before you "read" them. First you'll cover the whole page, then move the covering device (a sheet of paper will do nicely) down till the first "paragraph" shows. Then quickly "read" it, using the circling hand movement. Look up and tell yourself what it "says." That's all there is to it.

EXERCISE NO. 22

Materials: *A sheet of paper or cardboard to cover the paragraphs on the next page*
Pencil or pen

1. Cover all the paragraphs on the next page; be careful not to look at them before doing this exercise.
2. Slip the paper down to expose the first paragraph.
3. Quickly use the circling hand movement, look at the first paragraph, underlining the first line from left to right and then dropping down and circling from right to left.
4. Look up quickly and write down on the paper what you saw.

How did you do? Did you find it quite easy? Did you catch the hidden word in paragraph D? ("Horse" appears amidst the dogs and cats.) This, of course, isn't very difficult, but it lets you "feel" what comprehension is like at very fast rates of reading. And even though all or most of the words in each paragraph were the same, you still had to see—and understand—what they all were. Obviously it's going to be harder when the words are mostly different, but with practice you'll learn how to get comprehension in those situations as well.

A. —————————————————————————

dog dog dog dog dog dog dog dog dog
dog dog dog dog dog dog dog dog dog
dog dog dog dog dog dog dog dog dog
dog dog dog dog dog dog dog dog dog
dog dog dog dog dog dog dog dog dog

B. —————————————————————————

cat cat cat cat cat cat cat cat cat cat cat
cat cat cat cat cat cat cat cat cat cat cat
cat cat cat cat cat cat cat cat cat cat cat
cat cat cat cat cat cat cat cat cat cat cat
cat cat cat cat cat cat cat cat cat cat cat

C. —————————————————————————

horse cow horse cow horse cow horse cow
cow horse cow horse cow horse cow horse
horse cow horse cow horse cow horse cow
cow horse cow horse cow horse cow horse
horse cow horse cow horse cow horse cow

D. —————————————————————————

cat and dog and cat and dog and cat and dog
and cat and dog and cat and dog and cat and
dog and cat and dog and cat and dog and cat
and dog and cat and dog and cat and dog and
cat and horse and dog and cat and dog

E. —————————————————————————

the horse and cow and dog and cat the horse
and cow and dog and cat the horse and cow
and dog and cat the horse and cow and dog
and cat the horse and cow and dog and cat
the horse and cow and dog and cat the horse

ADAPT YOUR HAND MOVEMENT TO THE PARAGRAPH

Always be certain to adapt the circling hand movement to paragraphs. That will help you to start working on your comprehension. Since the paragraph is the first unit of thought, as all its sentences help to form a single idea, this is the first unit on a page that we pay attention to when reading fast.

As a progressive step, since the first sentence of a paragraph usually tells you what the paragraph is about, we begin by reading the first line of a paragraph using the underlining hand movement, *then* drop down three or more lines and start circling the rest of the paragraph.

Try to take a whole paragraph at a time. If it is too long, repeat the circling hand movement two or more times. If it is only one or two lines, just use underlining in *both* directions. Once again you'll need to practice this a bit before trying to use it. Do this in the exercise below before doing your practice drilling; then you'll be ready to move ahead tomorrow.

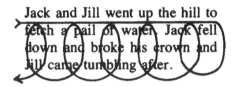

EXERCISE NO. 23

Materials: *Any book*

1. Start at the beginning of a chapter.
    Underline the first line of every paragraph (for single lines of dialogue you will just be underlining them).
    At the end of the line, drop down three or more lines and make fast circles coming back from left-to-right.
    Finish circling the paragraph until you reach the end.
2. Continue the new hand movement for about ten pages. Repeat the ten pages once or twice, as time permits.

CAUTION: Spend no more than two seconds maximum when circling. Less time is better. Be certain to read the single line you underline and just look at the words you circle.

While practicing Exercise No. 23, do not expect to get much comprehension—possibly none. At this point you are simply practicing the hand movement in order to get the hand movement smooth, even, and automatic. If it bothers you to be missing so much, simply turn the book upside down and work with the pages so that you can't possibly be reading anything. Then get some good practicing in so that you're ready to take the next step in getting comprehension at higher reading rates.

TURN TO PAGE 72 FOR THE PRACTICE DRILLS TO COMPLETE TODAY'S WORK.

16

HOW TO START GETTING COMPREHENSION AT HIGH SPEEDS

There are three basic rules which govern how quickly you can read and understand a passage. They will probably seem obvious to you at this point because you have already come a long way in the development of your reading efficiency and awareness. They need to be brought to your attention because they will help you to understand the process you'll be going through in the next few weeks as you learn to read visually.

THE THREE RULES WHICH GOVERN COMPREHENSION

RULE ONE: The more abstract words a passage contains, the harder it is to read quickly.

This is an obvious rule, because you can easily recognize that your mind can "understand" specifics such as "the brown dog" or "the woman with red hair" much more easily than it can such abstract sentences as "The complexity of brain rhythms challenges the capacity of man's ability for sustained thought." Therefore, when you are first learning to read at high rates of speed, it is best to start with material in which you can get comprehension. This would be material which is not written on a very complex level.

RULE TWO: The fewer ideas a passage contains, the easier it is to read fast.

This is also easy to understand. But some people are not aware that some passages present different ideas and thoughts more quickly than other written passages. Obviously, fewer ideas per 100 words, for example, means more structure words—words that are very easy to recognize and read quickly. And the more ideas per 100 words probably means the more you must slow down to get meaning.

RULE THREE: The more prior knowledge of the subject of a written passage the reader has, the easier it is to read fast.

If you are a nuclear physicist, you should be able to read books in your field with great ease. If I were to read them, I would have great difficulty and have to go (relatively) slowly. That's because I wouldn't know what many of the words meant, and the ideas would be new to me. And that makes it very difficult to "think" in the subject. This affects lots of people.

When I teach doctors to read faster, they should learn how to breeze through their medical journals very quickly. If they return to their medical textbooks, they would also find them relatively easy to read. But they have spent many years developing their medical vocabulary and learning medical concepts that have now become second nature. These once abstract terms and ideas have as much concrete meaning for doctors as "the brown dog" does for the rest of us. Therefore, they just need training in the skills of rapid reading in order to go quickly.

On the other hand, a first-year medical student would have much more trouble. For that individual, it is like reading a foreign language. It is very difficult to go fast before you know the words and concepts. But still, with dedication and practice, the average student should be able to increase his study reading rate at least 50 to 100 percent. And when you're spending long hours pouring over medical tomes, that's a big savings of time.

BACK TO THE FIRST GRADE

When you start learning to read visually, you're putting yourself back in the first grade. First, you must learn to read and understand on a very easy level, in material that is written with few abstract words, with few ideas per 100 words, and preferably in fields in which you have a lot of knowledge. Once you can get comprehension on an easy level, then start moving up until you can understand on whatever level you wish. This, of course, comes with a lot of practice.

To prepare for the visual practicing, which will begin at the end of this week, get yourself some easy books. Borrow a few from your children or nephews or nieces. Invade the children's section of the public library, even on the pretext that you have young children. Or, if you must, go to your bookstore and seek out some books that are written and printed for young people. There are many fine biographies (remember *Young Thomas Jefferson* and the like?) and other interesting stories. Another solution is to use easy books that you've read before, perhaps a year or two ago. Wherever you get them, round up a few books to practice in, because you'll need them in a couple of days.

PRACTICE AS MUCH AS YOU CAN

You've been practicing a few minutes with the variation of circling, reading the first line of paragraphs with the underlining step and then circling the rest of the paragraph, just looking at the words. In the next exercise, there are some more paragraphs to practice. Once again, do not look at them in advance. You will be covering them, then "reading" each one using the new hand movement.

When practicing visual reading, you must never go back and read the material the "old way," with linear or underlining reading (except for the first lines of paragraphs). It is most important to go through the material once, look up quickly and see what registers. Later, you may return, but only to again "read" it the new way.

If you go back and re-read passages the old way, you will surely find that you didn't get much from the passages, or that what you did get was incorrect. And that's just what I want. You've got to make many mistakes, just like when you first learned to walk, and the sooner you make them the quicker you'll learn. But if you keep confirming the fact that you're not able to do it, then you won't progress very quickly. So don't bother checking. Just keep working in very easy material, or material that you've read before. That way, you won't care so much, and it won't bother you. And when you're understanding, you'll know it. But for now, the greatest assets are practice and patience. So read the instructions below; then turn to the next page and do the exercise.

EXERCISE NO. 24

Materials: *A sheet of paper or cardboard to cover the paragraphs on the following page*
Pencil or pen

1. Cover all the paragraphs on the following page; be careful not to look at them before doing this exercise.
2. Slip the paper down to expose the first paragraph.
3. Quickly underline the first line and read it, then drop down to the bottom of the paragraph and circle coming back from right to left.
4. Look up quickly and write down on the paper the "meaning" of the paragraph.

The "answers" to these paragraphs are general ones. You shouldn't be able to remember every word; you never do with any reading at any rate. But you should have "seen" all of the words and realized that they all had a single thought. In paragraph A "Herbert goes to the garden and picks *a lot of vegetables*" is all it's really saying. And in paragraph B Gloria goes to the store and buys *a lot of groceries*.

I have used these to give you as good an idea as I believe possible of what it "feels" like to read very quickly and comprehend. But there is no substitute for the actual experience, so the last exercise is a very simple short story. Using the new hand movement, "read" the story several times. Just remember to go very fast, no less than one second per line when underlining the first line of a paragraph, and no less than three (try to make it two) seconds when circling. You may go back again and "re-read" the story as many times as you like, as long as you do it the new way. Just don't go back and read it the old way.

A. _____

Herbert went to the garden for his mother and picked many vegetables including peas, lettuce, tomatoes, cucumbers, carrots, potatoes, green beans, eggplant, squash, parsley, onions, spinach, corn and lima beans.

B. _____

Gloria went to the grocery store and bought milk, butter, cream, eggs, cheese, apples, pears, peaches, grapes and canned nuts, two bananas, cereal, bread, frozen pizzas, vanilla and chocolate ice cream, a cake, popcorn, Coca-Cola and orange soda.

C. _____

Raymond took his nephew and niece to the zoo, where they enjoyed seeing many of the animals. Some of their favorites included zebras, monkeys, giraffes, antelopes, elephants, tigers, water buffalos, deer, rhinoceroses, gorillas, bears, lions, cougars and jaguars.

D. _____

Susan was an athletic type who enjoyed watching as well as playing many different sports. She was on the swimming team and also liked to dive; she plays tennis, handball, field hockey, and track. She also likes to ride horseback and jumps as well. She really loves all sports.

E. _____

Autumn is a magnificent time in Vermont. Nowhere else do leaves achieve such bright colors as they do for two weeks in October. They go through several changes and become sunny yellows, fiery reds, golden ambers, rich purples, turning the area into a blaze of color.

EXERCISE NO. 25

Materials: *This book*

1. Underline the first line of each paragraph, beginning on the following page; then drop down to the bottom of the paragraph and come back, circling.
2. Quickly go on to the next paragraph.
3. Attempt to follow the story line. You may get only bits and pieces of the story, which is normal.

"PANTHER CUB"

Mark Purdy was on his knees on the grass putting live bait into little white boxes. It was Saturday afternoon, and there were plenty of jobs for him to do.

Mark listened for the sound of his father's motor-boat. Mark's father was a guide. He had taken two hunters out in the boat that morning. Mark looked toward the creek and saw his father bringing in the boat.

Mark hurried to the landing and fastened the boat. Then he noticed a small bundle near the feet of one of the hunters. It was an animal. Its fur looked shiny in the sunlight. "We found a panther cub," Mark's father said. "How did you get it away from its mother?" Mark asked.

"The mother was not around," said Mark's father. "We couldn't leave it to die so we brought it in with us."

The two hunters stepped out of the boat. Mark's father followed carrying the cub.

"We didn't catch a thing," said one of the hunters. "But you are a fine guide, Mr. Purdy."

The hunters picked up their guns and left.

Mark ran ahead of his father to the house. "Ma, come look! Dad brought us a panther cub."

Mark's mother came to the door. "Why," she said, "it looks just like a beautiful cat. The poor thing must be hungry. I'm going to warm some milk for it."

Mrs. Purdy went into the kitchen. She came back with a dish of milk. She put the dish near the cub. But the cub didn't move. Mark dipped his fingers into the milk. Then he patted the milk on the animal's lips. The cub licked its lips.

"It's just a baby," Mrs. Purdy said. "We should get it a bottle."

Mrs. Purdy found a bottle and filled it with warm milk. Now the cub knew what to do. It drank the milk, then settled back comfortably and fell asleep.

Mark smoothed its fur. "You sure are sleek," he said. "I know your mother took good care of you."

"What about its mother?" asked Mrs. Purdy. "Where is she?"

"She must be hurt somewhere in the Everglades," said Mr. Purdy. "No mother ever leaves her baby for long if she can help it."

The cub grew stronger day by day. It began to follow Mark all around the camp. Mark called it Sleek.

One morning before breakfast, Mark walked down to the creek. Sleek was close behind him. Mark sat down on the bank. Pretty white birds flew over the tall grass or rested on the banks. Hundreds of frogs called their noisy "Good morning." Birds sang. The Everglades was awake.

Sleek playfully nipped Mark's toes, and Mark scolded the cub with a light pat on its nose. "Don't bite, Sleek," he said.

Suddenly something growled and Mark looked up. About ten yards away he saw a large brown panther. It had come so quietly that Mark had not heard it. It stood still and watched the boy and the cub. Mark felt sure it was the mother. He didn't move an inch. "Mark, Mark!" called his father. "Come in for breakfast."

Mark was afraid to turn his head. "Look down the bank, Dad," he said quietly. "I think it's the mother panther."

"Don't move, Son. I'll get my gun," his father said softly.

Mark waited, without moving, as the panther crept closer. Sleek didn't see its mother. It was playing with Mark's toes.

The front door squeaked, and Mark knew his father was coming with the gun.

The panther headed for her cub. A fly lighted on Mark's face, but he could only twitch his nose. He knew he must not move.

The panther sniffed and sniffed. At first it looked as if she might not know her cub. The cub did not smell quite the same. Then the mother began to lick the baby's fur. Sleek rubbed happily against her. The panther turned around and headed for the thick bushes. She knew that her cub would follow her. It did.

Then Mark's father came up behind him.

"You were very brave, Son," he said. "I didn't want to shoot unless I had to. I was counting on you not to move and you didn't."

"I'm going to miss Sleek," said Mark. "We were just beginning to be good friends."

"It would have happened sooner or later," said Mark's father. "We would have had to turn Sleek loose in the Everglades when he grew bigger. But," he added, "some day you might see him again."

Mark knew just how it would happen. He would be in his boat going down a quiet creek when he would see Sleek. Sleek would look at him with yellow eyes and remember. And they would always be neighbors. They both were part of the beautiful wild world of the Everglades.

After you've gone through this story a few times you should be able to get a rough idea of what's happening. Don't expect it to ever be or feel like reading it the other way. It never will be. But, of course, with practice and the development of your skills, you'll get very good with it and gain the confidence that you'll require.

TURN TO PAGE 72 FOR THE PRACTICE DRILLS TO COMPLETE TODAY'S WORK.

1 7

READ WITHOUT SAYING EACH WORD TO YOURSELF—AND SOAR

If you've been practicing faithfully, and you've been able to read with comprehension around 500 words per minute, then you're ready to take the next step in learning to read rapidly. If you haven't experienced reading 500 words per minute, then you should take a vacation, at least from this book, but *not* from your practice drilling. It's important to be able to read with fairly decent comprehension at around 500 words per minute or faster (though this does not mean that you can read *everything* at that rate) before attempting to move into the higher speeds.

BE SURE YOU'RE READY TO MOVE AHEAD

If you've been moving up fairly regularly but are still under 500, then continue to do the practice drills from last week for a week before moving ahead. It will also help if you spend extra time just reading, with your hand, so that you will be comfortable at rates around 500 or more. Some people may spend several weeks at this stage, consolidating their efforts, before moving on. Occasionally, I've counseled students to drop out of the course and continue practicing and reading using their hand, using the underlining hand movement, for about six months before coming back and continuing. Usually this applies to those working in English as a second language, because their vocabulary in English isn't sufficiently developed. For this same reason, it can apply to those for whom English is their first language, but who have had considerable difficulty with reading. Don't insist on going on if you're really not ready. It won't allow you to become a faster or better reader any quicker. In fact, it could slow down your progress.

"PARAGRAPHING": THE NEW HAND MOVEMENT

Before you begin your high speed visual practice, you will need a new hand movement. This will just be an evolution of what you have been working with, the circling hand movement. As you know, the first thing that you should be getting from a passage of print is simply "seeing" all of the words. You should be able to recognize that all of the words are English, or whatever language you're reading. Proper names and italicized words will probably jump out at you. This has been easy to do when using the circling hand movement, and its variation of underlining and circling. By this time your eyes probably know what to do, so you won't need to make the circles any more to attract them to the right part of the page.

The paragraphing hand movement is done with the index finger and is exactly like what you have been doing, but *without making the circles*. The index finger underlines the first line of the paragraph, then drops down three or more lines and comes back to the left side of the page. If there's more to the paragraph, then you drop down again and take one more line across, drop down and take three or more lines, etc.

> **The paragraphing handmove-**
> **ment is done with the index**
> **finger and is exactly like what**
> **you have been doing but without**
> **making the circles. The finger**
> **underlines the first line of the**
> **paragraph, then drops down**
> **three or more lines and comes**
> **back to the left side of the page,**
> **and if there's more to the para-**
> **graph, then you drop down again**
> **and take one more line across,**
> **drop down and take**

It's important that your finger moves *down* the three lines or more in the margin. Your eyes are used to jumping back to the left side of the line and the movement of your finger, moving down, is necessary to keep them on that side of the page. As your finger moves back to the left side, *in about one second,* your eyes will be sweeping across the three lines of print and looking at all of the words.

The two hardest things to get all of my students to do are making certain that they run *down* the margin on each side and not cut across the lines; and that when they are moving their finger from left to right and then back from right to left, that they move *quickly,* about one second per sweep. You know why you should move carefully down the margin, and not cut across, but the need to move quickly needs a fuller explanation.

PUT YOUR EARPLUGS ON TO PRACTICE

Do you recall my story about the blind man being able to discern more from hearing the same sounds that you do? At that time I said that one way to learn to be able to discern more information from the sounds that you already hear would be to wear a blindfold for a month or so. That is exactly what you have to do in order to learn to read "visually," except that you must put in "earplugs."

Of course you do not really have to wear earplugs, but you are not listening to real sounds. You are only recalling the sounds of the words in your mind's ear. But in order to learn to discern information from what you see, without hearing it, you have to go faster than you can say the words to yourself. This usually means somewhere around 1,700 or 1,800 words per minute. Does that scare you? I tell my class 2,000 words per minute *minimum*, because that's a nice round figure and easy to remember.

Good linear reading, as you may recall, can be done from about 500 words per minute up to around 1,200. At 1,200 words per minute, linear reading does not suddenly stop and visual reading begin, but the faster you get, the fewer words you're able to subvocalize to yourself. Somewhere around 1,200 words per minute you're going so fast that you're reading most of the words visually. *But this is not fast enough for good practice.* That's because you can still vocalize too many of the words, and you may come to depend on those few words, trying to get any kind of comprehension at all.

I have found that the students who learn these skills most quickly do so by doing their practice reading (for visual reading) at 2,000 words per minute *or faster.* It's like jumping into the cold, icy water: it's easier just to jump in and get used to it quickly than to try to "warm up" to it. Often you just get too cold and give up. The same thing happens to students who practice at too low a speed. They don't get enough comprehension the old way, or the new way. It's very frustrating, so they usually don't get very far.

THE TWO KEYS TO SUCCESSFUL PRACTICE

You now know how to go about selecting the best materials to practice (in Chapter Sixteen), you know the proper hand movement, and you know why to practice very fast. (How to go fast enough simply involves spending no more than about one second going across the page, either way.) Knowing this, you are ready to begin, and there are only two more things that can help you. In order to succeed you need (1) to practice at high enough speeds and get lots of practice, and (2) get a lot of repetition over the same material. This helps in developing comprehension at high speeds, just as it helps to eliminate regressions at the lower speeds.

EXERCISE NO. 26

Materials: *Any book*

1. Open the book to any chapter.
   Practice the paragraphing hand movement through at least ten pages of the chapter. Be certain to underline the first line of every paragraph, then take three or more lines going back and forth till you have looked over all of the paragraph.
2. Repeat the section in order to get the hand movement smooth (never jerky! being careful to run down the margins) and automatic.

YOU'RE YOUR OWN BEST BET

Trusting yourself and being willing to take a chance is a most important aspect of learning to read rapidly. Within a few short lessons, one of my students was reading over ten times his beginning reading rate. When he began he was an "average" reader, he practiced just as much as was requested, and the only difference between him and his fellow students—besides his much higher reading rates at the end of the course—was his cheerful countenance and belief in himself. I think it's important to know that factors such as your attitude can control your performance in various skills.

The next drill, which will be a major part of next week's practice drilling, combines all of the elements necessary for successful practice. But you must ensure that the material you are practicing in is appropriate, and that you are going fast enough.

You will be doing the drill in a chapter of a book, or a section of about ten pages. Preferably the book should be fairly easy, on about a seventh grade reading level. The first step will be to use dusting, going about three seconds per page through the whole chapter or section. This acts as a good warm-up and prepares you for some really fast practice. At the same time as you are doing it, you should try to look the chapter over and perhaps find what it's about.

When you are going this fast, the first thing that you usually see is whether the passage contains dialogue or not. Quotation marks and indentation always stand out very easily. Or, you may notice if it's a passage describing or explaining something. If the material is fiction or a biography, you'll probably notice names while you're dusting through the chapter. When you complete this, you are to stop and put down anything at all that you might have noted on a recall pattern. Most people note very little. But that's how it begins.

After this step, you simply use the paragraphing hand movement two or more times over the passage, stopping at the end each time and trying to recall whatever you can. At first all you should expect is bits and pieces of the story, maybe just a *feeling* that something is there, and as soon as you stop, you may experience a lot of difficulty in trying to remember anything at all! Can you accept so little comprehension for a week or longer? If you want to learn this skill, you will probably have to. But when you've learned it, you will look back and realize how quickly it happened.

EXERCISE NO. 27

Materials: *Very easy book or a book you've read before*
       Paper
       Pencil or pen (or PC)
       Timing device

1. Select a chapter or section of about ten pages.
    Using dusting, pace down the pages about three or four seconds per page, going margin-to-margin with your whole hand.
    At the end of the section stop, and without referring back to your material set up a recall pattern, drawing a diagonal line, and jot down *anything* at all that you remember or *think* you remember. If you prefer, write it down in a word processing program.
2. From the beginning of the section, using the paragraphing hand movement, practice read through the entire section going no slower than one second over and one second back with the hand movement.
    At the end of the section stop, and without referring back to your material add to your recall pattern anything you can.
3. From the beginning of the section again practice read through the material using the paragraphing hand movement.
    Time how long it takes you to cover the entire section.
    After noting the amount of time it took, add to your recall pattern.
4. Compute your "reading" rate, and record it in your progress profile. First compute the total number of words that you read.

    A. Obtain the average number of words per line.
    B. Count the total number of lines on a full page.
    C. Multiply "A" times "B" to get an average number of words per page. Round it down, i.e., 277 becomes 270.
    D. Multiply the average number of words per page ("C") times the number of pages read, i.e., 8.5 pages times 270 = 2,295.
    E. Divide the total number of words read ("D") by the amount of time, i.e., 1.5 minutes into 2,295 = 1,530 words per minute.

5.   Optional: Practice read through the section again, stopping to recall after each time, till you feel more satisfaction.

CAUTION: **Do not go back and read the section the old way!**

Now that you're fully initiated into the mysteries of visual reading, you need to work on comprehension. And you need to get as much practice as you possibly can. The comprehension techniques will soon follow. The practice, of course, is up to you. Good luck!

TURN TO PAGE 72 FOR THE PRACTICE DRILLS TO COMPLETE TODAY'S WORK.

18

HOW ARE YOU COMING ALONG?

I've always noticed an odd thing about students taking this rapid reading course. Students in other rapid reading courses may spend just as much time practicing, or even much more, and end up feeling quite satisfied with a rate increase of 50, 100, or 200 words per minute. Yet, in this type of course, many students have already doubled their rates at this point. But they seem very unhappy that they haven't done far better. Perhaps it's just because they are beginning to appreciate how far they can go.

It's important to always remember that you have to compete only with yourself. In learning this skill, and most others, the only real competition is you, because we all learn different things at different rates and in our own way. While healthy competition can often push some people on to greater efforts, often the hardest problem for a person learning in a group is to realize that because others are progressing faster, it does not mean that he or she is stupid, a poorer student overall, or inferior in any way. Perhaps, and only perhaps, they are not as good in learning that particular skill or aspect of the skill, but that is all it means.

At this point, your reading rate should be significantly higher than when you began; possibly it is already double your initial rate. And you should know as much as I have to teach you about linear reading. That does not mean that you will not continue to improve, which you will with all of the further practice and drills. But beginning with the practice drills section for the coming week we will do most of our work with visual reading, which you have been introduced to in the past few chapters.

This is the time, midway through the course, to find out how you are progressing. This will determine whether you should continue to do the practice drills from this past week, or move ahead with the new ones. So let's find out.

RE-TEST YOURSELF

As in Chapter Two, assemble the materials necessary to re-test yourself so that you can have a comparison of how you are doing now with when you started. You'll need your testing book, and the other usual materials.

Mid-Course Reading Evaluation

Directions: *Read through the four steps carefully. When you understand everything, come back to the first step and begin.*

1. Select a section of your testing book that is about 30 pages long and that you have not read.
2. Read as far as you can in the material for three minutes. Use your timing device, either a tape or a recording device on your computer.
3. At the end of the three minutes make a mark where you stopped reading, then close the book.
4. On a piece of paper write down everything you can remember from the reading *without looking back at the reading selection.*
   Number the items as you write, giving every main idea and/or detail its own number. You may take up to six minutes; use your timing device.
5. Compute your reading rate and record it on your progress file.

Now, compare your results with your beginning course evaluation. Are you surprised? Has your rate shot up? Has your retention improved a bit? Of course everyone's doesn't. Some people get "test fever" and block as soon as they know they're being tested. And others just have a bad day. If this has happened to you, then test yourself again in a day or so in a new passage. But don't get discouraged. Everyone can improve, if he or she is willing to work at it.

This is also the time to check to see if you have become familiar with the other concepts and skills which this course entails. Go through the following list and check to see what you are familiar with. If you're unsure of anything, go back to the pages indicated and review it.

Mid-Course Review

Do you know how to compute your reading rate? (Page 7)

Can you read with the underlining hand movement? (Page 17)

Can you read a paragraph and find out what it's about? (Page 30)

Can you make a recall pattern? (Page 52)

Do you know the best reading posture? (Page 16)

Do you know how to test whether the light is too dim or too bright? (Page 16)

Have you learned how to read without making regressions? (Page 22)

When you practice read, can you usually make the mark? (Page 59)

Do you evaluate how important reading material is to you? (Page 42)

Do you know the basic form of nonfiction writing? (Page 61)

Do you know the basic form of fiction? (Page 63)

Can you break in a book properly? (Page 68)

Can you do the dusting hand movement? (Page 65)

Can you turn pages the new way (with the nonpacing hand)? (Page 69)

Can you do the Double/Triple Drill? (Page 58)

Do you understand how authors write, often moving from a general level to a more specific one? (Page 77)

Do you understand that all words do not carry the meaning? (Page 94)

Can you do the circling hand movement? (Page 89)

Can you do the paragraphing hand movement? (Page 105)

When you practice read, do you *try* to understand something? (Page 67)

Do you understand why some reading passages are harder to read than others? (Page 77)

Do you understand that we can't eliminate subvocalizing and we don't even try (and why)? (Page 25)

ARE YOU READY TO MOVE ON?

Whether or not you are ready to move on with the second part of the course is simple to determine. *You must be able to read and get what you consider to be fairly good comprehension some of the time at rates in excess of 500 words per minute.*

If you can do this, then continue, even if you did not know or remember everything on the Mid-Course Review. If you didn't remember everything, look over those pages once again. If you have not yet reached 500 words per minute, at least some of the time, then you should not yet go on to the next part of the book. What you should do is continue with the last week's practice drills until you can achieve these reading rates. It may take a week or so of extra practice. For some people it may take two or three months. This depends entirely upon how well developed your reading skills were when you started this book.

When I taught the Evelyn Wood course, I would sometimes ask a student to drop out of class after the first two or three lessons. I did not want to get rid of that person, but I was doing the best thing I could do to help them. (At that time a student could drop out and reenter with no additional cost.) I would advise him to do a drill similar to the Double/Triple Drill at least once a day for six months, and, in addition, to spend at least half an hour a day just reading. Like any sport, reading is just a skill, and the more you practice it the better you will get. Then they were to come back and finish the course.

When I was teaching in Pittsburgh, Tom was the weakest student in one class. I saw this during the first lesson and I advised him against taking the course at all: I told him to go in and ask for his money back. But he had already tried several other measures, none of which worked, and all of which were frustrating to him. He was coming to us as a last resort, and it's pretty hard to refuse to help someone like that.

At the end of the first lesson, Tom was quite confused with all of the new ways of reading and drilling and computing rates. I stayed after class with him and that seemed to clear up things. But by the second lesson he was getting further behind, and by the third lesson (a similar point to where we are now in this course) it was a hopeless situation.

If he had stayed in the course, the experience would have been so frustrating that he would probably have never succeeded in reading successfully. Luckily, he agreed to drop out for six months and follow a reading plan similar to the one I just outlined. He had never read much and had just barely finished high school. I suggested that he start reading *whatever* was of interest to him; the important thing was to be reading. This he faithfully did, though when he found time to do it I can't imagine. He worked nights at the post office and held another job in a restaurant during the day. But somehow he made the time.

When he returned to class five months later, he started all over again. This time he found the first part of the course quite easy. In fact, he was quite delighted (and so was I) to find himself almost at the top in reading rate. He was certainly the best in understanding the drills. When another student started to have trouble following directions, I asked him to sit next to Tom. I think that this was the first time in his life that he was best at something in school.

Tom didn't finish first in the class, but he did finish with the top group. He then liked to read so much that he wanted to come back in another six months and take the course over again. I left Pittsburgh to go to New York by that time so I don't know what happened. I hope he did return though, because he was such a fine example of how easy it can be, with a little extra effort, to get to the top even when you start at the very bottom.

You must evaluate yourself

When you are teaching yourself a skill, such as this one, you have to be both the student and the teacher. That makes it a tougher job. If you've decided that you need more work, then set up a schedule. If you're ready to move ahead, then finish your practice drills for today and move on to the next ones tomorrow.

Turn to page 72 for the practice drills to complete today's work.

Practice Drills for Week 4

As soon as you have completed Chapters Thirteen through Eighteen, and have spent a good six days doing the second set of practice drills, then if you have achieved at least some readings with comprehension at 500 words per minute or more, you should begin doing this next set of drills for the next seven days. You should spend the first day just working on these practice drills. Beginning the second day, first read a new chapter, starting with Chapter Nineteen; *then* repeat the practice drills.

Always do the drills in order, after having finished the day's chapter. If you practice only twenty minutes a day, do the first drill; if you practice 40 minutes a day, do the first and second drills, etc. *Do not repeat any drills in any single practice session until you have first done all of the drills given.* Then you may repeat whichever drills you prefer.

Materials You Will Need for This Week's Drills

1. *A timing device.*
2. *Pen or pencil.* (or PC)
3. *Paper.* Preferably unlined, 8 1/2 × 11 inches.
4. *Several books* from your list in Chapter One.
5. *Paper clips* or small strips of paper.

Levels of Comprehension in High Speed Reading

As I told you at the beginning of this book, in learning some skills the practice is more important than an understanding. Sometimes the understanding only follows the ability to perform the skill. To a large degree this is true with reading over 1,200 words per minute. And as you start practicing these skills—and I've asked you to practice over 1,800 words per minute to be most effective—it is sometimes hard to keep the faith.

Below is a chart which represents an attempt to describe the various stages you will be moving through as you develop the ability to perceive more and more information when viewing words at a very fast rate. Look it over carefully and try to remember it as you do your practicing every day. If you feel discouraged, look back at the chart to find what stage you're in. If you find after several days practice that you need to get more comprehension, select easier books to work in. When a high level of understanding starts to come through, you can begin to use more difficult materials.

Levels of Comprehension in High Speed Reading

As you develop your ability to perceive information at the higher rates, you will probably move through these levels:

1. WORDS. You are able to see all of the words and recognize that they are all English words—or whatever language you're reading in.
2. ISOLATED PHRASES. Words and phrases seem to "jump" out at you but you have almost no idea of what is going on.
3. MEANING OFF AND ON. If you're practicing in fiction, you begin to know what's going on, *now and then;* if it's non-fiction, you know what it's about.
4. BARE STORY LINE: CONNECTING THE MEANING. You can follow the bare story-line of the plot (fiction) or generally follow the main points (nonfiction) but are missing a lot.
5. READING. You know what you are reading *while* you are reading, even though you may not be able to remember what you've just read (that will come with lots of practice).

DRILL NO. 9

Materials: Basic List

Estimated Time: 10 Minutes

Purpose: Learn to quickly find what "level" the third sentence of a paragraph is on.

Objective: See how many paragraphs you can analyze in 6 minutes

---

DO THIS DRILL ONCE PER PRACTICE SESSION

1. Select a paragraph of at least three sentences. Using your hand, read it as quickly as you can to find what it is about.
    Draw a linear recall pattern and write down, without looking back at the paragraph, what it is about. Do not add any details.
2. Look back at the paragraph and analyze the first three sentences.
    Complete the linear recall pattern reflecting the levels of the first three sentences. See example below:

EXAMPLE: (a) Wordsworth believed that every man could attain the vision of joy and harmony of life in nature, which for him transformed the whole of existence. (b) Spurgeon calls his poetry a series of notes and investigations devoted to the practical and detailed explanation of how this state of vision might be reached. (c) Wordsworth's description of the method of realizing this condition emphasizes the practice of a passive attitude.

Level 1	*Wordsworth's belief about all men*
Level 2	*Spurgeon: poetry explanation of this state of vision*
Level 3	*This condition*

OR to save time:

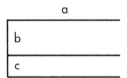

3. Continue, analyzing the first three sentences of different paragraphs (not sequential ones). See how many you can do in six minutes. Record on your progress profile.

DRILL NO. 10

Materials: Easy Books   Purpose: Practice Visual Reading at high rates
Estimated Time: 10 Minutes   Objective: Attempt to follow every story line,
at least bits and pieces of it while going
at high rates

THIS DRILL MAY BE REPEATED

Diagram:

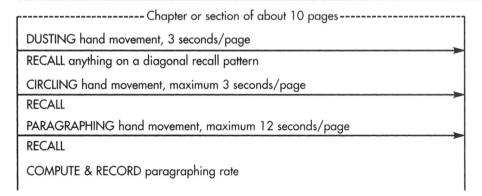

Explanation:

1. Select a chapter or section of a chapter approximately ten pages; this should be in a relatively easy book or one that you've read before.
2. Using the dusting hand movement, dust down the page, spending no more than three seconds per page (you may wish to count at first: one—and, two—and, three—and, etc.). Set up a diagonal recall pattern. Recall anything you can remember or even *guess* that you remember. You will probably not remember much more than proper names.

3. Using the circling hand movement, repeat the entire section, underlining one line, then dropping down and circling three or more lines coming from right-to-left, spending no more than twenty seconds per page (about seven complete hand movements per page). Add to your recall pattern anything that you can.

4. Using the paragraphing hand movement, repeat the entire section, underlining one line, then dropping down three or more lines and coming back from right-to-left, spending no more than twelve seconds per page (about six complete hand movements per page).

Reading Purpose: Attempt to follow story line in bits and pieces, on-again, off-again, while maintaining visual reading rate (1,600 or more).

5. Compute your practice reading rate in step 4, recording it on your progress profile. Find the total number of words in the section or chapter by first finding the average number of words per full page, then multiplying by number of pages: i.e., 240 words per page × 8.5 pages = 2,040 total words. Divide the total number of words by the amount of time: i.e., 2,040 words/1.5 minutes = 1,360 WPM.

CAUTION: Make certain to maintain a practice reading rate in step 4 over 1,600 WPM (in the example it is not high enough!).

DRILL NO. 11

Materials: Easy Books   Purpose: Practice visual reading at very high rates
Estimated Time: 15 Minutes   Objective: Make the marks when practice reading

THIS DRILL MAY BE REPEATED

Diagram:

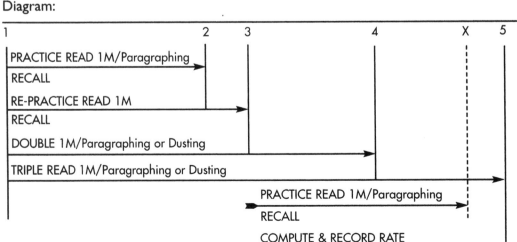

Explanation:

1. Make a mark, "1," where you will begin using paragraphing hand movement. Practice read from the "1" for one minute, no slower than six hand movements per page.
   Mark where you stop with a "2." Begin a recall pattern putting "what it's about" on a diagonal line.

2. Re-practice read the same passage going faster and farther. Mark the new ending point with a "3." Add to your recall.

3. Mark a new passage from "3" to a new point, "4," that is approximately equal to the amount from "1" to "3."
   Practice read from "1" to "4" in one minute using paragraphing or dusting.

4. Mark a new passage from "4" to a new point, "5," that is approximately equal to the amount from "3" to "4."
   Practice read from "1" to "5" in one minute.

5. Go back to point "3" and practice read, using paragraphing, as fast as you can while attempting to follow the story line (but not necessarily always succeeding) for one minute.
   Make an "X" where you stop reading. Add to your recall pattern.
   Compute your reading rate, from point "3" to "X," recording it on your progress profile.

DRILL NO. 12

Materials: Basic list & books
     from Chapter One
Estimated Time: 15 Minutes

Purpose: Practice reading at triple your initial reading rate

Objective: Maintain a reading rate of triple your initial reading rate with some comprehension

THIS DRILL MAY BE REPEATED

Diagram: Find initial reading rate and round down to nearest tenth.
Set up five sections six times, each the amount above.

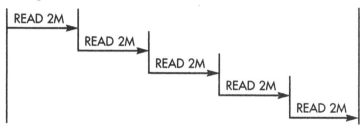

Compute & Record any 2M section.

Explanation:

1. Take your initial reading rate from Chapter Two: i.e., 248 WPM. Round this amount down to the nearest tenth: i.e., 240 WPM. Multiply this result times six: 6 × 240 = 1,440 words. Set up five sections of words approximately equal to the final amount. Mark the end of each section with a paper clip or small strip of paper sticking out from the page.

2. Using your hand as a pacer, attempt to read the first section in two minutes. You may use any hand movement you choose.

Reading Purpose: Barely following the story line, make the mark even at the loss of comprehension.

3. Continue, reading each part in two minutes or less. Be certain to make the mark!

4. Compute the reading rate of any section and record it on your progress profile.

19

KNOWING READING SIGNALS HELPS SPEED YOU UP

There are two types of writing which you continually encounter, fiction and nonfiction. Most narrative writing, or fiction, is written on a level that you can understand immediately. Much nonfiction, such as news reporting, is also written this way. The words and ideas are everyday ones that are easy to grasp. But, if you are reading the philosophy of John Locke, John Stuart Mill, or anyone who writes on a fairly abstract level, you may find they don't always use ideas or words that are concrete enough for you to recognize them readily.

One aid to understanding abstract writing is to become aware of transition words. These are words which *signal* that the writer is going to shift ideas or do something other than what he has been doing. Perhaps he is going to give you an example of what he's been talking about, or maybe he will say "on the other hand" and change ideas. She might say "as a result of" and tie the whole thing up, or "secondly" and give you a new thought. In many different ways the author can signal you that he is changing thoughts. Authors give you the signal because they want you to stay with them through the shift. Once you become aware of these words you will start noticing them more frequently, especially when the writing becomes more difficult to read.

WHY SIGNAL WORDS HELP YOU UNDERSTAND

Signal words aid you in *anticipating* that something new is coming. You see the signal word, you anticipate that something is to come, and you keep a "space" ready for whatever it is. Then you find that what's coming just falls into the reserved space. For example, sight reading in music is somewhat similar. When a musician sight reads music, he is always looking just a little bit ahead of what he is actually playing. As he reads ahead, he is setting up the anticipation for what he is going to play. The same thing can happen with reading and the signal words help when the writing is difficult.

THE MANY KINDS OF TRANSITION WORDS

There are several different types of signal words. One group which you are already familiar with is that of *time*. This relates one part of a paragraph to another in terms of when it takes place. In the brief exercise below, see how quickly you can recognize the time signal words.

EXERCISE NO. 28

Directions: Find the signal word or words which indicate *time* in the following paragraphs.

1. When Janelle went into the restaurant business, many of her friends were surprised. Formerly she had been an ad executive.
2. During the strawberry season Terry sprained his wrist. After that he was never able to pick as many berries.
3. To start with, the hunters had not come expecting snow. They did not have any snowshoes or proper cold weather equipment. They had a very limited supply of fuel. Soon they ran out of food. Next they decided to go home.
4. New York City is well known for its parades. St. Patrick's Day parade is one of the noisiest. Later in the year comes the Puerto Rican Day parade. Finally comes the best of all, the Thanksgiving Day parade.
5. Before the doorbell rang, Lori had already put on her coat. Then she started looking for her purse, which she had lost. Earlier she had misplaced her shopping bag. Now she was in no mood to go shopping at the mall with her friend.

Did you immediately recognize most of the signal words? In the first paragraph they are "when" and "formerly"; in the second "during" and "after", in the third "to start with," "soon," and "next"; in the fourth "later" and "finally"; and in the fifth "before," "then," "earlier," and "now."

Another type of signal word is what a writer uses when he wants you to *consider both sides* of a situation. Can you find them in the paragraphs below?

EXERCISE NO. 29

Directions: Find the signal word or words which indicate that you are to consider *both sides* of a situation.

1. Some people are eager to make their first trip by plane. Nevertheless, when they finally take off, they may wish they were still on the ground.
2. The United States has often been cited as the land of golden opportunity. However, opportunity seldom comes to those who sit and wait.
3. Emily was a truly attractive young woman. On the other hand, she was unbearably spoiled.

4.   Paul thought it could be very pleasant to have a dog as a pet. On the contrary, he found it a nuisance to have to walk the dog so frequently.

The words signaling that you should consider the other side are "nevertheless" in the first paragraph; "however" in the second; "on the other hand" in the third; and "on the contrary" in the fourth.

Words which indicate that a writer has *more to say* about a subject are usually obvious. See how many you can identify.

EXERCISE NO. 30

Directions: Find the signal word or words which indicate that the writer has *more* to say.

1.   Jo was a very unusual young woman. She was very good in sports. At age fourteen she was headed for the Olympics both in swimming and track. Moreover, she was a very good student.

2.   The city government was nearly bankrupt. Social services had been almost terminated. For example, the community health program had been cut back from ten employees to only one.

3.   Mrs. Henry had a great many pets. She kept dozens of parakeets and several cats. She had only one dog but seven goldfish. Also she had a ferret.

4.   Margaret couldn't understand why her grades weren't better. She spent lots of time studying and reading. Besides, she'd memorized all of the dates, even the unimportant ones.

5.   Dennis likes to write. He has won several awards for his plays and stories. In addition, he writes screenplays for movies and maintains his own website to promote his work.

6.   Karen works very hard at her job. She arrives before 8:00 A.M. and always leaves after 5:00 P.M. Furthermore, she sometimes works on Saturdays and even telecommutes.

The signal words in Exercise No. 30 are "moreover" in the first paragraph; "for example" in the second; "also" in the third; "besides" in the fourth; "in addition" in the fifth; and "furthermore" in the sixth.

Word signals indicating *order* are also common, such as first, second, lastly, etc. They are easily identified and help you to know what to expect. Also they can help you to organize what you are reading. For instance, in a long paragraph you can pick out signal words which will help you to break up the material into parts. This helps to categorize and understand it more easily. Look at this paragraph:

When Dr. Locusi went into the laboratory, he carefully checked out all of his instruments and equipment; then he began his daily work. First he ran an experiment on genetics. He was trying to find if curly hair is dominant or recessive. He verified that it is a dominant trait. Next he ran some tests to help out a friend who had fallen ill. These tests were routine blood tests on some mice. The tests had to be conducted daily. They were part of some cancer research. When he finished he e-mailed the results to his friend. Finally, he returned to another experiment he was working on. It was part of his research for a cure for Parkinsons Disease.

If you identified all of the signal words of order you were able to "divide" the paragraph into four parts: the introduction beginning with "when," and the following parts which begin with "first," "next," and "finally."

Another set of word signals commonly encountered tells you that the writer is going to *summarize* or *draw a conclusion*. These are not difficult to identify and will tell you to anticipate an ending. Find the summary word in this paragraph:

Hawaii has a great deal to offer the modern traveler. It always has a warm and pleasing climate, not too hot and not too cool. It offers great opportunities for surfing and swimming and other sports. It is the ideal locale for simply lying on the beach and sunbathing. You might also just wish to relax at your hotel and read or pop in a CD and listen to music. The friendly people make almost everyone feel very welcome. As you can see, whether you are eighteen or eighty, it is a perfect vacation spot.

Some of the common signal words indicating a summary are "in short," "therefore," "for this reason," and as in the paragraph above, "as you can see."

FASTER READING IN HARDER MATERIALS

You can learn to read quickly through most novels, but it is usually more difficult to read a textbook. If you are reading philosophy and abstract materials, it is often imperative to watch for the signal words in order to anticipate what is coming next. In setting up this anticipation, a skilled reader can usually stay on top of abstract reading at a pretty fast rate. But *only* by maintaining this awareness can you expect to understand difficult material at rapid rates. Remember that when you read above 1,000 words per minute you begin to read out of expectancy order. When you do this you must respond to the words and ideas almost automatically. You will become more aware of whole thoughts and complete events rather than individual words. This is similar to your present ability to recognize an entire word rather than look at each letter individually. The words have become almost like symbols or pictures. In visual reading you will soon be looking over whole groups of words and responding to the idea or event to which they all contribute a small part.

At visual reading rates, over 1,000 words per minute, you obviously cannot stop and analyze. So don't expect to read an abstract book with ideas which are new to you at rates over 1,000 words per minute. If you can reach such a rate in these difficult materials, then consider yourself a very gifted reader. Five or six hundred words per minute is an excellent rate in such material.

Don't think that this means that you can't read difficult material faster than you once could. You certainly can, but I have found that at the beginning of a rapid reading course the best readers usually drop to rates of 100 to 200 words per minute when the material is really hard. To read these materials around 600 words per minute, or higher, is really an accomplishment.

HIGH-SPEED PRACTICE HELPS LOWER-SPEED READING

While you undoubtedly recall that we work on comprehension and rate development separately, you should also know that to develop lower reading rates you must practice at high speeds in easier materials. *Developing the ability to recognize words and ideas rapidly is best done in easy materials at high rates.* As your range in easy materials gets faster and faster, you will find that the bottom of your range, in truly difficult materials, will also improve.

Almost everyone will always face two kinds of reading. Some books contain very simple words and ideas. These books can be read very quickly. Other books contain very abstract and difficult ideas. This type of book often requires analytical reading in order to understand it. Reading and analyzing as you go along can be difficult to do. So don't feel that you should be doing this when you are asked to speed up in an exercise or drill. But practice it enough so that when the material you are reading is difficult, you will know how to handle it. Slowing down is only one way (and you won't have to slow so far down as you become skilled). Recognizing the transition words is another. Becoming aware of how writers move from the general to the specific is a third.

These are only *some* of the ways to improve your comprehension in reading. Next you will learn other ways. But as in dealing with all skills, learn this one well, because it is the foundation for the more difficult techniques to follow.

TURN TO PAGE 115 FOR THE PRACTICE DRILLS TO COMPLETE TODAY'S WORK.

20

THERE'S MORE THAN ONE WAY TO "READ"

By this time you are already reading in new ways, ways they didn't tell you about in school. It's important to be aware that you have several alternatives in reading. Just like skinning the proverbial cat, there's more than one way to read, and you should know about them. In this chapter, we'll look at some of the various choices open to you.

In school, you probably felt that reading meant to pick up a book, or whatever you wanted to read, and begin going through it word by word by word. If you went to the end of the book first you might even have felt that you were "cheating." I hope that at this point I have convinced you that reading means meeting *your* purpose while viewing the print in a book or other source of reading. Just because you were taught only one technique in school is no reason to suppose that it should be sacred.

OLD-FASHIONED SPEED READING

Many years ago, schools used to teach their students how to skim. This was an old-fashioned method of getting through a book more quickly. It's really too bad that this valuable skill isn't still being taught because it can be very useful. I'll show you a way to do it, and it will become one of your reading alternatives.

Skimming is simply selective linear reading. In other words, it is reading on a word-by-word, line-by-line basis, but you do not read every word. When taught to skim you are usually taught to read the first line of every paragraph. This can be a good way to get an idea of a story or article, but it does have some obvious drawbacks. It is certainly not complete and sometimes it is misleading.

The best way to skim a chapter is to read the first paragraph or two, then begin reading the topic sentences of all of the paragraphs as quickly as you can. Use an underlining hand movement. Try it in the following exercise just to establish in your mind how it is done.

EXERCISE NO. 31

Directions: *Skim the following selection by reading the underlined material with your hand. Then go back and read the entire passage (using any hand movement) to see if your impression of the material was correct.*

As the moving van pulls away and you stand on the porch surveying your very own piece of property, you are suddenly struck with a thought . . . "What am I going to do with this sand patch surrounding me?"

In many cases, as the moving van pulls away it also is taking your last buck. When many of us move into a new home, we have used up just about all of our savings. Plus, by the time you make the down payment, the closing costs (which no one can figure out), and pay for the gas, water, phone, electric hook-up, and the miscellaneous items needed for privacy, you're lucky if you can buy a loaf of bread and a quart of milk. But since you have a reputation to build in your new neighborhood, you decide to plant a lawn. Where do you start and what do you do?

You usually begin by swearing at the builder, whom you don't like anyhow, because you expected the Taj Mahal and he built a house that you are sure isn't as well constructed as the clubhouse you built in the back yard when you were only twelve years old. And now, with your shovel in hand, you begin to dig and find that he must have contracted with the city sanitation department to dump all of the old trash in your yard to get what he called a "finished grade."

Nonetheless, it is yours, all yours, to do with as you please. And contrary to the beliefs of many, you can have a good, healthy, lush, green lawn, no matter what the soil content is, unless there is some chemical present. For instance, sometimes fill is brought from a construction site that had a heavy overflow of gasoline, oil or salt deposits. To make sure that this is not the case, smell the soil from various locations in your yard. If there are any strange smells that you cannot identify or which smell like petroleum, go to your local nurseryman and ask if he does soil tests or can get one done for you.

Assuming that all is well, let's proceed. Put down your shovel. You won't need it for a day or two. Begin by picking up every loose object that you can lay your eyes and hands on: stones, bricks, tar paper, lumber, tree stumps, and glass. Do not pass over anything. If just a corner is in sight, work it out of the soil or it will haunt you later.

When you are sure you have picked up every rock, stone and pebble, ask your wife and mother-in-law to look it over. With their eyesight, you'll be amazed at what you missed. Then I want you to apply fifty pounds of Grand Prize Garden

Gypsum per 1,000 square feet of soil to the surface. Finally, add fifty pounds of any garden food with a low nitrogen content—4-12-4 or 5-10-5 will do nicely. You don't want a big burst of growth; you want fat grass and healthy roots.

Here is where you will have to stretch your budget and rent a power tiller to grind up thoroughly the soil and the material that we have spread on top. Mix this all down from six to ten inches. Till back and forth, then criss-cross the area. When that's done, go over the same area from corner to corner and criss-cross that also. The secret is to get the soil as fine as possible in order to save you a lot of hand work.

Before you do anything else, take the rented machine back to save money. I have received mail galore for that simple suggestion. The rent goes on whether you use it or not.*

After skimming this selection, did you know what it was about? In many cases you would know what it is about, but in others you can receive a totally false impression. This does not mean that skimming isn't useful. But it certainly is not a substitute for reading.

SCANNING IS ANOTHER READING ALTERNATIVE

Sometimes the words skimming and scanning are used interchangeably. Most people probably aren't certain what either of them really means. But even reading experts are not in agreement over the meaning of these words. So I'll give the definitions of these two words as I use them.

Scanning is a totally different process. In scanning material, you are usually *looking for something*. Therefore you have to look over everything to see if what you are looking for is there. Finding a name in the telephone directory is the most common example of scanning. You are looking for a specific name which makes the reading task fairly easy. But you must also see all of the names to verify that they are not the one you are trying to find.

Therefore, scanning is somewhat like visual reading. You are seeing all of the words. Of course in visual reading you do not necessarily know in advance what to expect, and you are expecting to follow the entire story, not just search for an item or two. The more specifically you know what you are looking for, the easier it is to scan. Try this next exercise as an example of a scanning task."

---

*From *Plants Are Like People* by Jerry Baker. Reprinted by permission of Nash Publishing Corporation.

EXERCISE NO. 32

Directions: *Find who the characters in the story are as quickly as you can, using your hand, any hand movement.*

Early one morning, a miner named Neil O'Dea stepped onto the cage of the *St. Vincent* mine. He signaled to be lowered. Cold air whistled around his ears as he dropped down the timbered shaft to the five-hundred-foot level. As he stepped out onto the station, he found it deserted. It was early.

The night-shift men were trudging down Bermuda Road. The day-shift men were swallowing the last of their porridge and coffee. Shortly they would swell the parade uphill to their jobs in the *Bermuda, Never Sweat* and *St. Vincent.*

The *Bermuda* dominated the summit of the south slope. The *"Sweat,"* as it was popularly called, was slightly down-hill to the west, and the *St. Lawrence* to the east. The *Bermuda* and *St. Vincent* adjoined underground in a confusing maze of levels and crosscuts. The strong draft that was sucked down the *St. Vincent* shaft swept through its openings into the *Bermuda.*

Lighting a candle, O'Dea entered the dark mouth of a crosscut. A hundred feet farther he paused, and sniffed nervously. It seemed to him that he smelled smoke.

He hastened farther along the crosscut, his heartbeat quickened. Nothing terrified a miner more than the threat of fire or gas explosion underground. But perhaps it was only some oil-soaked rags smoldering because a careless man, going off shift, had dropped a lighted match on them.

O'Dea forged ahead. The blackness turned gradually to a dull reddish glow. Then he heard crackling noises. Aghast, he saw that flames were eating up the wall timbers ahead. Even the overhead caps were ablaze.

Instead of rushing off to safety, O'Dea tore off his shirt. Fortunately for him, most of the smoke was being drawn off in the direction of the *Bermuda.* He beat the flames with his shirt, but they worsened. Smoke swirled about his head. He was choking from the sulfurous gas formed by the heated rocks.

He stumbled back to the station. Several miners were just stepping off the cage. "Fire in the crosscut!" he gasped.

They dropped their lunch pails and grabbed a huge roll of canvas hose. Hauling it down the crosscut, they connected it to a water standpipe. After dampening rags to tie over their faces, they trailed O'Dea to the fire. The fight had begun.*

---

*From *The Copper Kings of Montana* by Marian T. Place. Reprinted by permission of Random House, Inc.

You should have been able to complete this task very quickly using a visual hand movement (paragraphing or dusting) and found that there is only one main character, Neil O'Dea, but other "miners" are mentioned at the end.

FOUR WAYS OF READING

The four methods of reading are:

1. *Linear Reading.* Reading word by word and line by line, as you were originally taught. This is an effective method in difficult materials and for reading rates up to around 800 words per minute.
2. *Skimming.* Selective linear reading, reading preselected paragraphs or first lines of paragraphs.
3. *Scanning.* Looking over all of the material to find something specific such as a name or number.
4. *Visual Reading.* Reading by groups of words, out-of-expectancy order, from left to right *and* from right to left in a generally downward movement pattern. This, with practice, becomes an effective method for moderately difficult reading tasks and easy ones, and for rates over 1,000 words per minute.

All of these methods of reading should be a part of your techniques as an efficient reader. And you will probably find yourself using most of them in many different reading situations. How to do this will be the subject of the next chapter.

LEAVE YOUR GUILT BEHIND!

Although our schools do not teach skimming any more, many people assume that anyone can do it. I have never found this to be so when questioning my students. When asked how to skim, the answers are quite numerous, and most of them are just guesses.

The most difficult thing in learning to skim, scan or read for a limited purpose, is to learn when your purpose is satisfied and quit. Very often, students of rapid reading techniques feel guilty because they haven't "read" *everything.* This is a very unrealistic, not to mention inefficient, attitude, and one which must be overcome if you are to become a good rapid reader.

Your bookshelves are probably filled with books that you have read, linearly, probably slowly, spending many, many hours with them. Look at them and select some book that you've spent fifteen to thirty hours reading. Now, many months or years later, how much do you remember?

You'll never be able to remember everything, of course, and probably never a lot of detail if you're trying to remember the book even a few months after reading it. *The important thing is to first decide your purpose,* what you want to be able to remember from the book, *then use a system for getting out of the book as quickly as possible whatever it takes to meet your purpose.* Once you've met your purpose, you've read that book. Once you've learned the technique of doing that, you must learn to feel guilt-free about using it.

Now that you've learned what skimming and scanning are, you are ready to move on and learn how to use all of your new techniques in attacking reading materials. This will be the subject of the next chapter. Before moving on, however, be certain to get a good hour's practice in.

TURN TO PAGE 115 FOR THE PRACTICE DRILLS TO COMPLETE TODAY'S WORK.

21
ADVANCE ORGANIZERS CAN HELP YOUR COMPREHENSION

Reading and listening are generally considered to be passive communication activities, while writing and speaking are active ones. One of the keys to rapid and efficient reading is to learn to become active when reading. In fact, we have been taught to read in a "receptive" manner, simply going through the material and taking in what is presented to us, in a somewhat passive way. Much of speed reading is learning how to become more aggressive in your approach.

An "advance organizer" is a precise name for the process of trying to organize something before you read it. The purpose of it is to increase your comprehension and also your retention of the information you will read. The more common name for an advance organizer is "preview" and some people call it an "overview" or a "survey."

The reason an advance organizer can help you understand is fairly easy to appreciate. If you were going to drive to a new city, you would find it much easier if you studied a map beforehand and knew what to expect. If you were expecting the road to split and knew which branch you would be taking, you might save yourself the time of having to slow down, maybe even pulling out a map, and making the decision. If, in your reading, you always knew what was coming, it would obviously make it easier to read faster and better.

Working with advance organizers helps in other ways. If you preview and then read a passage, you are going over it more than one time. You would assume that someone who reads something twice should understand it better than if he had just read it once. This, of course, is useful only to a rapid reader, who can go through the material two or more times *in at least one-third* the time of the slower reader. It should be remembered, then, that a multiple reading process is an integral part of how a rapid reader gets better comprehension than a slow reader.

Although going over a piece of material more than once has its obvious advantages, what you are doing when you go over the material is very important too. *You are not simply re-reading something two times.* As the name implies, you should be attempting to *organize* the material, and the better you are able to do this, the quicker you should be able to read the material.

FROM WHOLE TO PARTS

When you first look at a map before setting out on a trip, you are looking over the whole journey. When you drive you are covering the terrain in detail. You might look at an aerial map of a city, for instance, and actually see the roads you will be traveling. Then when you start driving you will see a great deal more. And you will be able to relate it easily to the overall route you are taking: *you will know where things "belong" in relation to the whole.*

When you are reading, you must try to do the same thing. You look over the *whole*, trying to discover where you're going and what you'll be getting from the material, then you begin your journey and discover all of the *parts.* Usually when you are able to see the whole of something first, then examine the parts, you can develop a better grasp of whatever it is you are looking at. It should be apparent why you would get better comprehension: first you are going through the material more than one time; and second you are attempting to organize it through the way you are approaching it.

FINDING THE AUTHOR'S "MAP"

If you understand that using advance organizers can help you comprehend better, perhaps you would like to know how to use them. Unfortunately, authors don't supply real "maps" to their books. But they often give you a lot of clues which you can use to begin your journey. Even if they don't, there are means you can take to help organize the material in advance. It sometimes takes a little more effort, but it isn't very difficult to become good at it. And when you can do it easily you will find that it gives you a big advantage in your reading.

HARD BOOKS ARE OFTEN THE EASIEST

Books that are supposedly most difficult are usually the ones in which the author provides a "map" textbooks. Most textbooks are organized to help you. The main "roads" are pointed out through signs which are called subheads or bold face headings. Often these subheads have second subheads of their own. These, of course, point out smaller "roads." A chapter of a textbook might be organized in the following way, here illustrated without any of the actual text:

LIFE IN NEW YORK CITY	Chapter Title
THE CITY HAS MADE A REAL TURN-AROUND!!	Subhead
Crime Rate Is Now Lower Than You'd Believe	Second Subhead
Some Areas Are Safer Than Others	Second Subhead

IT'S EASIER TO LIVE IN THAN TO VISIT	Subhead
Tourist Life Can Be Hectic	Second Subhead
Residential Areas Are Different	Second Subhead
City Services Can Make Life Easy	Second Subhead
Mass Transportation Eliminates Need To Be A Chauffeur	Third Subhead
CULTURAL & SOCIAL ADVANTAGES ARE MANY	Subhead
Theaters and Movies Abound	Second Subhead
Times Square Is Now a Jewel	Second Subhead
Music, Education, Social Opportunities	Second Subhead
Sports and Recreation Advantages	Second Subhead

In this example if you just read all of the subheads, you would have a pretty good idea of where the author is "going" and what you'll be reading about.

PREVIEWING NONFICTION

The purpose of "previewing," which is the first step in a multiple reading process, is to organize in advance. If you are given a nice "map" as illustrated above, then you are ready to take the next step—finding out more about the material. This is fairly easy to do and, upon reflection, obvious. As you learned in Chapter Eleven about the form of nonfiction, key information tends to lie at the beginning and ending of sections.

To preview nonfiction, first look over the material to see how it is organized (broken up into various parts). Next, find out what the main points are *by skimming the beginnings and endings of the major sections*. To skim a section of nonfiction effectively, read linearly the first few paragraphs of the chapter and look for what the author will be talking about in the chapter. Be certain to relate this to the chapter title. After all, it should be highlighting the main idea of the chapter. The purpose of nonfiction is always to communicate, and the chapter title is where most authors begin doing this.

After completing this, you may have two choices. You may skip (yes skip!) to the end of the chapter and look for summarizing paragraphs. This might be the last one or it may be several paragraphs before the end. Signal words often tip you off, words such as "in short," "thus," "therefore," "as you can see," or even "to summarize." Sometimes there isn't a summary paragraph, but you should still note what the author is talking about.

If there are divisions through subheads or any other device, you can then exercise a second choice. You may go through the chapter, reading beginnings and endings of the major parts of the chapter. This should give you a good idea of how the author will develop his ideas.

After you have organized the selection *in advance*, through this type of previewing, you are ready to read.

WHEN THERE IS NO APPARENT "MAP"

It isn't always so easy to find the author's map. But knowing what you now do about the way nonfiction is written, you should always look for beginnings and endings and any other obvious signs of organization. There is always the paragraph, which is the first indication of organization. Sometimes there will be a large blank space between paragraphs. This indicates a break or shift in ideas and you should look out for these blank spaces.

Your ability to *visualize the organization* of material will help you to understand and retain it. Understanding might even be viewed as the mind's organizing and categorizing information. When the mind receives information, it checks it out against what has already been stored. If the material is all new, it is necessary to set up new "files," or else the information will be left in chaos. Without the new places for the new information, everything will be in a big jumble. It will be rather difficult to find things and very easy to lose or forget them. The more you can consciously help to organize the information, the better you can help yourself think.

Now try this new previewing technique in the following selection from the book *You, Inc.* by Peter Weaver.

EXERCISE NO. 33

Directions: Preview the chapter (from *You, Inc.*) by (1) looking over the entire chapter just to find out how it is organized (are there any divisions?), then (2) skim it by reading the beginning and ending paragraphs of the major divisions (if more than one), trying to find what the chapter is going to be about.

When you have finished previewing the chapter, go back and attempt to read it, using the paragraphing hand movement and find out if the author does what you would expect after having previewed it. You may read it twice if you feel the need to do so, but only using the paragraphing hand movement.

WHY LEAVE?

Why should anyone shun the security of working inside an organization—company or government—for the insecurity of trying to make it alone on the outside?

It's usually the first question that those who still work for the establishment ask. Usually, they're trying to rationalize their own vague feelings of restlessness or unhappiness with the fact that they "know where the next paycheck is coming from" and they get all those "fringe benefits." They're taken care of from cradle to grave by the establishment. It may not be the greatest, they say, "but it's secure."

Is it secure? Today, maybe. But tomorrow? Ask some of those aerospace engineers and others who lost their jobs what it's like to be lulled into a false sense of security by all the money flowing from government contracts. Now you see it, now you don't. The government giveth, and the government taketh away. The flow stops and, suddenly, you're out on the street blinking in bewilderment.

If it isn't cutbacks in government spending, it's another recession or a merger. "Sorry, you know how it is . . . but we're phasing out your department." Yeah, you know how it is. You know that now you're out of a job and all those fancy medical plans, sick leaves and pensions don't mean a damn.

Then there's the problem of "human obsolescence." You may be plugging away at your job and suddenly realize "they're phasing me out." Why? Because the stuff they taught you back in high school or college is old hat. New techniques are needed and those young squirts they recently hired seem to know all the angles. Can't happen to me, you say? Hah! Listen to what Dr. James Schulz, Brandeis University economist, has to say:

"Technology is moving at a faster clip. They're now talking about engineers who become obsolete at age thirty-five. They say engineers burn out. Their education becomes outmoded by new technology. Some are shifted off into dead ends or, like burnt-out light bulbs, they're unscrewed and thrown out."

Dr. Schulz isn't the only one who speaks out against the dangers of getting unscrewed ("screwed" seems like a better word). Dr. Harry Levinson, industrial psychologist at Harvard and Boston University, says:

"It's dangerous to cling to an organization too long. Reductions in forces are happening every day. There's a built-in manipulation to make people obsolete. Some employees are automatically down-graded as they grow older to attract new talent at the front end."

Then, says Levinson, "there's the new-broom syndrome." By this he means a new boss who comes in, doesn't like the way you part your hair, and you're swept out.

The "security" of an established job, of working for an organization, is not all that secure. You've got to prepare yourself to be able to leave before the "unscrewing" begins. You've got to start making more of the decisions about your life and stop having them made for you by a series of bosses who always seem to say, "You know how it is," when they give you the shaft.

Says Levinson in his book *Executive Stress:*

"Mentally healthy people use their resources in their own behalf and in behalf of others. . . . They are in charge of their activities, the activities are not in charge of them. . . . If a man does not manage his own life, then it will be managed inadvertently by others . . . . Your life is yours. You have to take charge of it, manage it, assume responsibility for it."

So far, we've talked primarily about the economic and technological reasons why you should, at least, seriously consider leaving an established job to head out on your own. There are even more important reasons for shunning the organizational way of life. A scientist might describe these reasons as "psychological." A humanist would describe them as "soul." Everytime they turn down one of your ideas without really considering it.

Every time you're told what to do, what not to do and when to do it your soul gets scarred and shrivels a little. Your intellectual growth withers. You can't even make your own mistakes. They make them for you.

This is what really got me. Without giving too much thought to it, people above me would dismiss a series of suggestions with a wave of the hand and would tell me "this isn't for us . . . you know how it is."

Peter Nagan, who now runs his own successful company, Newsletter Services, Inc. (which writes and publishes business newsletters), can sympathize. The same thing happened to him before he got out to start his own business. He says:

"When I was working for a big corporation, my immediate supervisor was a fellow who was competent enough but I felt he didn't have any God-given right to order my life. I'd present a carefully thought-out, deeply felt idea and—with a shrug—he'd just mow me down."

I guess what we're all grumbling about is our lack of freedom. For the somewhat dubious security the establishment offers, we have to give up much of our intellectual freedom. Humans—even animals—don't like giving up their freedom, so, in order to get you to do a lot of things you'd rather not do, organizations bribe you and keep raising the ante whenever you or your colleagues get uppity and threaten to leave. These bribes are sometimes labeled "raises," or "expense accounts," or even "free parking space."

So you stay on and wonder why you get an ulcer, growl at your family and friends or can't sleep nights. You don't like yourself. Nobody does when they have to accept a bribe. If this makes you unhappy, you've got lots of company. Listen to how labor expert Sam Zagoria, author of *Public Workers and Public Unions,* analyzes the current job scene:

"American workers—male and female, black and white, manual, clerical, technical and managerial, old and young—are being infected by a malaise... Some employers, jarred by lower productivity, higher absenteeism, occasional in-plant vandalism and even drug addiction, recognize that just below the surface is the fact that a growing number of employees see themselves engaged in joyless, dehumanizing chores."

Changing from one establishment job to another usually doesn't work. The bribe may be bigger. Working conditions may be easier to take at first. But, after a while, many of those "joyless, dehumanizing chores" seem to keep crawling back into your work week.

Sometimes you're lucky. You hit a really good job. You get a relatively free hand to do what you want. The boss is a prince and things look bright. "What, me worry?" you say. "I've got a deal . . . they're paying me to do what I like best." I hate to be a bore but things might not always be coming up roses. Remember those economic disasters? Whole industries, whole cities have been ravaged by the whims of government spending or some flip-flop in technology.

Even if you're in a job you love and the odds are against any economic upheaval, you should still consider making a side bet on a little business of your own that takes only part of your time.

"Starting a venture on the side," says Professor Richard Beckhard, Sloan School of Management, M.I.T., "will make you a better person where you're working." Beckhard ought to know. He started his own sideline consulting business and says it makes him a better teacher, helps him keep more in touch with the real world. He encourages self-satisfied management to become involved in outside projects to sharpen their skills, get a better perspective.

There's a great deal of satisfaction to be had in working on your own project outside the organization. It's like planting a seed, watering it and watching it grow. This relevancy of one's creative efforts often becomes blurred inside a large organization. Also, when you have your own project going and it's a success—not necessarily a big success—you gain confidence in yourself. This confidence is reflected in your work inside an organization. I know, I did better work after I started up my first sideline news columns. I was cooler. I was less dependent on the organization and a little more relaxed.

According to Dr. Levinson, "people need a wider variety of sources of gratification. You can't afford to have all your eggs in one basket. If you drop the basket, then you've got scrambled eggs."

A young man who's still on the inside working for a major corporation, cites his own experience:

"I found that I had more guts in meetings. When something was wrong, I would say so even if I knew it wasn't what my superiors wanted to hear."

In a very real sense, this man's company is benefiting from the confidence he gained by starting up a little business outside its walls. Any organization benefits when it hears the truth and not just what some boss wants to hear.

Before we leave the "why" of starting up your own little business, let's not forget that final blow everyone in all organizations must face. I call it the "final firing." They call it "retirement." You may be sublimely happy with your job. The days go by. Pretty soon the years go by and then they give you a nice little luncheon, a little gift, maybe, and wish you well in your new "leisure." Zapp! They cut you off. For many, this cutoff comes as an economic disaster. When you feverishly open up your Social Security and pension package, you find very little in it. For most employees retirement means a sudden, brutal drop in annual income.

Any good doctor will also tell you when a man or woman stops working, they often start going to pieces. Their children no longer depend on them. Now their organization no longer needs them. Somehow, little aches and pains seem to grow into serious illness.

If you have had something going for you on the outside, when you retire you can devote more time to it and make it grow. Your little business needs you. People who buy your product or services need you as do those who may be working for you.

So, if you're happy with the job you now have, look at a sideline business as sort of a "lifeboat." Even though the seas are calm and a captain has a big and powerful ship underneath him, he never sets sail unless he knows he has enough lifeboats and they're all in working order. He even conducts lifeboat "drills" to make sure that, if disaster strikes, he'll be ready for it.

You should do the same thing. Build a little business, a little lifeboat. Outfit it. Conduct periodic drills to make sure it will work right when, and if, you ever need it. You may even find it's more fun being in charge of your own lifeboat than it is being just another member of the ship's crew.*

When first looking over the chapter, did you notice the break, indicated by a larger space between the last two paragraphs, on page 137? This means there are two parts to the chapter. Did you find the summarizing paragraph at the end of the chapter? It begins with the signal word "So," and is the second paragraph before the end.

If you read the first two or three paragraphs, the final one on page 137 before the break, the first one after the break, and the last two paragraphs at the end of the chapter, then you previewed the chapter well. When you went back and "read" the chapter, using the paragraphing hand movement, could you see that the author was merely illustrating and developing his main points?

How carefully you would read this chapter would, of course, depend upon your reading purpose. If you were reading the book to find the main points, the "reading" of this chapter might be good enough. But if you were a student and had to be able to cite various examples and illustrations, you would have to "read" it more carefully. So, purpose always determines your reading techniques, and practice makes you better, as well as faster, at them.

TURN TO PAGE 115 FOR THE PRACTICE DRILLS TO COMPLETE TODAY'S WORK.

---

*From *You, Inc.* by Peter Weaver. Weaver Communications, Inc. Reprinted by permission of Doubleday & Company.

22

CHANGE YOUR ATTITUDE AND INCREASE YOUR SPEED

At this point in the book you are a little more than halfway through this course. If you have been doing the drills as directed, you have undoubtedly made a certain amount of progress. Perhaps you have even experienced reading over a thousand words a minute—probably with fairly good comprehension. Certainly you have experienced practice reading at very high rates. Are you amazed at what you are able to get at such high practicing rates? Or do you feel that you are just turning pages and looking at words without *anything* coming through?

Most students at this point in the course are progressing at about the same rate. Some are very excited at their progress and others are discouraged. When, as an instructor, you see two people at the same point with such very different feelings, you sometimes wonder why. With a little experience you soon learn who will do well and who will not, just on the basis of a student's attitude.

The situation is somewhat similar to the proverbial glass of water which is filled halfway: is it half full or half empty? The student who views it as half full obviously has positive feelings about it, while the student who views it as half empty tends to regard things in a slightly negative manner. Through experience the teacher soon learns how helpful a positive, optimistic attitude is to a student. We learn it through experience: the students who regard their work in the positive way generally do better.

WHAT A BASKETBALL EXPERIMENT TAUGHT ME

Years ago, while reading the celebrated plastic surgeon Maxwell Maltz's book *Psycho-Cybernetics* I found out why this happens. He describes an experiment with a basketball team in which the team was randomly divided. All team members were tested to see how many baskets they could throw from a certain point. Then the interesting part of the experiment began. One-half of the team was to practice throwing baskets for one hour each day for two weeks. The other half was instructed to lie on cots for ten minutes each day for the two-week period. But the second half was also given a simple instruction: to imagine themselves *successfully* shooting baskets.

At the end of the two-week period both halves of the team were again tested. None of the players were exactly Michael Jordan, but the results were startling: the half that had performed the actual practice had improved 25 percent, as I recall; the half that had performed the imaginary practice had improved 24 percent.

The point of this is not to stop doing the drilling and to start imagining yourself reading faster. On the contrary, the point of this true experiment is that *what you picture yourself doing in your mind is actually a form of practice.* It may not be as efficient as real practice, but it is practice nevertheless. To understand this fully, you would have to read Maltz's very interesting book. For our purposes it is sufficient to appreciate that a negative attitude implies picturing yourself failing. And picturing yourself failing is a form of practicing failure. If you find yourself doing this, it would be better to stop for a while rather than continue this type of "practice."

It is important to *believe* that you will soon be reading faster. It is also important to picture yourself able to breeze through books, studying more efficiently, and in general, *succeeding.* A conscious effort to do this should not be difficult. If you think that you harbor a negative attitude, plan to change it. At least once a day for a few minutes, consciously see yourself succeeding at speed reading. And whenever you catch yourself doubting your progress, again begin picturing your success. If you *know* how much a negative attitude can keep you from progressing, you can do something about it if you really wish to read faster.

HOW YOU'RE MAKING PROGRESS WHEN YOUR RATE STAYS THE SAME—OR EVEN DROPS

When you are learning a new skill, such as this one, you go through many stages. Some are exciting when you make great progress and others can be discouraging when nothing seems to be happening. These latter ones are sometimes referred to as learning plateaus. That means that you make some progress, then it seems like you have come to a halt and possibly you feel that you are even regressing! Although they can be frustrating, if you understand them they can be very helpful.

Contrary to your feelings, this is an important period in your progress. It is during this time that you are *consolidating* your gains and preparing to move further ahead. With all of the progress you've made, you have to take some time to get used to the tremendous changes.

Some people practically double their reading rate overnight and then are dissatisfied that they can't keep up the same rate immediately. But you have been accustomed to reading at half that speed, your brain has been used to processing printed information much more slowly. Give it a chance to catch up. Certainly it is capable of going much faster, but this process is something new. Your brain may be a computer, but it's not as simple as adding new memory or a faster chip. Learning doesn't work that way. So relax and enjoy the periods of "no progress" or plateaus; they're just as important as the times when you suddenly shoot way up.

REMEMBER THE VALUE OF PRACTICE READING

You've spent over two weeks working on visual reading. It's sometimes important to review what you are doing and why you are doing it. Learning visual reading can be quite trying for some people; you may feel that you are just "turning pages" or just "looking at words" and nothing is coming through. As long as you're *trying*, though, something is happening for you.

As I explained earlier in this book, learning visual reading is somewhat similar to a person who is suddenly blind learning to perceive information from hearing alone. Although you and I hear the same sounds as a blind person, he or she can discern more information. At this point your eyes can see everything mine can on the page but yours do not yet discern as much information—possibly very little at this point—while you are practicing at a high rate of speed.

The key to success is lots of practice *depending* on getting information in this manner, visually. If you wanted to learn to discern more information from hearing, you would wear blinders for a period of time, maybe a month or more. If you want to learn to discern more information from seeing words, and not "hearing" them all, you will have to put in "ear plugs" for a month or so. Please do not rush out and buy a pair of real ear plugs; they will do you no good whatsoever. Your practicing at high rates of speed is all that is necessary.

Practicing at high rates of speed, preferably over 2,000 words per minute, forces you to depend on a visual signal to the brain to perceive information. When reading at average rates, your reading involves sending the brain both a visual signal as well as an auditory one, because you are "saying" the words to yourself as you look at them. You already know that it is possible to simply see the words (or symbols) and understand them without saying them to yourself. Obviously the best way to learn to do this better is to practice going very fast and force your brain to depend on this visual signal.

You've been practicing all of your reading life receiving two signals in order to comprehend what you have been reading. That might be anywhere from ten to seventy years. Certainly you can't expect your brain to adjust to something new overnight. It might, in fact, just take one or two months of practicing at high rates of reading speed. Depending on your age and attitude, it might take several more months of using your new skills to become comfortable with them. But don't let this discourage you. Whatever effort and practice you expend will reap its reward. Just reading 50 words a minute faster means reading 3,000 more words in an hour—or about ten extra pages in a novel.

MY "BEST" STUDENT

The best student I've ever had the privilege of having in my classes was named Mary. Her brother, Alexander, who was in class with her, was already a very good reader. In comparison, Mary was quite slow, well under average, and her comprehension score on a standardized reading test was low. Alexander let me know in no uncertain terms at the first lesson that he *knew* rapid reading "worked," he needed no proof, he just wanted to get down to work, which he did.

Mary was more modest. She quietly set about her work and diligently did her practicing. At first the results were meager; though her rates went up, her comprehension dropped or stayed the same, which was clearly unacceptable. But Mary didn't discourage easily, even sitting next to a brother who was obviously the star of the class and with her initially disheartening results. Instead of practicing six hours a week she would practice ten, twelve or even more.

Finally, toward the end of the course both her rate and her comprehension began to climb. At our final session she had of course improved her rate, about six times as I remember, but her comprehension score had shot up about 50 points, from about 30 percent to 80 percent. I wish I could take credit for this but Mary really did it through her own efforts which were truly considerable. I just felt lucky to have been there to point the path she should follow.

HANDLE EACH DAY'S PRACTICE BY ITSELF

It is important to begin each day with a firm resolve to learn these skills. Learning a new skill, especially by yourself, takes a great deal of determination and discipline. Just as it is important to have a positive attitude toward your new skill, it is also important to have one about establishing the new habit of practicing these skills for a month or so.

The best time to practice something new is as soon as you get up. If you cannot arrange to practice upon rising, at least go over in your mind what you intend to do for your practice during the day and when you will do it. This will begin your positive mental set. Also, just before you go to bed, again contemplate your successful practicing on the following day. Decide when you can do it, what you will do, and see yourself doing it *successfully*.

These are simple techniques, but techniques which have been proven to work. If you're having any difficulties, simply go along with my suggestions and see if they don't make it easier. I, too, once struggled to learn this skill and I've helped thousands of others like you to learn it as well. If you disregard this as just so much "positive thinking," you might also find this book sitting on the shelf very soon and you not reading much faster. Since you do want to read faster, or you wouldn't have picked up this book, why not go along with its ideas? After all, you have nothing to lose by following my instructions, except learning to read more efficiently.

EXERCISE NO. 34

1. Before going to sleep, either before you go to bed or while in bed, take several minutes to successfully imagine your next day.

2. Close your eyes and visualize a large movie screen. Decide now the time you plan to do your practicing tomorrow. Visualize a huge clock and turn its hands to the hour you will begin to practice. Then watch yourself sit down at your desk and begin to practice.

3. Continue to visualize yourself using your new skills. "Watch" yourself reading with your hand, watch yourself reading various books while practicing, and watch yourself reading your newspaper and magazines very quickly.

The more often you visualize yourself practicing and using these skills successfully, the sooner and more easily you will be able to succeed with them. Therefore this exercise is to be used as often as possible.

TURN TO PAGE 115 FOR THE PRACTICE DRILLS TO COMPLETE TODAY'S WORK.

23

PREVIEWING FICTION IS ALWAYS VERY FAST

Most people seem to consider a novel the easiest type of book to read. But if you are looking for a "map" of the action, you usually can't find one. Usually, there is no table of contents, often not even any chapter titles. And of course it is highly improbable that you will find subheads in a work of fiction.

Fiction is an art form which makes it differ considerably from nonfiction. If the purpose of nonfiction is generally to communicate information, the purpose of fiction is to involve us with a story and give us a meaningful, vicarious human experience. Being an art form, the structure or organization is usually well hidden. In fact there may be as many forms of fiction as there are authors.

In Chapter Eleven, I suggested that if there is any general pattern to the organizational form of fiction, it would be that we are presented with a character or characters who usually are about to do something. Soon a problem arises; later the problem is resolved.

If the purpose of a preview is to organize in advance, this can prove to be difficult when reading fiction. With a good preview of nonfiction, you can sometimes find all of the information you need, completing your reading purpose. But this would rarely happen with fiction. Perhaps the most information you will be able to get in previewing fiction would be the basic story elements. These would be the major characters, and when and where the story takes place. Occasionally you will also find out what is happening, but often when you get that much you are actually reading the story.

USE SCANNING TO PREVIEW FICTION

If we are to limit our purpose in previewing to find the basic story elements of characters, setting, and time, then we have a fairly specific reading task. Thus it is usually possible to find this information through scanning.

Using the kind of preview we do for nonfiction, skimming the beginnings and endings of major divisions, usually will not render much information in fiction. We may find the setting of the story and the time, but not much more. Authors simply don't put the main points of their story, let alone a summary, at the beginning or the ending. Not unless you're reading something like *Aesop's Fables*.

To preview a work of fiction, look over the whole book for any clues as to what the story will be about. This will include a careful reading of the outside covers, including any advertising blurbs, reviews, online information, etc. Next look over the entire work for any aids, such as chapter titles or other organizational divisions.

Following this preliminary step, begin going through the material using a very fast dusting hand movement. You should be able to move at a rate of two to three seconds per page because you're looking only for characters, setting, and time. You will probably also become aware, especially if you are dealing with a lot of pages, of how difficult the writing is, how much dialogue or exposition there is, and possibly even a feeling for the style of the writing.

READ FOR ENJOYMENT

Following a preview you should begin reading, and read to become involved with the story because that is what the author is trying to get you to do. Your reading rate will depend on several factors, primarily your current skill level (affected by your regular daily practice) and also how difficult the material is. Because most fiction is written about human experience, and we all have background in this, our wealth of experience helps us to identify and think quickly in the material. This usually supports a fairly fast rate once you have developed your reading skills.

Be careful when reading to get a good footing in the beginning of each new division. A new aspect to the story will begin with each new chapter or break in the text. Novelists often use spaces between paragraphs as an organizing device. Pay attention to them, slowing down when there is a new part. Once you know what is happening, you can afford to increase your rate. In general you can speed up and slow down according to what's happening. It's usually easy to speed up over descriptive passages and also often over dialogue. But sometimes when subtle plot features are being developed, you must slow down to catch the details. With experience you'll find yourself doing this easily and naturally.

BEWARE OF READING PROBLEMS

The major problems which face the reader of a novel are usually those of characters. This is common in Russian novels, where a single character will have several different variations of name, something well known to those who are familiar with the language. But the westerner may think he's reading about another character when a different name is used. It is therefore important when previewing to establish firmly in your own mind who the major characters are and what their various names are.

You may discover other problems in other books; it is hoped these will become apparent while previewing. Once identified, try to solve the problem before beginning the book. If you are able to do this, such as having all of the characters clearly in mind, it will be easy to read the book quickly and "organize" it as you are going.

REVIEWING: THE THIRD STEP

The last step in a multiple reading process is to go over all of the material again for a general review. This completes the organizing process when reading nonfiction. You have started with a view of the whole; then gone over the parts; and as a final step you "stood back" and reviewed everything, pulling it together again quickly in your mind.

Interestingly, when reading fiction the review step is when you analyze the material. This is directly opposite to the nonfiction procedure. But in nonfiction the organization is usually readily apparent in the preview step. However, in fiction, as we've seen, it is not apparent. So after establishing the major story elements in a preview, then reading and following the story line through to its conclusion, you are in a position to analyze the book or story as you review if this suits your purpose. For most people this step is not necessary, as they read fiction only for their own enjoyment. But if you are a student in a literature course, then to do justice to the work you should plan to preview, read, and then do a careful review of the material.

See how well you can apply these techniques to the following story, *The Cop and the Anthem*, by O. Henry.

EXERCISE NO. 35

Directions: *Preview this story by dusting through the entire story very quickly, about three seconds per page, just to find out who the major characters are, the setting, the time the story takes place, and the general style and difficulty of the writing.*

When you have finished previewing the story, go back and read it as quickly as you can. Attempt to use the paragraphing hand movement, speeding up and slowing down, as fast as you can stay with the story line.

Finally, if you wish, review the story and analyze it, looking for the major problem and its resolution.

THE COP AND THE ANTHEM

On his bench in Madison Square, Soapy moved uneasily. When wild geese honk high of nights, and when women without sealskin coats grow kind to their husbands, and when Soapy moves uneasily on his bench in the park, you may know that winter is near at hand.

A deaf leaf fell in Soapy's lap. That was Jack Frost's card. Jack is kind to the regular denizens of Madison Square and gives fair warning of his annual call. At the corners of four streets he hands his pasteboards to the North Wind, footman of the mansion of All Outdoors, so that the inhabitants thereof may make ready.

Soapy's mind became cognizant of the fact that the time had come for him to resolve himself into a singular Committee of Ways and Means to provide against the coming rigor. And therefore he moved uneasily on his bench.

The hibernatorial ambitions of Soapy were not of the highest. In them there were no considerations of Mediterranean cruises, of soporific Southern skies, or drifting in the Vesuvian Bay. Three months on the Island was what his soul craved. Three months of assured board and bed and congenial company, safe from Boreas and bluecoats, seemed to Soapy the essence of things desirable. For years the hospitable Blackwell's had been his winter quarters. Just as his more fortunate fellow New Yorkers had bought their tickets to Palm Beach and the Riviera each winter so Soapy had made his humble arrangements for his annual hegira to the Island. And now the time was come. On the previous night three Sabbath newspapers, distributed beneath his coat, about his ankles, and over his lap, had failed to repulse the cold as he slept on his bench near the spurting fountain in the ancient square. So the Island loomed big and timely in Soapy's mind. He scorned the provisions made in the name of charity for the city's dependents. In Soapy's opinion the Law was more benign than Philanthropy. There was an endless round of institutions, municipal and eleemosynary, on which he might set out and receive lodging and food accordant with the simple life. But to one of Soapy's proud spirit the gifts of charity are encumbered. If not in coin you must pay in humiliation of spirit for every benefit received at the hands of philanthropy. As Caesar had his Brutus, every bed of charity must have its toll of a bath, every loaf of bread its compensation of a private and personal inquisition. Wherefore it is better to be a guest of the law which, though conducted by rules, does not meddle unduly with a gentleman's private affairs.

Soapy, having decided to go to the Island, at once set about accomplishing his desire. There were many easy ways of doing this. The pleasantest was to dine luxuriously at some expensive restaurant; and then, after declaring insolvency, be handed over quietly and without uproar to a policeman. An accommodating magistrate would do the rest.

Soapy left his bench and strolled out of the square and across the level sea of asphalt, where Broadway and Fifth Avenue flow together. Up Broadway he turned, and halted at a glittering cafe, where are gathered together nightly the choicest products of the grape, the silkworm, and the protoplasm.

Soapy had confidence in himself from the lowest button of his vest upward. He was shaven, and his coat was decent and his neat, black, ready-tied four-in-hand had been presented to him by a lady missionary on Thanksgiving Day. If he could reach a table in the restaurant unsuspected, success would be his. The portion of him that would show above the table would raise no doubt in the waiter's mind. A roasted mallard duck, thought Soapy, would be about the thing—with a bottle of Chablis, and then Camembert, a demi-tasse and a cigar. One dollar for the cigar would be enough. The total would not be so high as to call forth any supreme manifestation of revenge from the cafe management; and yet the meat would leave him filled and happy for the journey to his winter refuge.

But as Soapy set foot inside the restaurant door the head waiter's eye fell upon his frayed trousers and decadent shoes. Strong and ready hands turned him about and conveyed him in silence and haste to the sidewalk and averted the ignoble fate of the menaced mallard.

Soapy turned off Broadway. It seemed that his route to the coveted island was not to be an epicurean one. Some other way of entering limbo must be thought of.

At a corner of Sixth Avenue electric lights and cunningly displayed wares behind a plate glass made a shop window conspicuous. Soapy took a cobblestone and dashed it through the glass. People came running around the corner, a policeman in the lead. Soapy stood still, with his hands in his pockets, and smiled at the sight of brass buttons.

"Where's the man that done that?" inquired the officer excitedly.

"Don't you figure out that I might have had something to do with it?" said Soapy, not without sarcasm, but friendly, as one greets good fortune.

The policeman's mind refused to accept Soapy even as a clue. Men who smash windows do not remain to parley with the law's minions. They take to their heels. The policeman saw a man halfway down the block running to catch a car. With drawn club he joined in the pursuit. Soapy, with disgust in his heart, loafed along, twice unsuccessful.

On the opposite side of the street was a restaurant of no great pretensions. It catered to large appetites and modest purses. Its crockery and atmosphere were thick; its soup and napery thin. Into this place Soapy took his accusive shoes and telltale trousers without challenge. At a table he sat and consumed beefsteak, flap-jacks, doughnuts, and pie. And then to the waiter he betrayed the fact that the minutest coin and himself were strangers.

"Now, get busy and call a cop," said Soapy. "And don't keep a gentleman waiting."

"No cop for youse," said the waiter, with a voice like butter cakes and an eye like the cherry in a Manhattan cocktail. "Hey, Con!"

Neatly upon his left ear on the callous pavement two waiters pitched Soapy. He arose, joint by joint, as a carpenter's rule opens, and beat the dust from his clothes. Arrest seemed but a rosey dream. The Island seemed very far away. A policeman who stood before a drugstore two doors away laughed and walked down the street.

Five blocks Soapy traveled before his courage permitted him to woo capture again. This time the opportunity presented what he fatuously termed to himself a "cinch." A young woman of a modest and pleasing guise was standing before a show window gazing with sprightly interest at its display of shaving mugs and inkstands, and two yards from the window a large policeman of severe demeanor leaned against a water plug.

It was Soapy's design to assume the role of the despicable and execrated "masher." The refined and elegant appearance of his victim and the contiguity of the con-scientious cop encouraged him to believe that he would soon feel the pleasant of-ficial clutch upon his arm that would insure his winter quarters on the right little, tight little isle.

Soapy straightened the lady missionary's ready-made tie, dragged his shrinking cuffs into the open, set his hat at a killing cant, and sidled toward the young woman. He made eyes at her, was taken with sudden coughs and "hems," smiled, smirked, and went brazenly through the impudent and contemptible litany of the "masher." With half an eye Soapy saw that the policeman was watching him fixedly. The young woman moved away a few steps, and again bestowed her ab-sorbed attention upon the shaving mugs. Soapy followed, boldly stepping to her side, raised his hat and said:

"Ah there, Bedelia! Don't you want to come and play in my yard?"

The policeman was still looking. The persecuted young woman had but to beckon a finger and Soapy would be practically en route for his insular haven. Already he imagined he could feel the cozy warmth of the station house. The young woman faced him and, stretching out a hand, caught Soapy's coat sleeve.

"Sure, Mike," she said joyfully, "if you'll blow me to a pail of suds. I'd have spoke to you sooner, but the cop was watching."

With the young woman playing the clinging ivy to his oak, Soapy walked past the policeman overcome with gloom. He seemed doomed to liberty.

At the next corner he shook off his companion and ran. He halted in the district where by night are found the lightest streets, hearts, vows, and librettos. Women in furs and men in greatcoats moved gaily in the wintry air. A sudden fear seized Soapy that some dreadful enchantment had rendered him immune to arrest. The thought brought a little of panic upon it, and when he came upon another po-liceman lounging grandly in front of a transplendent theater he caught at the im-mediate straw of "disorderly conduct."

On the sidewalk Soapy began to yell drunken gibberish at the top of his harsh voice. He danced, howled, raved, and otherwise disturbed the welkin.

The policeman twirled his club, turned his back to Soapy and remarked to a citizen:

"'Tis one of them Yale lads celebratin' the goose egg they give to the Hartford College. Noisy; but no harm. We've instructions to leave them be."

Disconsolate, Soapy ceased his unavailing racket. Would never a policeman lay hands on him? In his fancy the Island seemed an unattainable Arcadia. He buttoned his thin coat against the chilling wind.

In a cigar store he saw a well-dressed man lighting a cigar at a swinging light. His silk umbrella he had set by the door on entering. Soapy stepped inside, secured the umbrella, and sauntered off with it slowly. The man at the cigar light followed hastily.

"My umbrella," he said, sternly.

"Oh, is it?" sneered Soapy, adding insult to petit larceny. "Well, why don't you call a policeman? I took it. Your umbrella! Why don't you call a cop? There stands one on the corner."

The umbrella owner slowed his steps. Soapy did likewise, with a presentiment that luck would again run against him. The policeman looked at the two curiously.

"Of course," said the umbrella man—"that is—well, you know how these mistakes occur—I—if it's your umbrella I hope you'll excuse me—I picked it up this morning in a restaurant—if you recognize it as yours, why—I hope you'll—"

"Of course it's mine," said Soapy, viciously.

The ex-umbrella man retreated. The policeman hurried to assist a tall blonde in an opera cloak across the street in front of a streetcar that was approaching two blocks away.

Soapy walked eastward through a street damaged by improvements. He hurled the umbrella wrathfully into an excavation. He muttered against the men who wear helmets and carry clubs. Because he wanted to fall into their clutches, they seemed to regard him as a king who could do no wrong.

At length Soapy reached one of the avenues to the east where the glitter and turmoil was but faint. He set his face down this toward Madison Square, for the homing instinct survives even when the home is a park bench.

But on an unusually quiet corner Soapy came to a standstill. Here was an old church, quaint and rambling and gabled. Through one violet-stained window a soft light glowed, where, no doubt, the organist loitered over the keys, making sure of his mastery of the coming Sabbath anthem. For there drifted out to Soapy's ears sweet music that caught and held him transfixed against the convolutions of the iron fence.

The moon was above, lustrous and serene; vehicles and pedestrians were few; sparrows twittered sleepily in the eaves—for a little while the scene might have been a country churchyard. And the anthem that the organist played cemented Soapy to the iron fence, for he had known it well in the days when his life contained such things as mothers and roses and ambitions and friends and immaculate thoughts and collars.

The conjunction of Soapy's receptive state of mind and the influences about the old church wrought a sudden and wonderful change in his soul. He viewed with swift horror the pit into which he had tumbled, the degraded days, unworthy desires, dead hopes, wrecked faculties, and base motives that made up his existence.

And also in a moment his heart responded thrillingly to this novel mood. An instantaneous and strong impulse moved him to battle with his desperate fate. He would pull himself out of the mire; he would make a man of himself again; he would conquer the evil that had taken possession of him. There was time; he was comparatively young yet; he would resurrect his old eager ambitions and pursue them without faltering. Those solemn but sweet organ notes had set up a revolution in him. Tomorrow he would go into the roaring downtown district and find work. A fur importer had once offered him a place as a driver. He would find him tomorrow and ask for the position. He would be somebody in the world. He would—

Soapy felt a hand laid on his arm. He looked quickly around into a broad face of a policeman.

"What are you doin' here?" asked the officer.

"Nothin'," said Soapy.

"Then come along," said the policeman.

"Three months on the Island," said the Magistrate in the Police Court the next morning.

TURN TO PAGE 115 FOR THE PRACTICE DRILLS TO COMPLETE TODAY'S WORK.

24

A DIFFERENT HAND MOVEMENT CAN HELP YOUR COMPREHENSION

You've been working with visual reading for only a few days, but possibly you're feeling slightly bedazzled by this type of practicing (assuming you've been following the directions). Maybe you're wondering if something more is supposed to happen or if you're doing something wrong. And in spite of your confusion here, I am introducing *new* hand movements, as though the old ones weren't enough. This chapter probably won't end your present feelings but it should help.

Most students need two or three weeks, sometimes much more, of determined practicing with visual reading before it makes much sense. I hope that you can ask that much of yourself because the rewards are well worth the little amount of trouble. In this chapter I want to show you some different hand movements and give you some drills to use them in. They probably will not solve all of your problems, but they will provide some interest and variety in your drilling. Above all they should help you get a little better comprehension and that's probably the most important thing for you right now.

THE GOOD REASON FOR NEW HAND MOVEMENTS

Apart from the fact that different hand movements can make your drilling more interesting, there is a definite reason why you should know and use different hand movements when reading. In teaching rapid reading we find that changing hand movements can help people get more comprehension from the same selection. In other words, two different people may find two very different hand movements are best suited for them in a certain passage. And you may find that changing from your current favorite hand movement to another in a selection that seems difficult will help you. At other times, you may find that your favorite hand movement no longer works well for you, and when you change, suddenly you find yourself comprehending much better.

It is important to become acquainted with at least several different hand movements. To do this you must use each one several times. Until a hand movement is automatic (you cannot be thinking of what your fingers are doing) you will not be able to "read" with it.

THE TWO TYPES OF HAND MOVEMENTS

There are two kinds of hand movements , those *with the individual fingers not moving,* and those which use some combination of fingers *constantly changing.* The underlining hand movement is an example of the first type: the hand moves *as a whole,* the fingers remain stationary. Dusting is another type of "whole hand" movement; although you use all of the fingers and the hand moves rapidly back and forth, the individual fingers are not moving. Paragraphing is also a whole hand movement. The type of hand movement in which the fingers move will be introduced in this chapter.

It is always important to keep in mind how important the hand's use as a pacer is. It helps you maintain your concentration, it attracts your eye to the page, and it helps you to avoid regressing.

Generally speaking, the more motion in the hand the better. The reason is simply that the more motion in the hand, the less movement there is with the eye. From our experience, this promotes both better speed as well as better comprehension. That is the reason for hand movements with the fingers *moving.*

Although it may be somewhat distracting in the beginning, you will soon find the two-finger hand movements easy and comfortable. Follow the illustration in Figure 12 with your middle, then index fingers. Go over this many times until it feels normal, comfortable, and you can do it automatically.

"UNDERLINING" WITH TWO FINGERS

When you have become accustomed to changing your fingers, attempt to read a page this way—it should be quite easy. Once you are able to change your fingers reading linearly, then you are ready to learn the new hand movements for visual reading.

FIGURE 12. UNDERLINING WITH TWO FINGERS

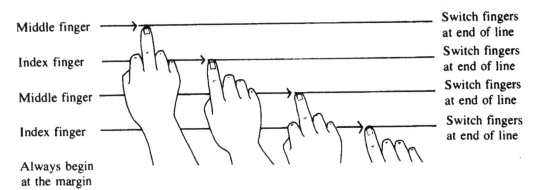

Middle finger —————→ Switch fingers at end of line

Index finger —————→ Switch fingers at end of line

Middle finger ————→ Switch fingers at end of line

Index finger ————→ Switch fingers at end of line

Always begin at the margin

It is easy to remember that in all of these hand movements *the middle finger always goes from left-to-right*. After changing fingers, *the index finger always goes from right-to-left*.

THE SLASHING HAND MOVEMENT

There are two new hand movements to learn. Slashing is the first one, and it's easiest to learn. When slashing, you move your middle finger from left-to-right, then switch to your index finger and *slash* diagonally down from right-to-left, coming down about four to five lines, and looking at all of the words that you "slash" through as you go. As with paragraphing, you should pay attention to the paragraphs, always beginning a new paragraph by going across from left to right. The pattern of slashing looks somewhat like the letter "Z" and with that in mind it is quite easy to remember. Run your fingers over the illustration in Figure 13 many times until you can do it very comfortably and almost without thinking.

Before going on to the next hand movement, practice slashing over several pages of reading material just to get used to it. Remember that you must practice a hand movement for several minutes to let it become automatic before you can even think of trying to use it to help you read. So practice a few pages, then come back and go on to the next one.

FIGURE 13. THE SLASHING HAND MOVEMENT

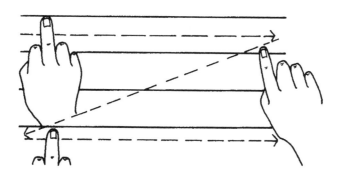

THE CRISS-CROSSING HAND MOVEMENT

Criss-crossing is just as easy to learn as slashing, because it also follows the pattern of a letter. This time it resembles an "X."

Once again your middle finger will move from left-to-right, but it will start out moving *down* several lines. This is the first time you haven't moved across the page linearly when going from left to right. Once again, move your fingers over the illustration (Figure 15) many times until you develop the "feel" for the criss-crossing hand movement. Be certain to come out into the margins when you are changing fingers. Cupping your hand as in Figure 14 will often help you to be in a position to change fingers easily.

Now practice doing the criss-crossing hand movement.

"CRISS-CROSSING"

Before going on to the exercise, be certain to practice criss-crossing on several pages so that you won't have to be thinking of what your fingers are doing. In this hand movement try to begin it with new paragraphs, but as it is a generally downward movement all the time, this starts breaking away from a paragraph orientation and begins to focus more on the page as a whole.

Once you've practiced these two new hand movements , try them in the following new reading drill in Exercise 36.

FIGURE 14. HAND POSITION FOR CHANGING FINGER HAND MOVEMENTS

"Cup" your hand when you do a
changing finger hand movement

Remember to tuck the fingers
you aren't using under your hand

FIGURE 15. THE CRISS-CROSSING HAND MOVEMENT

Now practice doing the criss-crossing hand movement:

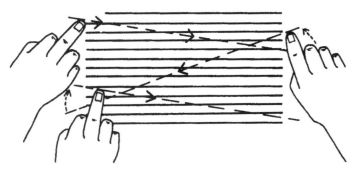

EXERCISE NO. 36

Materials: *Book*
        Timing device

1. Select an easy book, one suitable for high speed drilling. Using circling or paragraphing, "read" as fast as you can for one minute. Make an "X" mark where you stop reading. Compute your rate.

   On the chart below, find the amount (or portion of page(s)) according to the reading rate you have just computed to use in the drill below:

IF YOUR READING RATE IS:	THEN THIS IS THE AMOUNT TO USE:
Under 500 WPM	1/3 of a page
500 to 800 WPM	2/3 of a page
800 to 1,200 WPM	1 page
1,200 to 1,800 WPM	2 pages
Over 1,800 WPM	3 pages

2. Practice read, using paragraphing, the entire section you read in Step No. 1 above *plus* one amount of page(s), in one minute. Be certain to make your mark.

3. Practice read, using slashing, the entire section you read in Step No. 1 above *plus* two amounts of page(s), in one minute.

4. Practice read, using criss-crossing, the entire section you read in Step No. 1 above *plus* three amounts of page(s), in one minute.

5. Practice read, using either paragraphing, slashing or criss-crossing, the entire section you read in Step No. 1 above *plus* four amounts of page(s), in one minute.

6. Go back to the "X" mark, where you finished the first reading, in Step No. 1 above. Read *from* that mark for one minute, as fast as you can, using any hand movement except underlining.

7. Compute your reading rate in Step No. 6 by figuring the total number of words in the final section read.

   Record this on your progress profile.

Once you've done this drill, go back to your practice drills for the week and do as many of them as you can. While you're doing them you may also want to try doing the paragraphing hand movement using two fingers: the middle finger goes from left to right across the top line of the paragraph, then you switch to the index finger when coming *down and around* the rest of the paragraph. Be certain to switch back to the middle finger again when you start across the next line from left to right.

AND WHY NOT STRAIGHT DOWN THE PAGE?

Many students wonder why we do not teach them to move their hand straight down the page, and some try to do this on their own. There is a very good reason for this. If you start to come straight down the page, you are very apt to establish incorrect eye movement patterns. You will probably teach yourself to take in phrases from the *center* of each line. This will give you some comprehension and you may think you are learning the skill of visual reading. Most likely you will not. Moving the hand back and forth across the page causes your eyes to follow the hand and to see *all* of the words. This is the way the eyes of natural speed readers move and the only way you can be certain you are seeing all of the words and not just skimming. Although skimming is useful, as you've already learned, it's not a substitute for reading.

TURN TO PAGE 115 FOR THE PRACTICE DRILLS TO COMPLETE TODAY'S WORK.

Practice Drills for Week 5

As soon as you have completed Chapters Nineteen through Twenty-four and have spent at least six days doing the third set of practice drills, you should be ready for this next set. As before, spend one full day just working on these practice drills without doing another chapter. Then the next day read Chapter Twenty-five and follow it by repeating the practice drills. Continue on each day doing another chapter and repeating the drills.

Always do the drills in order, after having finished the day's chapter. If you practice only a short while, do the first drill; if you practice longer, do the first drill followed by the second, and so forth. Do not repeat any drills in any one day until you have first completed all of them. You may, however, do only the first or first and second drills on one day and on the following day begin with the third drill.

Materials You Will Need for This Week's Drills

1. *A timing device.*
2. *Pen or pencil.*
3. *Paper.* Preferably unlined 8 1/2 × 11 inches.
4. *Basic list of books.*

DRILL NO. 13

Materials: Nonfiction book of moderate difficulty, pencil, paper
Estimated Time: 15 minutes

Purpose: Develop the ability to analyze paragraphs quickly
Objective: Attempt to cover more paragraphs each day in the same amount of time

DO THIS DRILL ONCE PER PRACTICE SESSION

Diagram:

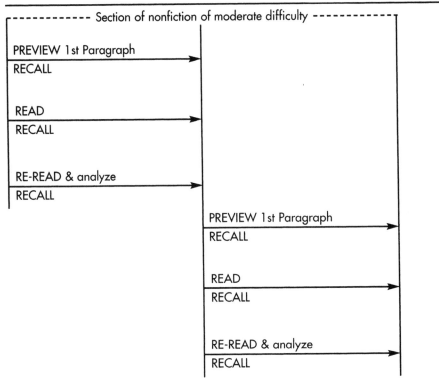

Explanation:

1. Select a section and start with the first paragraph.
    Preview the first paragraph, using your hand, *just for the purpose of finding what it's about*. Draw a diagonal recall pattern and put down what the paragraph is about without looking back.

2. Read the same paragraph carefully, using any hand movement you wish, *for the purpose of understanding it well*. Without looking back at the paragraph, add to your recall pattern.

3. Re-read the same paragraph, using an underlining hand movement, and *beginning with the third sentence* find out if the sentences relate back to the previous sentence or if they refer back to the first or second sentence.
    You need not make a diagram of the paragraph (unless you wish to do so).
    Without looking back at the paragraph, add anything more that you remember to your recall pattern.

4. Continue on, one paragraph after another, doing as many paragraphs as you can in 15 minutes. Record the number of paragraphs on your progress profile.

DRILL NO. 14

Materials: Basic List
Estimated Time: 12 minutes

Purpose: Practice using various hand movements
Objective: Do hand movements in required amount of time

THIS DRILL MAY BE REPEATED

Diagram:

```
┌---------------------- Chapter or section of about 12 pages ----------------------┐
| DUSTING HAND MOVEMENT                                    3 seconds/page           |
|----------------------------------------------------------------------------→      |
| RECALL anything on a diagonal recall pattern                                       |
|                                                                                   |
| PARAGRAPHING HAND MOVEMENT                              12 seconds/page            |
|----------------------------------------------------------------------------→      |
| RECALL                                                                             |
|                                                                                   |
| SLASHING HAND MOVEMENT                                  10 seconds/page            |
|----------------------------------------------------------------------------→      |
| RECALL                                                                             |
|                                                                                   |
| CRISS-CROSSING HAND MOVEMENT                            8 seconds/page             |
|----------------------------------------------------------------------------→      |
| RECALL                                                                             |
|                                                                                   |
| COMPUTE & RECORD criss-crossing rate                                              |
└-----------------------------------------------------------------------------------┘
```

Explanation:

1. Select a chapter or section of a chapter approximately 12 pages long.

2. Using the dusting hand movement, move down each page, spending no more than three seconds per page (count if you wish to help maintain the correct speed). Set up a diagonal recall pattern. Recall anything you can remember (which may be very little).

3. Using the paragraphing hand movement, repeat the entire section, spending no more than twelve seconds per page (about six complete hand movements per page).

READING PURPOSE: Attempt to follow the barest story line.
    Add anything you can to your recall pattern.

4. Using the slashing hand movement, repeat the entire section, spending no more than ten seconds per page (about five complete hand movements per page). Add to your recall.

5. Time yourself (how long this entire step takes to do).
   Use the criss-crossing hand movement to repeat the entire section, spending no more than eight seconds per page (about four complete hand movements per page). Add to your recall.

6. Compute your practice reading rate in Step 5 (criss-crossing). Find the total number of words in the entire section, then divide that by the number of minutes taken to do the criss-crossing through the material.

CAUTION: Make certain to maintain a practice reading rate in step 5 over 1,800 WPM. Record your rate on your progress profile.

DRILL NO. 15

Materials: Assorted books
        paper and pencil
        timing device
Estimated Time: 15 minutes

Purpose: Develop confidence in using rapid
        reading techniques in different materials
Objective: Adjust the techniques according to
        the materials and your purposes.

THIS DRILL MAY BE REPEATED

Diagram:

```
|-------------------- Chapter or section of about 6-10 pages --------------------|
| PREVIEW according to the form                                                →  |
| RECALL                                                                          |
| PRACTICE READ (Paragraphing, slashing, or cris-crossing)    10-12 seconds/page  |
| RECALL                                                                          |
| READ (Choice of hand movement) time yourself                                 →  |
| RECALL                                                                          |
| COMPUTE & RECORD criss-crossing rate                                            |
| REVIEW (Paragraphing, slashing, or criss-crossing)          6 seconds/page   →  |
| RECALL                                                                          |
```

Explanation:

1. Select a chapter or section of a chapter of about 6-10 pages. Each day use a different type of book, alternating between fiction, nonfiction, and biography.

2. Preview the entire section according to its form: (1) nonfiction, skim the beginnings and endings of sections, (2) fiction, scan—using the dusting hand movement—the entire section, (3) biography, treat as though it were fiction.

READING PURPOSE: (1) Nonfiction: find main point of section, (2) Fiction or (3) Biography: find characters, general time, location, or what it's about.

Begin a diagonal recall pattern.

3. Practice read the entire section using paragraphing, slashing or criss-crossing hand movement and spend no more than ten seconds per page (about five complete hand movements per page). Add to your recall pattern.

4. *Read* the entire section as quickly as you can using any hand movement (underlining is acceptable). Time yourself on this section.

READING PURPOSE: Barely follow the story or line of thought.

Add to your recall pattern.

5. REVIEW the entire section using paragraphing, slashing or criss-crossing and spending no more than six seconds per page (about three complete hand movements per page, or more than three if using less than two seconds each).

Add to your recall pattern.

6. Compute your reading rate in Step 4. Find the total number of words in the entire section, then divide that by the number of minutes taken for that section. Record your rate on your progress profile.

DRILL NO. 16

Materials: Assorted books
           Timing device
Estimated Time: 10 minutes

Purpose: Stretch your rate according to your present level of comprehension

Objective: Make each mark in one minute

IF YOUR FIRST READING IS:	THEN ADD THIS AMOUNT:
Under 500 WPM	1/3 of a page
500 to 800 WPM	2/3 of a page
800 to 1,200 WPM	1 page
1,200 to 1,800 WPM	2 pages
Over 1,800 WPM	3 pages

THIS DRILL MAY BE REPEATED

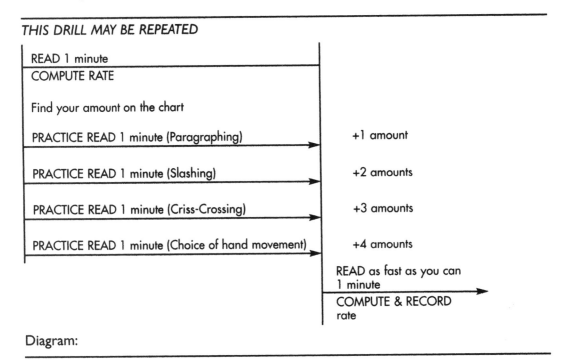

READ 1 minute	
COMPUTE RATE	
Find your amount on the chart	
PRACTICE READ 1 minute (Paragraphing)	+1 amount
PRACTICE READ 1 minute (Slashing)	+2 amounts
PRACTICE READ 1 minute (Criss-Crossing)	+3 amounts
PRACTICE READ 1 minute (Choice of hand movement)	+4 amounts
	READ as fast as you can 1 minute
	COMPUTE & RECORD rate

Diagram:

Explanation:

---

1. In an easy book read as fast as you can for one minute, any hand movement. Make an "X" mark where you stop reading.

2. Compute your rate.
   On the chart above, find the amount of pages you are to add for each practice reading. For instance, if you read over 500 words per minute but under 800, you would add one-half page to each practice reading.

3. Practice read, using paragraphing, the entire section plus one amount of page(s) that you are to add, in one minute.

4. Practice read, using slashing, the entire section plus two amounts of page(s) that you are to add, in one minute.

5. Practice read, using criss-crossing, the entire section plus three amounts of page(s) that you are to add, in one minute.

6. Practice read, using your choice of hand movements , the entire section plus four amounts of page(s) that you are to add, in one minute.

7. From the "X" mark, where you finished the first reading in Step 1, read ahead for one minute as fast as you can, using any hand movement used in this drill.

8. Compute your final reading rate by figuring the total number of words in the final section read. Record your rate on your progress profile.

DRILL NO. 17

Materials: Books listed in Chapter One   Purpose: Practice reading at four times
          Timing device   your initial reading rate
Estimated Time: 15 minutes   Objective: Maintain a reading rate of four times
          your initial rate with comprehension

THIS DRILL MAY BE REPEATED

Diagram:

      Find initial reading rate and round down to nearest tenth
      Set up five sections eight times the amount

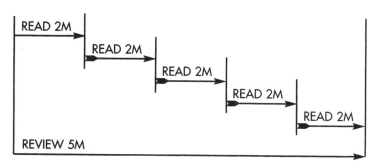

COMPUTE & RECORD rate

Explanation:

---

1.   Take your initial reading rate from Chapter Two.
     Round this amount down to the nearest tenth. Multiply this result by eight.
     Set up five sections of words approximately equal to the final amount.
     Mark the end of each section with a paper clip or small strip of paper sticking
     out from the page.
2.   Using your hand as a pacer, attempt to read the first section in two minutes. You
     may use any hand movement you choose.

**READING PURPOSE: Attempt to follow the story line. Make the mark even at the
loss of comprehension.**

3.   Continue, reading each part in two minutes or less.
4.   Review the whole in five minutes or less.
5.   Compute the reading rate of any section and record it on your progress profile.

25

MAKE STUDY READING A GAME

Study reading is really just an intellectual sport if you understand the basic laws of learning. It has always amazed me that we require people to attend school for 12 years, continue on for another four years, and increasingly go on to graduate school, and yet during all this time rarely teach them *how* to learn. In this chapter, you will find out some of the basic fundamentals of learning.

Some may surprise you, all should interest you, and you should definitely discover some shortcuts to learning while reading. Some people never realize that they are *always* learning. It's not something that just happens in a classroom. Every time you meet someone and remember their name, when you watch the news on television and then tell someone about it, whenever you master a computer program—these are all instances of learning. We are all good learners and concentrate easily in *some* area: a favorite sport, a certain hobby, perhaps an intellectual subject. To find out why and how you are a good learner in *any* situation is the purpose here, so that you can find out how to apply it to other situations and become more efficient.

WHAT'S HAPPENING WHILE YOU'RE LEARNING

To learn something we must first get information about it. This must be information we see, hear, touch, smell or taste. That's the usual way we receive information, and it all comes through the various senses first as stimuli to the various nerves.

In a certain sense, learning is a process of dealing with many different stimuli. And you are constantly receiving many stimuli from different sources.

How many things do you "feel" right now? The touch of your clothes, the floor you are standing on (you can feel it *through* your shoes and socks as well), the pen you are holding, the table your arm is resting on, the warmth or coolness of the air, and on and on. Simultaneously you are also hearing many sounds—outside traffic, breathing, the clicking of a keyboard, a creak in the building, the hum of a printer, people talking faintly in the next room. There are so many stimuli being received at any given moment that it is difficult to list them all.

THE MIND CAN'T HANDLE EVERYTHING THAT COMES TO IT

Even if you relax and attempt to become aware of all the various stimuli you are hearing, touching, seeing, tasting, smelling, you will soon realize that though they are there you are not *dealing* with *all* of them all of the time. You are tuning most of them out and paying attention to only a few things. In fact, it is not possible to be aware of all of these stimuli at one time. We tend to unconsciously select stimuli to be aware of. For example, if you picked up a hot pan handle from a stove, believing it to be cool, you will immediately process those feelings. In effect you are "learning" this information.

It is important to become aware that it is never possible, nor efficient, to take in 100 percent of what you are dealing with. In informal learning you almost unconsciously select the stimuli. In a more formal situation you must *learn to select what it is that you want to learn.*

CONCENTRATION IS A TRICK

After you isolate specific things to be learned, you then must concentrate on them. Concentration is a word that is usually used to remind us of something that we are not doing. Actually we are always concentrating on something, unless we are asleep or in a state of semi-consciousness. Concentrating simply means to be *involved* with something. The student "not concentrating" in the classroom, daydreaming or looking out the window, is certainly concentrating. He is involved with his thoughts or involved with some action outside.

The way to consciously concentrate on something is to find simple ways to become actively involved with the object. Try to use all channels for receiving stimuli that you can: touch, sound, sight, taste, smell. In most instances sight, touch, and sound will be all that are practical. To become involved you must find things to *do*. For instance, if you wanted to concentrate on a painting, you might see how many different colors were used (that you could determine), or count the number of persons depicted in a crowd scene. Such *activities* would easily allow you to keep involved. It is certainly much better than staring at the painting with an intensely furrowed brow.

In concentrating and learning verbal information, you must also learn to become active, to find an activity to help your concentration, to learn to *use* this information.

THE TWO RULES OF LEARNING

The two primary rules in learning something efficiently are: first, you must set a purpose, which will help you to isolate what it is that you wish to learn. The more specifically you can do this, the easier it will be. Second, you must know how to involve yourself with what it is you wish to learn. Completing this chicken-or-egg proposition can best be done when the information to be learned is well defined.

Being able to determine your purpose is probably the hardest aspect of learning. It involves knowing how to pick out what it is that you wish to learn, which we will deal with extensively in the next chapter. If you have understood that you can't ever deal with 100 percent, that you can't learn "all there is," so therefore you *must* select, then you are well on your way to becoming a more efficient learner.

WAYS TO INCREASE YOUR CONCENTRATION

To involve yourself with written information, first it is important not to let the subject overwhelm you with its magnitude. If you are studying a difficult 30-page chapter, break it into manageable sections. How large or small will depend both on the difficulty of the material as well as your purpose for reading it. If the author offers no subheads or other easy aids to break it up, divide it arbitrarily into five, six, or ten parts. You can always adjust your "sections" as you read, placing them where they might logically be.

The next important step is to develop activities that use the information, involving as many of the senses as possible. This sort of traps your concentration, if a lot of your channels of reception of information are involved with a certain subject, and then it is more difficult to lose your concentration to something else. In reading you see as well as have the motor activity of the moving hand. The use of the hand definitely contributes to your concentration in a major way. These are only two of the ways you can involve yourself.

THE TRUE TEST OF LEARNING

Recalling, another activity, is certainly a student's "best friend." It is the only indication that you have learned something. It gets information out of the book and into, or at least through, you. Processes like underlining and copying only postpone learning. Underlining basically leaves the information *in the book*. Recalling, without referring to the book, but from your memory and in your own words, causes you to learn very efficiently. It's possibly the best way of knowing whether or not you've learned something.

READ AGGRESSIVELY

William James, the great psychologist who did a lot of research on memory, wrote that "All improvement of memory consists in the improvement of one's habitual methods of recording facts." That's an important statement with a lot to think about. It implies that you should be actively reading, *organizing as you read,* and doing whatever contributes to improving the recording or initial reception of the information. Passive reading usually requires a duplication of the time spent to learn the information. Reading to recall and reading to organize the information are active steps which help you to learn more efficiently. If you know you are going to try to recall the information afterwards, more information tends to stick.

"USE" THE INFORMATION WELL

The only way you can become involved with information you wish to learn is to *use* it in some way. Basically your choices are few: they run from rote repetition of the information to some meaningful organization or synthesis of it. The former makes for rather dull learning and the latter for very interesting learning.

The first thing to do is to look over the whole and then break it up into parts. When you have it broken into parts you then begin by reading and recalling each part. To become even more efficient you should also begin to organize: preview and recall first to find the main point, then begin reading and recalling to find out more. Finally you may review and recall to check yourself. How thoroughly you do each step depends of course on your purpose. Possibly your purpose would be met with a simple previewing?

There are many ways to become involved with material, but be certain that you take small enough parts with which you can succeed. In this next exercise it is assumed that the purpose has been established and the material divided. Now you are to practice the involvement techniques.

EXERCISE NO. 37

Materials: *Paper and pen or pencil or a word processing program on your PC.*

Directions: *When studying difficult passages, they sometimes must be studied paragraph by paragraph. Assume the following paragraphs are difficult for you. First preview a paragraph quickly just to find what it's basically about; cover the paragraph and begin a recall pattern. Then read the paragraph for the purpose of understanding it; cover the paragraph and see how much you can recall. If you feel you need to know more, or that your recall is not adequate, re-read the paragraph, cover it, and recall again.*

1. Psychology derives its name from two Greek words, psyche, meaning spirits, and logos, meaning speech or sayings. In classical terms, then, psychology is a collection of words about the spirit or mind. The Greeks liked to differentiate between the physical side of man—his corporeal being—and his mental or spiritual side.

From this ancient dualism has come the most troublesome spector ever to haunt a science, namely, the mind-body problem. Does the mind affect the body's behavior or vice versa? Even today, psychology has not completely solved this dualistic dilemma.

2. The Trying Twenties confront us with the question of how to take hold in the adult world. Our focus shifts from the interior turmoils of late adolescence— "Who am I?" "What is truth?"—and we become almost totally preoccupied with working out the externals. "How do I put my aspirations into effect?" "What is the best way to start?" "Where do I go?" "Who can help me?" "How did *you* do it?" In this period, which is longer and more stable compared with the passage that leads to it, the tasks are as enormous as they are exhilarating: to shape a dream, that vision of ourselves which will generate energy, aliveness, and hope. To prepare for a lifework. To find a mentor if possible. And to form the capacity for intimacy, without losing in the process whatever consistency of self we have thus far mustered. The first test structure must be erected around the life we choose to try.

3. Although one of man's most powerful drives is his need for love, he is full of another emotion which has not been clearly brought to public attention until the recent acts of violence and hostility. This emotion, anger, probably has a greater influence on a human being's behavior and mental and physical health than the drive for love.

4. Carl Rogers's conceptions of personality and psychopathology and his techniques of therapy have gained increasing acceptance in the United States. Chronologically, Rogers developed his technique of treatment first. Only considerably later did he begin to develop an integrated, inclusive theory about personality and psychopathology. Rogers assumed first that man's nature is innately good and that he will naturally become kind, concerned, friendly, and effective in the process of actualizing his nature unless he is diverted from the course of his normal development.

5. Light reaching the eye is focused on the retina, where it elicits complex neural responses. The light first passes through the cornea, then the aqueous humor, then the pupil, then the lens, and finally the vitreous humor before reaching the retina. The lens by changing its shape—accommodation—focuses the light on the retina. The lens thickens in order to focus near objects and returns to its flatter shape to focus far objects (twenty feet or farther away). Near-sightedness (myopia), the inability to distinguish far objects clearly, results when the lens is not flat enough to focus the light rays on the retina. Nearsightedness usually is not the fault of the lens; the retina is too far from the lens, so that the far object is focused on a plane in front of the retina and the retinal image is blurred.

TURN TO PAGE 161 FOR THE PRACTICE DRILLS TO COMPLETE TODAY'S WORK.

26

READ WITH
DEFINED PURPOSES

At this point, I hope that you no longer believe that you should cherish every word in everything you read. There are so many reasons for reading, but few people vary their reading techniques to suit their reading purposes. Everything so far should have led you to an understanding of why you should do this. This chapter will show you how to set different purposes, so that you can plan your reading techniques and become a more efficient reader.

READING PURPOSES VARY WIDELY

If you are a student, and students as a group probably do the most serious reading, your reading purposes can vary enormously. You might be assigned a chapter in a business management textbook that is only 20 pages long; you might also know that you will have a 20-question quiz on the chapter at the end of the week. You may also be aware that your teacher expects you to be familiar with the new words and concepts, to understand and know the examples and discussions—and possibly to be able to recall them. Probably this is as *responsible* a reading as you will be asked to do in your career as a student, or at any time.

But you might also be enrolled in a graduate seminar. In this hypothetical course, 15 books are assigned for the term, and one book is discussed each week. Certainly the instructor does not expect you to be as responsible in reading each chapter as your biology professor does. This time you should be reading to find the thesis of the book, to find how it is developed throughout the book, probably to become familiar with some of the main ideas of the various chapters. This ultimately requires a good, intelligent reading of the material.

WHEN YOUR PURPOSE IS PLEASURE

You might also be reading a mystery or a novel for your own enjoyment. Your purpose is certainly not to take a test; it is only to become involved and enjoy the book. You have no need to remember anything that you don't wish to.

You might also be in business, reviewing reports, reading long e-mails from clients, some important and some routine. You might be going through many books and journals to find support for points you are going to make in a speech or paper. There are so many different reasons for reading anything, and just as the reasons differ, so should your reading approach to the various materials.

A STOCK BROKER FINDS THERE'S MORE TO IT THAN SPEED ALONE

In a class at the successful brokerage house of Donaldson, Lufkin and Jenrette, where I trained about 30 executives, one of these well-educated men, John, stayed after class to tell me that he really appreciated what he was learning. In group classes such as this one, I teach a special course which involves no outside practicing because many business and professional people are far too busy to find time for practicing. So I teach a very practical version of rapid reading which just aims for a doubling of reading speeds with all of the work done in the materials from their work.

In spite of a successful career and an outstanding education at one of this country's top universities, John felt that learning to determine his purpose in a reading and finding out that he didn't "have" to read everything the same way was positively revolutionary. He was not only able to more than double his reading rate within a few class sessions; in addition he was able to save an equal amount of time just by carefully deciding his purpose. This resulted in "reading" almost five times as fast as he had originally.

READ SMARTER AND FASTER

It's especially important to understand that good reading is not just faster reading, it's also smarter reading—knowing when to speed up, when to slow down, what to read and what not to, and all the other good "tricks" an efficient reader uses.

The more specific you can be in defining what your purpose is for reading something, the more efficiently you can read it. Sometimes this is simple. In reading a mystery your only purpose is enjoyment, so read it in the most comfortable manner, taking as long or short a time as you wish. Sometimes it is more difficult. A teacher may give a reading assignment without stating a purpose; then it is necessary for you to set one.

DON'T LET CHANCE DETERMINE YOUR PURPOSE

In the case of an unspecified purpose, do not give up in the beginning and just "read" it. You will soon find that if you have a defined approach with a predetermined purpose, you will end with what you want. If you have no system, what comes out will be hit or miss. *You make a decision even when you do nothing.* It's either making an intelligent choice or guess, or leaving it up to chance.

LEVELS OF READING AND LEARNING

Here is a way of approaching general information and text books which you may find helpful. Determine in advance, or as early as possible while reading the book, *what level of information* you need to obtain from the book.

The first level of information for any piece of material would be the work's thesis or main idea or overall point. Naturally, if this is all you need to get from it, it is probable that you could do so with a good overall preview.

The next level of information would be to learn the main point of each chapter or unit of the book. The third level would be to know the main points of sections within chapters, and so on. Only rarely do you need to work at the fifth level, the memorization level. First year medical students certainly spend a lot of their time studying for this level of information. "Reading" when your learning purpose is so demanding is very difficult to do at high rates. However, the dedicated student can usually cut this learning time in half by learning both the rapid reading skills and the study techniques well.

Levels of Information in Reading

1. Book's thesis or main idea
2. Main point of each chapter
3. Main point of each section within chapters
4. Main point of most paragraphs
5. Details within each paragraph (memorization)

It is also important to realize that a very valid level of information in reading a book is just to be able to know the subject areas covered in the book—in other words, what book has the information you're seeking on a particular subject. You can't learn everything you read, nor should you be expected to do so. Part of setting your purpose in any reading situation is simply to determine whether you wish to learn anything from the material at all, or if you just want to find out what's in the book.

HOW TO DEFINE A PURPOSE WHEN STUDYING

Let's go back and look at the first example in this chapter. Our student has been assigned 20 pages in a business management textbook. This is not the first assignment, there have been several, and every week he has found that there is a 20-question quiz on that week's reading. He has several choices.

If there is a chapter summary, vocabulary words, or questions about the reading at the end of the chapter, this should be read first and used as a guide to the chapter. After all, this is the author telling you what is important. Some readers feel that to look at the end first is in some way cheating, but that is nonsense. Your purpose is to learn and any way that you can do it efficiently is certainly all right.

If there is no chapter summary or questions, there are other approaches. Think of the quiz from the teacher's point of view: what *kind* of questions does he ask? Details, conceptual, problem solving, vocabulary? If *you* were going to write the quiz how would you do it? You might look for one good question per page (20 questions, 20 pages, or adjust it accordingly). There might be five main divisions in the chapter, of equal or unequal length. You might try to find the main ideas or points in each section. This is the moment to decide at what level of information you need to read and study the material.

WHEN YOU'RE NOT CERTAIN

If you can, discuss with your teacher what he expects you to know, what "counts" most—lectures, textbook, whatever. Of course your teacher may not tell you. Maybe this is your first assignment and you feel too shy to ask. Then you must approach it in some sensible way, guessing the purpose. Begin with the length of the selection to be read: what level information would you expect your students to know from such an amount of reading assigned over a given period of time? Remember, *any intelligent approach is better than an approach that is just left up to chance.* It not only results in better learning (and grades) but also in less time spent studying.

If you had to read a passage which contained ten paragraphs of equal length, and even upon questioning your instructor you could not determine how responsibly you should read the material, you should still set a purpose. If you had read the material your former way, going once through, how much would you be able to recall at the end of your reading? Five points, maybe eight or ten? And would that have been enough?

Simply predetermine what you would think is enough: perhaps two or three points per paragraph, maybe only a point for every two or three paragraphs. Whatever you decide, then divide the material up according to this predetermined purpose. For instance, if you felt you should be able to recall two or three points per paragraph, then break the passage into paragraphs.

If you felt that a point for every two or three paragraphs would be enough, then break it up into sections of two to three paragraphs.

DRAW THE RECALL PATTERN IN ADVANCE

When you are first learning this system it is best to set up a recall pattern in advance with a branch for each piece of information you have predetermined you should be able to recall. This tells you how much you should get and also when you have gotten enough from the passage.

HOW TO LEARN THE CORRECT INFORMATION

Once you've defined your purpose for a passage, you might wonder: how do I find the information I want? You already know these techniques and you only need apply them to meet your newly-defined purposes. If the material was divided into five main divisions, you would begin by previewing the first division. Stop and recall its *main* point. Go back and read this section carefully, again stopping at the end to recall whatever you can. When you are able to recall the main ideas and points in this section, you are ready to move ahead to the next one. But you should read, re-read, and re-read again *until you have met your purpose*. You might be re-reading only to find a certain item, or reviewing it, but continue until your purpose is satisfied: that you can recall as many points as you set out to get in your own words.

If you were the student enrolled in the graduate seminar, then your purpose could vary. Possibly there are no quizzes or tests at all, just a discussion of the books read. Possibly you are also asked to write a paper or two for the course. In this case you would first preview the entire book for its main thesis, then you would stop and recall it. Maybe your purpose would be met with this one step.

You might actually meet your purpose with a good twenty- to thirty-minute preview. Or you might need more; you might continue and preview each chapter, or read the first and last chapters and preview the rest. I cannot give you the correct formula for each book—you must determine that yourself. I can only give you the techniques to use to meet your purposes and solve your reading problems.

HOWEVER YOU CAN LEARN MOST EFFICIENTLY IS THE RIGHT WAY

Possibly you think that this is not fair. Maybe you are thinking that you really should *read* the book, the whole book. Let me tell you one of my experiences. In one of the last graduate seminars I attended, there were about ten of us in the class. We were assigned a book each week. I allotted thirty minutes just prior to the seminar to "read" the book. I gave it a good preview, made up a quick recall pattern, and went into class. I usually found that out of the ten persons only one person had "read" the book (a very studious person with lots of time—maybe fifteen or so hours to spare). Several others had intended to read the book and had read one or two chapters. Several had not read it at all nor had even made the attempt. The result was usually a three-way discussion between the instructor, the studious person, and me. Unfortunately those who read only one or two chapters (usually starting from the front and word-by-wording it onward) had very little idea of the scope of the book and therefore were hard pressed to enter into a discussion of the book.

And if you are in some other situation—business, research, or self-improvement—you must adapt your reading techniques to suit your purpose. Here is a drill to help you begin.

EXERCISE NO. 38

Materials: *Paper and pencil or pen or a word processing program on your PC.*

Directions: *On a separate piece of paper, set up a recall pattern for each of the reading situations given below. First read what the problem or situation is, then look over the reading passage. From those two conditions determine: (1) how you would divide the passage, and do it by making a recall pattern which has a main branch for each part; (2) how many items you think you should be able to recall from each part, then put small subbranches onto the recall pattern.*

PROBLEM A. *You are a first-year medical student.* You will be given a quiz on this material tomorrow. This is the total material assigned. Usually the quiz has five questions.

DIFFERENTIAL DIAGNOSIS OF CONDITIONS INVOLVING EPISODIC WEAKNESS AND FAINTNESS BUT NOT SYNCOPE

ANXIETY ATTACKS AND THE HYPERVENTILATION SYNDROME. These are discussed in detail in Chaps. 14, 19, and 344. The giddiness of anxiety is frequently interpreted as a feeling of faintness without actual loss of consciousness. Such symptoms are not accompanied by facial pallor and are not relieved by recumbency. The diagnosis is made on the basis of the associated symptom, and part of the attack can be reproduced by hyperventilation. Two of the mechanisms known to be involved in the attacks are reduction in carbon dioxide as the result of hyperventilation and the release of epinephrine. Hyperventilation results in hypocapnia, alkalosis, increased cerebrovascular resistance, and decreased cerebral blood flow.

HYPOGLYCEMIA. When severe, hypoglycemia is usually traceable to a serious disease, such as a tumor of the islets of Langerhans or advanced adrenal, pituitary, or hepatic disease. The clinical picture is one of confusion or even a loss of consciousness. When mild, as is usually the case, hypoglycemia is the reactive type (Chap. 97), occurring 2 to 5 h after eating, and is not usually associated with a disturbance of consciousness. The diagnosis depends on the history, the documentation of reduced blood sugar during an attack, and the reproduction by an injection of insulin of a symptom complex exactly similar to that occurring in the spontaneous attacks.

ACUTE HEMORRHAGE. Acute blood loss, usually within the gastrointestinal tract, is an occasional cause of syncope. In the absence of pain and hematemesis the cause of the weakness, faintness, or even unconsciousness may remain obscure until the passage of a black stool.

CEREBRAL ISCHEMIC ATTACKS. These occur in some patients with arteriosclerotic narrowings or occlusion of the major arteries of the brain. The main symptoms vary from patient to patient and include dim vision, hemiparesis, numbness of one side of the body, dizziness, and thick speech, and to these may be added an impairment of consciousness. In any one patient all attacks are of identical type and indicate a temporary deficit of the function in a certain region of the brain due to inadequate circulation.

HYSTERICAL FAINTING. Hysterical fainting is rather frequent and usually occurs under dramatic circumstances (Chap. 344). The attack is unattended by any outward display of anxiety. The evident lack of change in pulse and blood pressure or color of the skin and mucous membranes distinguishes it from the vasodepressor faint. The diagnosis is based on the bizarre nature of the attack in a person who exhibits the general personality and behavioral characteristics of hysteria.*

EXERCISE NO. 38 CONTINUED

PROBLEM B. *You are studying to become a nurse.* You also have been assigned the above passage to read. You will be taking a quiz on the material tomorrow. This is only one of five passages assigned to be read. Usually the quiz has five questions.

PROBLEM C. *You are a bon vivant visiting New York City.* You must take an important person to dinner this evening. You wish to check on a certain restaurant and have obtained a restaurant guide. The passage below is a critique of one of these restaurants.

Il Monello Deserves Michelin Mention

By Peter Kump

A recent lunch at Il Monello in the heart of the upper East Side reminded me of many pleasant meals on quiet afternoons spent in Italy. From the white linen napery to the cheerful Italian staff you know you are in good hands. In fact, with

---

*From Harrison's *Principles of Internal Medicine*, Revised Eighth Edition, by Wintrobe et al. Used with permission of McGraw-Hill Book Company.

its comfortable red banquettes, warm paneled walls, and wine bottles for atmosphere, the restaurant is a good deal more attractive than many in Italy.

At Il Monello, with careful choosing, you can enjoy one of the best Italian meals to be found in New York. The menu offers a great variety from the Italian culinary palette and prices are moderately expensive.

Il Monello offers a nice variety of pastas and we began by sampling the house specialty, Fettucini Monello. I was assured it was just like the famous Fettucini Alfredo but with green noodles as well as the traditional white. I recently dined at Alfredo's in Rome where the dish originated, and Il Monello's sauce holds up well. But the chef apparently realized that and used extra to mask the limp egg noodles.

The other pastas sampled followed the same pattern, with a new twist. They were very nicely sauced—albeit too much—but the sauces were inauthentic. The spaghetti carbonara, a famous Roman specialty, had a very good sauce in the carbonara *style*, but what were the tomatoes doing in it? And where was the wonderful sharp taste of Italian bacon (pancetta)? Il Monello's pesto, I am sad to report, was a bigger disappointment.

Pesto is possibly Italy's finest culinary inspiration, a rhapsodic tribute to the vibrant flavors of the Mediterranean. Its chief ingredient is basil—a recipe for only four persons will generally begin by listing two packed cupfuls of fresh basil leaves. Il Monello's "pesto" was a delicious parsley and garlic sauce, but if there was any basil in it it was only a few withered leaves.

Happily, the entrees fared much better. The veal dishes were excellent—good quality meat, well cooked, nicely sauced. The one chicken dish tasted was also delicious. You can simply choose any of the veal or chicken dishes according to your sauce preference; the only one to avoid is anything including artichokes as they obviously were the marinated, canned variety. Special mention must be made of Friday's delicious fish stew. Though not exactly similar to what I've had in Livorno, as this one was billed (the same fish are not available), it was quite outstanding.

The only vegetable sampled separately, fried zucchini, was very good and nicely representative of the sensational vegetable dishes the Italians can produce. A rugola salad was refreshingly good, but the mixed green salad had a sauce that tasted of bottled "French" dressing, complete with sugar.

Desserts are passable; a fair chocolate mousse pie, a Gateau St. Honore whose pastry had known fresher times, and a decent Zuppa Inglese—the Italian version of an English Trifle, laced with rum. But, as the Italians do, I would stick to fresh fruit and cheese—except that no cheese is available. Adequate espresso is served with that tell-tale sign of Americanization, the lemon peel. In Italy that would indicate that you are not feeling well!

If the Michelin people had a guide to New York restaurants I would nominate Il Monello for a listing and a candidate for its first star, pending improvement of its pasta. The *New York Times*, whose current reviewer is known to have a heavy hand with stars, generously gave it three. I find this curious with the inconsistency in their pastas and service that, albeit friendly, can include waiters not only stacking dishes but also scraping them at the table. But recommend it I do. And I'm looking forward to a return visit just for the fish stew.

Are you curious about the correct answers to the exercise? It is not possible to be correct or incorrect; it is only possible to make good choices. My choices would be as follows:

(A) I would divide the five paragraphs into five parts, set up a recall pattern with five large branches. Because this is difficult material and the test is detailed, I would try to recall about three items in each of the five parts: the main idea and at least two more points (Figure 16A.)

FIGURE 16A.

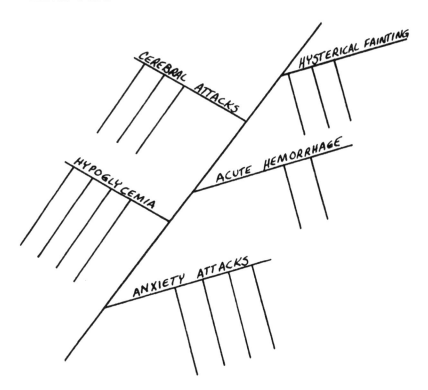

(B) With this purpose, over the same passage, I would read the entire passage and study it as a whole rather than dividing it up into five parts. I would try to recall the main point of each section. This, together with the same amount from the other four passages assigned, should suffice. (Figure 16B.)

(C) The purpose is to find if this restaurant would be a "candidate." Therefore a very simple recall pattern with a branch for each restaurant looked at (only one restaurant is given here), and possibly one to three points: yes or no (if it is acceptable), and if yes perhaps some noteworthy feature(s) or recommendations. This information would probably come from a good and simple preview. (Figure 16C.)

FIGURE 16B.

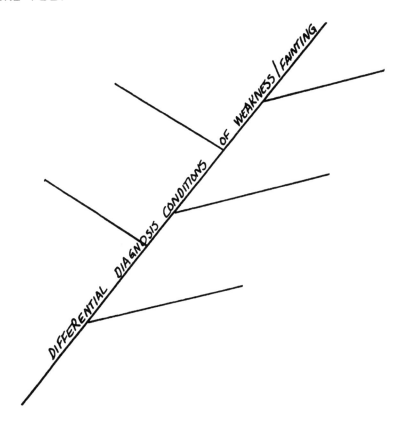

FIGURE 16C.

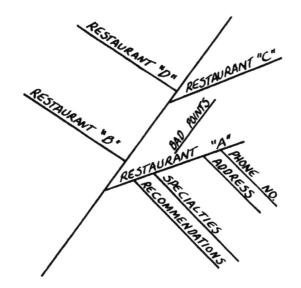

FIGURE 16. RECALL PATTERN ANSWERS

TURN TO PAGE 161 FOR THE PRACTICE DRILLS
TO COMPLETE TODAY'S WORK.

"PROGRAM" YOUR READING TO LEARN MORE EFFICIENTLY

The secret of programmed materials which seem to help students learn very efficiently is simple. A large and overwhelming amount of material is broken up into small parts. Then, step by step you use each piece of information many times. In concept this obeys many of the rules of learning. Using good learning techniques in your own studying is simply a matter of learning to "program" for yourself.

SPEND LESS TIME TO LEARN MORE

Before we get into a specific program, it is time to bring up another principle, that of "reminiscence." This means that the mind will work *unconsciously* on information, even solving problems, if you know how to use it properly. To feed the mind information, *give it time to work*, and almost like a computer it will process and react to the information. A good example is if you have ever tried to remember a name and find you are unable to, you are feeding the mind a question. You have undoubtedly experienced having the name come back to you a while later, maybe after thirty minutes or an hour. The mind has unconsciously solved the problem. This is basically how reminiscence works.

The important factor to remember here is the time factor. You need time to learn most subjects. The more fact-oriented, like having to memorize vocabulary, the more time you need. More conceptual types of material often lend themselves to long bouts of intensive studying, but if you piece them out over several days, you will always come out ahead. It has been shown that eight hours of cramming is usually not worth four hours of space learning, e.g., one-half hour a day over eight days. This is because the mind is reviewing the information you have studied *in between* the study periods. Therefore, though these study techniques can help you to be much more efficient, the student who plans ahead and studies a bit each day (often spending less time), will usually come out ahead.

THE MOST EFFICIENT READING

Many studies have repeatedly shown that when an act of reading is followed by an attempt to recall the information, in writing or out loud, that the efficiency of the reading is greatly enhanced. One study randomly divided a group of people and gave them all the same passage to read in the same amount of time. One-half was instructed to divide the time between reading and recalling the information, the other half spent all of the time reading. When both groups were tested, the half which spent equal time reading and recalling did better on the test.

This knowledge presents an interesting paradox for the student. Although you have perhaps twenty minutes to read a certain passage, you might feel that there is only enough time for reading, and not enough time for recalling as well. Probably with your experience in this course you've discovered that recalling can take even longer than reading.

The wise student, however, would understand that what he would be able to remember well at a later time from spending the full 20 minutes just reading would be *less* than what he would be able to remember well if he had spent only ten minutes reading and ten minutes recalling—even though he might not be able to cover all of the material or to cover it as carefully. This is a very important thing to be aware of, so important that I suggest you re-read this paragraph and, yes, recall it.

A PLAN FOR STUDYING

Quite simply, the most efficient plan for studying would be equal parts of reading and recalling of a single subject in one- to two-hour periods, carefully spaced out over a period of days. To approach your own materials, follow these steps:

(1) Know your overall purpose or attempt to determine it. Are you reading for the main ideas? Must you know a lot of detail?

(2) Survey the material to be read. Look for organization aids, such as bold face headings, large spaces between paragraphs, signal words ("first," "second," etc.), introductions, summaries, questions at the end of the material. While doing this, *determine how you will break up the material.* Will you study-read it paragraph by paragraph? Page by page? Or can you take (and will your purpose allow) the entire chapter or section? *This is the "programming" step, perhaps the most important of all.* You might want to review the chart on "Levels of Information in Reading" on page 177 to help determine your purpose.

(3) Set up a recall pattern. Let it reflect any organization the author uses, such as a main branch for each main section. Then add subbranches which will tell you how much you expect to be able to recall from each paragraph or section.

(4) Then going section by section (handling each section in its entirety before going on to the next), follow these steps:

(a) Preview the section to find what it's about. Recall this information *in your own words* and without looking at the material.

(b) Read the section carefully to understand it well. Attempt to recall as much as you can. Did you recall enough? Did you fill all of the branches indicating you have learned enough from that section? If not, re-read the section and recall again. Repeat this until your purpose is satisfied.

(5) Review the entire section. Attempt to see the material as a whole again, with all of the small parts you've studied coming together to form this whole.

DON'T READ TO REMEMBER

A problem many students have when they first learn these techniques is learning to always read *in order to understand*. Never, never read in order to remember! If you do the latter, a strange thing happens—you won't remember as much as you will if you read to understand. It seems to be somewhat like gathering apples when you read in order to remember. You gather a few, reach for more, some fall out, and so on. But when you read for an understanding, then you find the structure of the material, and see how everything relates. When this happens you learn, and consequently are able to remember a great deal more.

In this next exercise you are to apply these techniques to a very simple passage from a book written on a fifth-grade level. I want you to begin on this level so that you will fully understand the techniques, then you will be ready to apply them in your own materials.

EXERCISE NO. 39

Materials: *Paper and pencil or a word processing program on your PC.*

1. You have been assigned, as a fifth grader, the chapter called "Air" to read from a textbook on the physical sciences. The following day you will be given a five-question quiz. Your purpose is to study-read the chapter well enough to pass the test.

2. Survey the material to be read. Decide how you will break up the material to study-read *according to your purpose.*

3. Set up a recall pattern. Have a branch for each section that the author has. *In addition, put more branches down indicating how much you have decided to be able to recall from each section in order to meet your purpose.*

4. Going section by section, first preview and recall in your own words, then read and recall in your own words, until you have filled all of the predetermined number of branches on the recall pattern.

5. When you have worked through the entire section, quickly review it.

CAUTION: Save this recall pattern for use in Exercise No. 40.

Once you have set up your recall pattern, see how quickly you can fill it by previewing-and-recalling, then reading-and-recalling each section. This is what begins to turn studying into an intellectual sport. The hardest part is defining your purpose and breaking up the material. The "studying" becomes a skill, one at which you become better and better.

"AIR"

Can you see air?

What do you know about this ocean of air you live in? Do you breathe it? Can you see through it? Do you feel it when it moves? The answer is yes. But it's hard to picture something you can't see. It's hard to believe something is real if you can't look at it and touch it. Are there ways of showing that air is real?

Does air take up space?

You might try turning a glass upside down and pushing it straight down into a bowl of water. There is something which keeps the water from filling the glass—isn't there? You thought the glass was empty. It wasn't filled with something to drink, but it was full. The glass was full of air. Only real things take up space. Air and water can't fit into the same glass any more than you and a friend can fit into the same clothes at the same time. The water can't get in the glass unless you tilt it to one side and let some of the air out.

Is air real?

Next try blowing up a balloon. When you pinch it, what do you feel inside? The only thing you put into the balloon was air. It must be air that you feel. If you feel the air, then the air is there. The air is real.

Can you squeeze air?

But you squeeze air every time you use a pump to blow up a basketball. If you held your finger over the end of the pump, it would be harder to push the handle, but you could at least push it part way.

Is air heavy?

How much does air weigh? It depends on when and where you measure it. The air in your living room may weigh as much as you do. Right now there is a column of air resting on your head and shoulders which is several hundred miles high. It weighs hundreds of pounds. How can you support such a weight? You couldn't bear it at all if the same air pressure in your body didn't also push in the opposite direction. The experiment described below helps to explain this idea.

Does air push in all directions?

Ask someone to hold a thin piece of paper in both hands. Now push your finger against one side of the paper. You've poked a hole right through. Take another piece of paper. This time use a finger on each hand. Push at the same spot from each side of the paper. Nothing happens. The pressure is equal on both sides of the paper. So, too, the pressure of air in your body is equal to the pressure of that column of air resting on your head and shoulders.

Can you squeeze water?

The tall column of air presses down on your head the way a tall column of water presses down on a deep-sea diver. But there is one big difference between these columns. You cannot squeeze water.*

How did you do? The way I would define my purpose for such a study-reading would be to first see that there are seven sections of the chapter. Knowing that I will be given a five-question quiz, there will probably be one question from five of the seven sections. That means I should at least know the main point from each section, and to be safe I'll be certain that I know at least two points from each section. But since some sections are very short, I'll adjust this and learn three things from the long sections and only one from the very short ones. Thus, my proposed recall pattern would look something like Figure 17. The final step is to fill in the blanks by previewing-and-recalling, then reading-and-recalling, section-by-section, until they are complete.

You'll probably find the B.E.M. principle helpful. It stands for the fact that we tend to remember "beginnings" of things best, next we remember the "end," and our memory will usually falter first on the "middles." Knowing this, be certain to pay special heed to the middles of things you're learning. Be sure to spend extra time reading-and-recalling them.

This method applies to anything you wish to know. You may be reading a chapter just to find out one or two things and perhaps a good preview will give you everything you want to know. Or you may be reading a magazine article only for pleasure when you come across a point you want to remember. But if you can't recall things, chances are you won't know them very long.

---

*From *The How and Why Wonder Book of Weather* by George Bonsall. Used by permission of Grosset & Dunlap, Inc.

Figure 17. Recall Pattern for Air (190)

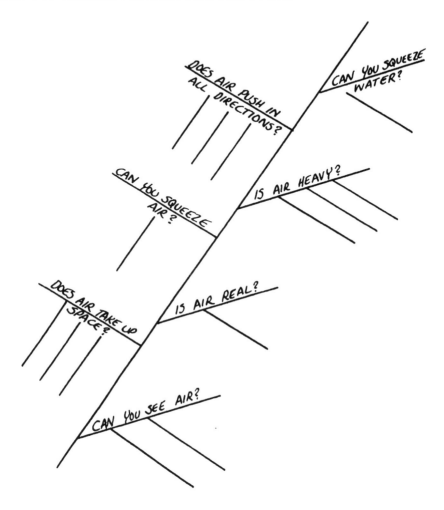

TURN TO PAGE 161 FOR THE PRACTICE DRILLS TO COMPLETE TODAY'S WORK.

28

CREATE VISUAL PATTERNS TO HELP YOUR RECALL

There is another step to take in the reading-studying-remembering path if you are interested in remembering the information for a long period of time. So far our concern with responsible reading has been to learn information we have to read. In this chapter we will deal with how to retain the information for long periods of time (more than a day or so) through a new use of the recall patterns.

So far you have been mainly working with one type of recall pattern for one purpose. This is the diagonal recall, for the purpose of the immediate feedback, or repetition, of the information that you have just read. This step in itself is one of the most important things that you can learn from this book. Every time you read something, as you have been doing in many of the drills in this book, and you follow it by making a recall pattern, you are increasing your reading efficiency. The chances that you will remember more and for a longer time are excellent.

I have often felt that if a student got nothing more from this course than learning to use his or her hand as a pacer and learning how to do a recall after a reading when he wanted to learn something, that it was worth every penny spent and hour practiced. With just those two skills you can certainly read twice as fast as your initial reading rate and twice as efficiently when you need to.

THE VALUE OF A RECALL PATTERN VERSUS AN OUTLINE

The visual recall pattern is useful in remembering information because it gives you a visual device in addition to the verbal information which you are storing in your memory. The recall pattern is a visual means of *picturing* both the organization and the relationships (association) of verbal information. Besides that, it is a more efficient way to write down the information. An outline does not have the obvious advantages of a visual pattern.

Probably when you have worked with a recall pattern it has ended up a mess. This is really as it should be because you are, in a sense, just practicing the information you are trying to learn. And these patterns do tend to be messy. That certainly belies their tremendous value in enhancing your reading efficiency.

TAKING THE SECOND STEP

When you wish to remember information for a long period of time, more than a few days, and you have completed the first steps of reading and recalling, then you are ready for the next step. The second stage is to reorganize your recall pattern, which is done without referring back to your book. Since the purpose is to remember the information for a longer period, it is best to be as creative as possible with the information. The first step in reorganizing a recall pattern and in trying to develop your own creative organization (try not to use the author's organization if you can) is to use a different type of recall pattern.

It is easily demonstrated that the more creative you are with the information, the quicker you will be able to learn it and the longer you will be able to retain it. You should try to clean up your messy recall pattern by (1) eliminating anything now seen as unnecessary, (2) making new associations of the information you have gotten out of the book, and (3) attempting to give it your own, original, organization in a new pattern.

RECALL PATTERNS CAN VARY

Besides the diagonal pattern there are several others which are generally used.

A circular pattern can be very useful for some information, such as fiction. Figure 18 illustrates two different ways of using it. In the first pattern, characters are "re-

FIGURE 18. TWO EXAMPLES OF A CIRCULAR RECALL PATTERN

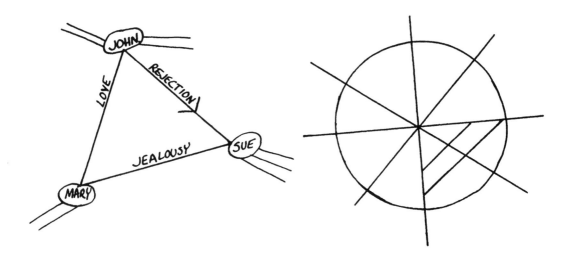

lated" to one another with the connecting lines. It tends to be most useful for fiction. Pertinent information would be added *where it relates* to the various lines. The second pattern resembles a sun or a target, perhaps even a pie. It is probably more useful in nonfiction.

A linear pattern is perhaps the most familiar to you. A flow chart is an example of one; sometimes a pyramidal form is used in English classes to demonstrate paragraph structures. It tends to be most useful in scientific materials and any business or professional materials where the material moves from one idea to the next in a logical manner. Two examples of the patterns are illustrated in Figures 19A and 19B.

Some persons enjoy trying a picture pattern, one which actually is representational of some related aspect of the information. I have seen students turn out such diverse offerings as a recall on the classic *Gulliver's Travels* which was a picture of Gulliver tied up by the Lilliputians, who were, of course, all words or phrases; to a picture of a

FIGURE 19A

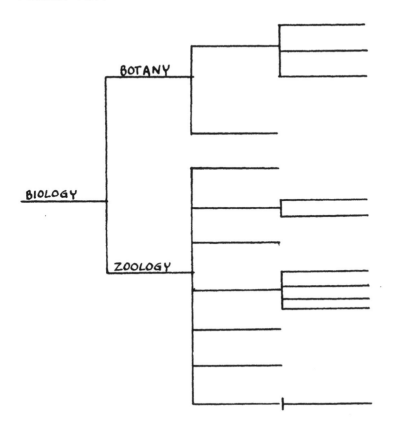

FIGURE 19B

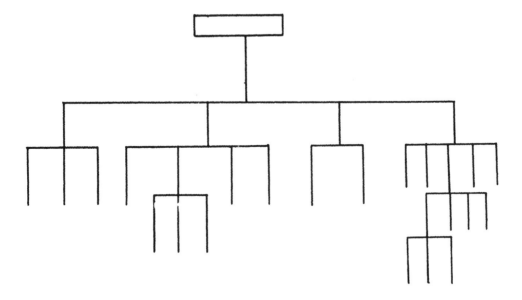

bridge which was made up of words depicting information from an engineering text-book. Here, in Figures 20A and 20B, are two rather ordinary examples which should give you a good idea if you care to use this.

The final type is your own device, any kind of random pattern. This is the best because you are being more creative, and the more creative you are with information, the more likely you are to remember it.

Often a recall pattern is developed in two distinct stages. First, a diagonal pattern might be used. If possible you would attempt to use the author's organization. For instance, look over the following passage:

SKIING: A SPORT FOR EVERYONE

Skiing is a sport that truly has something for everyone. Most people think of skiing only as downhill or Alpine skiing. There is also cross-country skiing which is quite different. Both types of skiing are good exercise as well as stimulating experiences. One is much easier to learn and lends itself to those who do not consider themselves athletically inclined.

FIGURE 20A

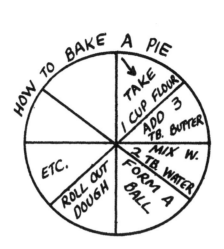

FIGURE 20B

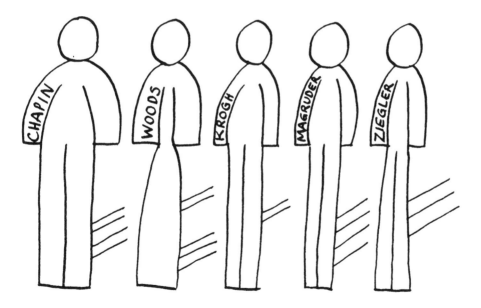

ALPINE SKIING

Alpine skiing is what most people think of as skiing, sliding down a hill with two boards attached to your feet to facilitate the sliding. It can be a very thrilling experience if you are willing to spend some time learning how to do it. Most people need to take lessons for several days. Fairly high speeds can be attained, as well as a variety of terrain enjoyed. Different sorts of snow offer different experiences.

CROSS-COUNTRY SKIING

Cross-country skiing has only recently come into vogue as a sport. Although you do attach "boards" to your feet to facilitate sliding on top of snow, the purpose is more one of travel—often across flat fields—rather than primarily downhill. There is great freedom to explore trails. It also can be done with very little instruction, as little as one-half hour, since you are basically walking. Anyone who enjoys the outdoors should enjoy one or another type of skiing. Both sorts of skiing are sports that you may enjoy at all ages. In fact, a whole family can enjoy skiing. You might not want to take up Alpine skiing at age seventy, but certainly cross-country skiing can be learned and enjoyed. Skiing definitely is a sport for everyone.

An attempt to use the author's organization might result in the recall pattern shown in Figure 21.

With this pattern you could begin to preview and recall, then to read and recall. It serves as a worksheet for learning the information by reading it and "feeding it

FIGURE 21. A DIAGONAL RECALL PATTERN FOR SKIING

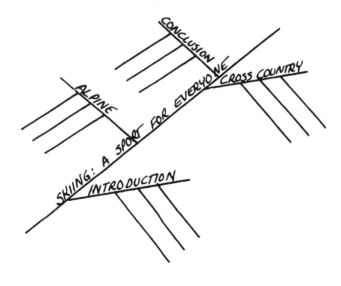

FIGURE 22. A RANDOM RECALL PATTERN FOR SKIING

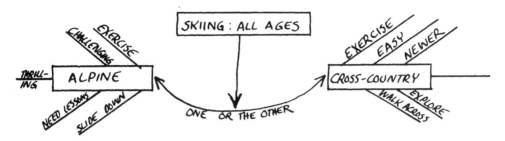

back" through a written recall. In the second stage you could go on and develop your own recall pattern for the information, something entirely different and more creative. Figure 22 is an example of the same information reorganized into a random pattern.

This is not necessarily the "right" way of doing it because there is no right or wrong. The best way is always *your* way, because if you organize it your own way, you will remember it much, much longer.

EXERCISE NO. 40

Materials: *Pencil and paper*
Your recall pattern from Exercise No. 39

1. Working only from your recall pattern (without referring back to the passage), reorganize the recall pattern by (1) putting it into a new pattern other than a diagonal pattern, (2) trying to make different or new associations of the information, (3) dropping anything that no longer seems important, including extra words which are not necessary for you to be able to remember the information.

2. When you have finished with the new recall pattern, take a new sheet of paper, and without referring back to either of the first two patterns, attempt to reproduce your new recall pattern. First recall and draw the pattern of lines, then fill in as much of the verbal information as you can.

3. When you have finished, check your new recall pattern with the one you were attempting to reproduce. See how much of the information you were able to remember.

This exercise is usually very important to students for two reasons. First because they are surprised that they were able to remember so much (often 100 percent); second that the "learning" of the information was so effortless and probably interesting.

If you had any trouble remembering the recall pattern, the reason is very simple. Most likely you were not creative enough when you were reorganizing from the first pattern. Be certain that you are using lines for *all* pieces of information, as the lines create the visual pattern. Be certain that you have attempted to reorganize the material, drawing new associations if possible. Even if you have been unsuccessful in finding a new form of organization, the *attempt* to do so is what adds the memory "glue."

In the next chapter, we will explore more ways of increasing your efficiency in remembering what you've read and in new ways to organize recall patterns. But first get a good amount of drilling done.

TURN TO PAGE 161 FOR THE PRACTICE DRILLS TO COMPLETE TODAY'S WORK.

29

REMEMBER MORE OF WHAT YOU'VE READ WITH THESE PROVEN TECHNIQUES

Most people can't remember something because they did not decide to remember it at the crucial time. The crucial time is when you are first encountering the information. The time most people decide they want to remember something is when they realize they can't recall it.

The simplest example is with names, something many people cannot remember well enough to suit themselves. These people decide they want to remember someone's name when they're trying to recall it. The time to make that decision is when you're being introduced. It has been suggested that you immediately repeat a person's name several times to yourself and also find some way to use it at least once out loud in your conversation with the person, even if it is just to say, "It was great fun talking with you, Lenore," or "How do you spell your name, Mr. Zeitgeist?"

The same principles that apply to remembering names also work for remembering what you've read. To efficiently remember what you have read, it is imperative to decide to remember it *before* you read it. This implies that you also be selective. It would be somewhat foolhardy to "decide" to remember a whole book prior to reading it. I'm sure that even the greatest memory whizzes would have difficulty recalling a total book—and moreover why would anyone bother?

THE THREE STEPS TO IMPROVING YOUR RETENTION

There are three basic steps to improving your recall skills or remembering ability. The first is learning to decide to remember something, and selecting what it is you wish to remember. That, of course, corresponds to defining your purpose.

ORGANIZE CREATIVELY

Once you know what it is you wish to remember, the second step is to organize it creatively. It is much easier to deal with information, whether it is finding it in a library or finding it in your brain, when it is well cataloged, well organized, and well filed.

In organizing information, first know "what it's about." This establishes its central point or theme, or in a filing system, where you will put it.

Second, if you have a series of points to be made, it is important to carefully examine them. It is difficult to remember more than a few items in a "category"—four or five items is usually enough. If you happen to have eleven items in a category, look for ways to subdivide them. There's always a way to break items up, even if it's just through arranging them alphabetically or numerically.

An excellent example of organization is a shopping list. A list of nineteen items or so might be rather difficult to remember:

canned tuna	broccoli	boiled ham
milk	rib steaks	laundry soap
peas	plastic wrap	glass cleaner
hamburger	chocolate ice cream	eggs
butter	cleanser	orange juice
green beans	sole filets	bacon
chicken		

But if you establish categories and organize the list, it no longer seems so formidable:

DAIRY	VEGETABLES	FISH
milk	peas	canned tuna
butter	green beans	sole filets
eggs	broccoli	MEAT
FROZEN	MISCELLANEOUS	hamburger
orange juice	plastic wrap	rib steaks
chocolate ice cream	cleanser	boiled ham
	laundry soap	bacon
	glass cleaner	chicken

This is certainly not the only way it could be done. The ice cream could be included under dairy; milk and orange juice might have been in a category called "beverages." The important thing is that a long list of items has been organized, broken down into manageable sections. When you want to remember information that you are reading, you should (1) select what it is you wish to remember, and (2) organize it.

If you use the reading process proposed for serious reading, it obviously helps you to organize: previewing will help you find what it's about and a few main points, reading will help you to find out more, and reviewing will help you check it over.

Associate information dramatically

The third step in remembering information is to learn how to associate information, or how to relate it to what you already know. This can be the most important step of all, because the more intimately you can associate information with what you already know and with what is important to you, the easier it is to remember it.

The classic example of this is to ask someone what he or she was doing on any random date—March 11, 1996, for example. Chances are they won't have the slightest idea unless it happens to be that person's birthday or some other special date. If you asked them what they were doing on the day that something traumatic in history occurred—such as when President Kennedy was assassinated or when an attempt was made on Ronald Reagan's life—maybe a flood of memories would come pouring back. If you can take information and associate it *meaningfully,* it will help greatly in remembering it. In fact, the more meaningfully you can relate it, the easier it will be to remember.

Compare and contrast

The way to begin relating information is to compare and contrast it with what you already know, to tie it in in some way, or attempt to, with any previous experience. If you wanted to remember a name, besides repeating it to yourself and finding some way of saying it aloud, compare and contrast it. Ask yourself if this "Jane Doe" reminds you of any other "Janes" you've known. Perhaps not. Perhaps you've never known another "Jane." Does this "Jane" in any way remind you of *anyone* else? Is she skinny like your sister? Wear the same colors as your aunt? Round-headed like your Uncle Harry? In some way you can relate to her by making such comparisons and contrasts.

More "recording" tricks

If you remember the passage I quoted from the great psychologist William James, the improvement of memory consists in the improvement of how you "record" the information (as you receive it, by implication). That of course affects your study-reading techniques, but tricks of "recording" information are also useful when you have isolated the information you wish to learn, drawn from the book, on your recall pattern and you are now ready to reorganize it.

It is definitely easier to remember items in odd lot quantities. So when you're breaking up a group of items, it's preferable to break them up into odd lot groups—three's, five's, and so on—when feasible and sensible. Also it is difficult to remember more than about seven items in any single category, and five is much easier. So as a general rule, if you have more than five items in a listing, find some way to subdivide them.

Enumeration is very helpful in remembering and it takes only a second to make this a part of your organizing techniques. For example, if you had a branch on your recall pattern which read "ways to do something or other," be certain to count *how many* ways and add that to your title. When trying to remember, it is easy to recall how many; then you have at least one association which will help you.

Mnemonic devices are useful, and well-organized recall patterns are an example of them. A mnemonic (pronounced ni-mon-ik) device is a system for remembering information which has little or nothing to do with that information. For instance, the rhyme "Thirty days hath September, April, June and November, / All the rest have 31 except . . ." is a good example. The rhyme helps us to remember the information, but in itself has nothing to do with the information.

Mnemonic devices are usually at the root of all good memory systems. The value of a recall pattern stems from the fact that, if creatively developed, it becomes a mnemonic device. If unorganized, messy, left to whim, its value is greatly diminished. It is important to remember that the best of these devices are ones which you create yourself. Creativity and originality in attempting to organize and synthesize information help you to remember it efficiently, probably better than anything else.

The main reason for attempting to reorganize a recall pattern into a new pattern is to get you to be more creative with the information. And there is often a way. An example I cite is of trying to reorganize a filing system of correspondence on your PC: you are given a filing system in which there is a slot for each person to whom a letter has been written, i.e., a file for Mr. Brown, for Ms. Clark, Ms. Davis, etc. You could "reorganize" this system by reorganizing the information according to the date it had been written, i.e., all the letters written on March 28, those on March 29, etc.

With these new organizing ideas in mind, take this exercise and follow a complete learning process with it, putting special emphasis on the reorganization of the recall pattern. Remember, the more cleverly you reorganize it, the easier it will be to remember it.

EXERCISE NO. 41

Materials: *Paper and pencil*

STAGE ONE

1. You have been assigned, as a freshman in a college biology course, to read a selection on body temperature. (The selection follows.) The following day you will be given a five-question quiz. Your purpose is to study-read the chapter well enough to pass the test.

2. Survey the material to be read. Decide how you will break up the material to study-read *according to your purpose*. Refer to the chart on page 177 and decide how much information you should be able to recall—at what *level* of information—to meet your purpose from each section or paragraph.

3. Set up a recall pattern. Have a branch for each section that you will handle by itself, i.e., one for each bold face heading, one for each paragraph, or however you have broken up the material. In addition, put any more branches down indicating how much you have decided to be able to recall from each section in order to meet your purpose.

4. Going section by section, first preview and recall in your own words, then read and recall in your own words, until you have filled all of the predetermined number of branches on the recall pattern.

5. When you have worked through the entire section, quickly review the entire material.

Body Temperature

Some people wear a fur coat "for warmth" in winter, but few will give it a thought that the fur in itself is not really warm at all. In fact it has the same temperature as its environment. It does not warm us but it keeps us warm.

Why we need a winter coat and why the sparrows and lizards do not

The source of heat is our body, not the fur. The heat is produced during slow oxidation processes that we call cell respiration. The fur is specially suited to preserve the heat and to prevent it from flowing off into the cold surroundings. Nobody would think of keeping the cold air out by wearing a coat made of tin sheet or for that matter a knight's armor. Metal is a good conductor of heat and therefore a bad protector against cold.

When we put a frying pan on the fire we know that its iron handle very quickly gets too hot to be touched, because iron conducts heat so well. We prefer our frying pans to have wooden handles since wood is a poor heat conductor. Water is a better conductor of heat than air; therefore we find a room of 68 degrees quite comfortable even if we wear just a bathing suit, while bath water of the same temperature is unpleasantly cool. The water drains our warm body of its heat much more quickly than the air. Another poor conductor of heat is the horn of our fingernails, and this can be easily proved. An object that is too hot to be touched for more than a split second with our hands or lips can be in contact with a fingernail for quite a time before the heat reaches the sensitive layer under the nail. Hair and feathers consist of the same horny substance as nails. They, too, are poor conductors of heat and a very good protection against cold. This effect is intensified by the layer of air caught between them.

This is the reason why a sparrow and a goose, a hare and even a bear in Siberia do not need a special winter coat. Nature has planted a fur coat right into their very skins. Man, having only a sparse remnant of a natural hair coat, has hunted animals for their fur since time immemorial, and we still use hair blankets and eiderdowns for cover.

Only mammals and birds have protective hair or feathers. All the other vertebrates, like lizards, frogs, and fish, and all invertebrates, like crabs, snails, and worms, have a naked skin. The body temperature of a lizard changes with the temperature of the environment. There exists a strange correlation: in hot sunshine the lizard is lively, during a cool spell it gets lazy, and during cold nights or in winter it will be rigid. Although the animal produces heat by oxidation in its body it cannot retain it and is thus to a high degree dependent on the temperature of its environment. All reptiles, amphibians, and fish, all insects and the lower animals change their temperature. One calls them cold-blooded, but this does not quite meet the case, because in the hot sun the blood of a lizard reaches a higher temperature than that of a human being. They are variably warm.

Birds and mammals are warm-blooded. They keep approximately the same temperature during summer and winter, by day and night, in sunshine and in rain. This is good, because it has made their metabolism and all their bodily functions independent of the environment. However, safeguards are needed to prevent a loss of body temperature to the surroundings, and one of the most important ones is a hair or feather coat. We, with a body temperature of approximately 98°F., have to wear clothes in order to maintain this temperature in all kinds of weather.

Prevention of heat loss alone does not explain how we can keep up a steady body temperature when the temperature of the environment changes. Special methods are employed to compensate for loss or gain of heat.

The regulation of the body temperature

When it gets cool we put on warmer clothes. Like our clothes, the thicker hair coat grown by animals in winter and lost again in spring can serve as a coarse temperature adjustment only.

The continuously necessary delicate adjustment is of a different kind. It functions independently of our will and often without our knowledge, whenever the temperature changes from the 98°F. to which the working of our cells is geared. When our body gets too warm the blood vessels in the skin dilate, our face gets red, and we give off heat. At the same time the oxidative processes in our body are cut down to a minimum and less heat is produced as we stop all vigorous movement. Morever, our sweat glands become active, we start sweating profusely, and heat is used up to evaporate the perspiration. This also cools the body. Dogs, which have no sweat glands, hang out their tongue instead and pant vigorously, using their tongue and lungs for cooling.

When on the other hand our body cools down, the blood is withdrawn from the skin into the internal organs reducing heat loss of the blood, food combustion increases, and if this is not enough we shiver with cold. This means that our muscles move involuntarily and thus produce heat.

Summer and winter this regulating mechanism is so accurate that our temperature rises only during a fever when an illness upsets the balance, or it falls a few degrees in a state of exhaustion. Some mammals have a slightly lower, most a slightly higher, body temperature than we. Birds generally have a normal temperature of up to 108°F., which Man never reaches except in a fatal attack of fever.

On the other hand, social insects cannot keep their own body temperature independent of their environment, but they do protect their most treasured possession, their brood, from overheating or from cooling down. On a hot day one can see field wasps flying busily to and fro between their nest and a nearby water puddle. The nest of the field wasps is an open one, usually built on stones, beams, or branches and exposed to weather intemperances. In their stomachs they fetch water and spit it over the pipeline substance of which their nest is composed. Then they sit down on it and, as living ventilators, start fanning vigorously with their wings. The water quickly evaporates and thus cools the nest. When, on the other hand, it gets cold they cluster over the nest and try to reduce the loss of heat by covering it with their bodies.

We find the most perfect thermo-regulation in the beehive, where the brood cells are kept day and night at a constant temperature of 95°F. Bees, like the field wasps, carry water, spread it in countless little puddles over the comb, and fan it when things get too hot. Quick and harmonious collaboration by many individuals makes this air-conditioning the more effective. When the temperature falls they heat the nest by crowding by the thousands into dense clusters all over the comb. Bees do not belong to the warmblooded animals but they can raise their body temperature about 20°F. above the temperature of the surroundings by speeding up the metabolic processes, and though this may not be noticeable in a single bee in the open air, it will be more effective when thousands of these little living stoves sit together in an enclosed beehive.

Under similar conditions other creatures too and even plants do generate heat. When, for malting, a pile of barley grains is brought to germination, the temperature close to the pile may rise by 10 to 20°F. above the room temperature. In plants the development of heat is usually masked by heat-consuming reactions such as photosynthesis. In the interior of flowers, however, the rise of temperature due to respiration may become measurably higher. Insects which often make the calyx of a flower their nightly quarters, find there not only protection but a warm, cozy little room. Many an alpine plant that flowers at the border of a snow field uses its warm breath to melt its way through hard crusts of ice and thus reaches the light and the warmth of the sun."*

---

*From *Man and the Living World* by Karl Von Frisch, copyright by Deutscher Verlag, Berlin; English translation by Oliver and Boyd. Reprinted by permission of Harcourt Brace Jovanovich, Inc.

EXERCISE NO. 41 CONTINUED

STAGE TWO

1. Working only from your recall pattern (without referring back to the passage), re-organize the recall pattern by putting it into a new pattern, trying to make different or new associations of the information, and dropping anything that no longer seems important.

2. When you have finished with the new recall pattern, take another sheet of paper, and without referring back to either of the first two patterns, attempt to reproduce your new recall pattern from memory. First recall and draw the pattern of lines; then fill in as much of the verbal information as you can.

3. When you have finished, check your new recall pattern with the one you were attempting to reproduce. See how much of the information you were able to remember. Note: if you wish to review at a later time, begin by looking over your recall pattern, then attempt again to recreate it from memory.

NOW APPLY THE TECHNIQUES FOR YOURSELF

Sometimes I have had people in my classes who complain about this part of the course. They tell me that they are out of school and have nothing to study and really don't want to be "studying" again. I try to point out to them that just because they are studying does not imply that they have to become as involved as a first-year medical student would. Actually, it should be quite enjoyable for the non-student. Just remember the first step—purpose setting. In the "study" drills for next week's practicing, the non-student should select any nonfiction book that is on a subject he would like to find out more about: scuba diving, foreign travel, career development, investing or whatever. Then with a chapter from your book set your purpose, which may well be only to learn the main idea of the chapter. Of course if you can meet that purpose with a good pre-viewing, then you are done.

I assume that you wish to remember something from some books or materials you read; these are the times to do a recall pattern and follow the learning techniques, *as far as your purpose dictates* that you should follow them. Please do not think that I want you to labor over study techniques or dull books just for their own sake.

A FINAL WORD

If you've felt that it takes too long to study this way, perhaps your problem is in setting your purpose. First of all, if you have a certain length of passage to read, you should know (and it has been definitively shown in many studies) that no matter how long you spend reading it, if some of that time is spent in recalling as well as reading, you will get more out of the material than if you just read it.

Second, if you take the time to predetermine what you will get from which parts of the passage, then you are determining what you will get out of it rather than leaving it up to chance.

Therefore, time is not the factor. Your old habits may be inhibiting you but the newer techniques do not, ultimately, take long. In fact, once you've practiced them you should be able to cut your study time significantly. Perhaps as much as by half.

TURN TO PAGE 161 FOR THE PRACTICE DRILLS TO COMPLETE TODAY'S WORK.

30

UNRAVEL DIFFICULT PASSAGES THIS EASY WAY

If you never come across difficult passages, passages which you read and then, upon reflection, aren't sure you understand, you probably should just skip this chapter. But if you do have to read difficult books or articles from time to time, then you may wish to avail yourself of this system for breaking through to comprehension. The techniques are also valuable for standardized tests which include difficult passages to read and then answer questions about. So if this is of value to you, proceed.

As I discussed in Chapter Thirteen, the reason certain passages are difficult to understand is usually due to the level of generality on which they are written—in other words, how abstract the words are. Of course a passage may also be difficult for you because it presents new ideas in a new field, or because it's poorly written. If you don't remember these concepts, then you would be wise to review Chapter Thirteen before continuing on with this one.

WHEN READING IN A NEW FIELD

The only way to deal with materials which are difficult because you have little background in the field and the ideas are new to you is to do as much reading in the field as possible. You'll need plenty of time to absorb the new ideas. Your brain will need time to reminisce, also. So plan lots of short (about an hour) study periods over as long a period of time as you can. If you must absorb a new field quickly, it sometimes helps to study-read for one to two hours, then take a half-hour's nap, allowing the brain time to reminisce and prepare for more new material, then work for another hour or so, followed by another brief nap.

It is also important to appreciate the importance of step-by-step learning when you are working in a new area and with new concepts. Be extra careful to break the material up into small amounts, and to preview/recall, read/recall with a very limited purpose. Learning is a building process and when you have little background knowledge, it is most efficient to build systematically. Take a bit at a time, adding as you go. Trying to tackle all at once is most foolhardy.

WHEN THE WRITING IS ABSTRACT

When the writing is abstract, what you must do to understand it is to apply your knowledge of signal words and levels of generality. This implies analyzing the writing as you go. At first it will seem difficult and probably slow you down, but with practice you can become quite adept at it. A skillful reader should be able to handle quite difficult material at reading rates around 1,000 words per minute. At first don't expect to do any analyzing-reading at rates much above 400 words per minute, if that.

What you must learn to do is become aware, as you read, of how one sentence relates to another. This is just as simple as what you were doing in Chapter Thirteen. You'll be asking yourself what in a sentence relates to the sentence just before it, *or* does this sentence relate back to the first sentence (topic sentence) of the paragraph? In other words, seeing the upward (difficult) and downward (concrete and easier) movement of the author.

You will also have to develop an awareness of the transitional words because they will relate various ideas and reveal the structure and organization of the writing. When you can understand the organization of a passage, you can usually follow and comprehend the writing. This also makes it easy to remember. Starting on page 214 is an exercise, very similar to one which I do with my classes. The passage which we will use is at the end of the section. Follow the steps in the exercise and the explanations will be included under the word "Discussion."

SUCCESS DOESN'T ALWAYS MEAN 100 PERCENT

I wish I could write that I've always been successful with every student, but such is not the case. I've read and heard that some of us are more visually oriented, some more auditorily and the rest in between. Those who are visually oriented usually find it very easy to learn these skills, those in between experience little difficulty, but some who are auditorily oriented can have a lot of trouble. If you suspect you're one of these latter, don't despair. As long as you want to learn these skills badly enough you can, if you persevere. Even if you're so wedded to hearing the sounds of words that you feel you just don't want to let go of them, you'll still be able to read faster by just using your hand (which assures at minimum increase of 10% and usually at least 30%) and diligently applying the smart reading techniques of always determining your purposes for all readings. That can easily save you 50% of your reading time. Combine those two figures and you'll soon be getting twice as much read in the same amount of time.

An outstanding doctor in cancer therapy at New York's renowned Sloane-Kettering Memorial Hospital came to me on a private basis after having taken the Reading Dynamics course twice. Her determination to succeed in spite of the fact that she was obviously very auditorily oriented and just couldn't feel comfortable with her comprehension when she speeded up, was truly admirable. Concentration was another problem for her, especially when reading certain medical texts.

After practicing observing the levels of generality in the writing while reading her texts and journals she reported that there was just no way her mind could wander when she was doing this. This relatively simple mental activity not only helped her to concentrate, but also to remember what she had read. This combined with diligent use of her hand resulted in considerable improvement. She can read difficult texts at double her initial rate which is quite a feat. And we're still working on higher rates.

HOW FAST CAN YOU READ?

How fast you read, as you know well by now, depends on many factors. When you are reading much over 1,000 words per minute and are reading words out-of-expectancy order, you must be able to think quickly in the material. It is obviously not possible to handle new ideas and analyze passages at these rates. But as I said, with practice you can expect to be able to do this type of difficult reading at rates from 600 to 1,200. That's probably the maximum, and for this type of reading it's very fast indeed.

This type of reading must be practiced. Read difficult materials and apply your new awareness. Whenever you begin to have difficulty with a passage, you must "shift gears" and move into your slower, analyzing reading. Usually this means using an underlining hand movement for much of the material. But don't hesitate to use a faster hand movement when you come to easily recognized examples.

WHEN READING TEST MATERIALS

When reading short passages in standardized tests, especially when you will have to answer questions without referring back to the passage, if time permits it pays off handsomely to use these techniques. First, quickly preview the whole passage to find what it's about and where it's "going." Then read the whole passage for a good understanding of the material. Next, come back and analyze-read the passage, noting signal words and how the sentences relate to one another moving up and down in levels of generality. Last, review the entire passage, again pulling all of the parts into the whole and attempting to see the whole relationship.

The analysis provides a structure to your understanding, and a structure, like a filing system which has a place for everything, makes it easier to remember the material as well. Luckily, you won't need these techniques most of the time. But when you do they're very valuable to have at your command.

TURN TO PAGE 161 FOR THE PRACTICE DRILLS TO COMPLETE TODAY'S WORK.

EXERCISE NO. 42

Materials: *Paper*
         Timing device

Have a piece of paper ready to cover the "Discussion" part of each step in this exercise until you have completed the instructions before it.

1. Set your timing device for one minute and give yourself this much time to look over the entire section at the end of this chapter entitled "The Symbolic Process."

2. Read the first paragraph quickly (lines 1 through 7) just to find what this passage is about. Take as much time as you wish, but try to read it once through.

Discussion

If you paid attention to the title itself (and you should because everything in a nonfiction passage should add up to and give meaning to its title), you may have discovered that the first paragraph is about the struggle for symbols. This may be expressed in different ways or with different shadings.

3. Re-read the first paragraph, paying special attention to the second sentence. Find out what the relationship is of the second sentence to the first.

Discussion

The second sentence drops a level of generality, becoming easier, and it gives an explanation of the first sentence. If you did not see this, go back and read it again.

It is important to understand that in a passage the first part, or paragraph, is often the most abstract and difficult to understand. Just as the sentences become easier to understand because they become more specific, the paragraphs tend to follow the same pattern.

When people are "turned off" by a passage, it is usually by the first part. Then they *expect* not to understand the rest, so they usually do not pay close attention and often give up. The wise reader will recognize the difficulty of the first part, and read on carefully, knowing that the later parts will soon explain and clarify, in easier language, the difficult parts.

4. Next, read the first two sentences of the second paragraph, lines 8 through 11, and see how the second relates to the first in terms of levels of writing.

Discussion

The second sentence becomes more specific and easier, giving an example, thus helping to clarify the difficult first sentence. It drops a level, to level 2.

5. Read the third sentence of paragraph two, lines 11 through 13. Note the signal words. What follows them?

Discussion

The signal words "for example" are indeed confirmed with the example, very easy to understand, of the two symbols "X" and "Y." This sentence, because it clarifies the one before, drops another level to become a level 3.

6. Read the next sentence, sentence 4, lines 14 through 16, and find what level it is on. How does it relate to the sentence before it?

Discussion

The sentence gives examples, all concrete and easy to understand. The sentence drops in levels of generality, to become a level 4.

It is important to begin recognizing that you can usually speed up your reading rate when you come to examples that are concrete and easy to understand. The wise reader slows down when he must "think" about ideas, and he speeds up when he can just recognize items easily.

7. Read the next sentence, sentence 5, lines 17 through 18, and try to determine whether it moves down a level or moves up.

Discussion

It becomes more difficult, usually indicating an upward movement. It relates back to the first sentence, lines 8 and 9, because it tells more about what human beings can do, giving an example. Therefore it moves up to a level 2.

8. Read the next sentence, sentence 6, lines 18 and 19, and see if it helps to clarify the one before it.

Discussion

It does clarify somewhat. It drops to become a level 3. It tells more about symbols.

9. Read the next sentence, sentence 7, lines 19 through 22, and see if this helps to explain. Look out for signal words.

Discussion

The signal words "for instance" tell us examples are coming, which they do, so the sentence moves down a level, becoming easier to understand.

10. Read the next sentence, sentence 8, lines 22 and 23, and see what this one does.

Discussion

The signal word "then" tips us off that more examples are coming.

11. Finally, read the last sentence, sentence 9, lines 23 through 25. What happens here?

Discussion

The sentence is more general, moving upward again, to a level 2 *or 1*. Basically it is a summary sentence, and whether summary sentences are on level 1 or 2 can usually be argued. Whatever the answer is, is unimportant: it is only necessary to realize that they move upward, becoming more abstract. Probably it is easy to understand because you have had so much explanation of the material.

12.   Move on to the next paragraph and read the first sentence. What do you expect to happen in the paragraph?

Discussion

Obviously you expect a series of examples.

13.   Read the rest of the paragraph and discover whether or not the author fulfills his promise of examples.

Discussion

Generally he does this. At this point you should be able to follow the argument of the passage because you have maneuvered from the abstract and difficult beginning, *understanding* the material, to the easier parts.

14.   Try to finish reading the entire passage, analyzing as you go along, noting the upward-downward movement of the author, noting how the signal words relate the information.

15.   Finally, go back to the beginning and re-read the first paragraph.

Discussion

The first paragraph should be much easier to understand now because you have worked through, and understood, the rest of the material. Note that the beginning and ending paragraphs of the passage are an introduction and a summary. They do give the main idea/thesis of the material; but it is hard to understand, in this case, without the development of the idea which is offered within the passage.

The Symbolic Process

1   Animals struggle with each other for food or for leadership, but they do not,
2   like human beings, struggle with each other for things that stand for food or
3   leadership: such things as our paper symbols of wealth (money, bonds,
4   titles), badges of rank to wear on our clothes, or low-number license plates,
5   supposed by some people to stand for social precedence. For animals,
6   the relationship in which one *thing stands* for something else does not appear to
7   exist except in very rudimentary form.
8   The process by means of which human beings can arbitrarily make
9   certain things *stand* for other things may be called the *symbolic process*.
10   Whenever two or more human beings can communicate with each other,
11   they can, by agreement, make anything stand for anything. For example,

12   here are two symbols:

13   *X Y*

14   We can agree to let *X* stand for buttons and *Y* stand for bows; then we can

15   freely change our agreement and let *X* stand for the Chicago White Sox and

16   *Y* for the Cincinnati Reds; or let *X* stand for Chaucer and *Y* for Shakespeare.

17   . . . We *are, as human beings, uniquely free to manufacture and manipulate*

18   *and assign values to our symbols as we please.* Indeed, we can go further

19   by making symbols that stand for symbols. If necessary we can, for instance,

20   let the symbol *M* stand for all the *X*'s in the above example (buttons, White

21   Sox, Chaucer . . .) and let *N* stand for all the *Y*'s (bows, Cincinnati Reds,

22   Shakespeare . . .). Then we can make another symbol, *T* stand for *M*

23   and *N*, which would be an instance of a symbol of symbols of symbols. This

24   freedom to create symbols of any assigned value and to create *symbols that*

25   *stand for symbols* is essential to what we call the symbolic process.

26   Everywhere we turn, we see the symbolic process at work. Feathers

27   worn on the head or stripes on the sleeve can be made to stand for military

28   rank; cowrie shells or rings of brass or pieces of paper can stand for wealth;

29   crossed sticks can stand for a set of religious beliefs; buttons, elks' teeth,

30   ribbons, special styles of ornamental haircutting or tattooing, can stand for

31   social affiliations. The symbolic process permeates human life at the most

32   primitive and the most civilized levels alike. Warriors, medicine men,

33   policemen, doormen, nurses, cardinals, and kings wear costumes that sym-

34   bolize their occupations. Vikings collected their victims' armor and college

35   students collect membership keys in honorary societies to symbolize vic-

36   tories in their respective fields. There are few things that men do or want to

37   do, possess or want to possess, that have not, in addition to their mechanical

38   or biological value, a symbolic value.

39   All fashionable clothes, as Thorsten Veblen has pointed out in his

40   *Theory of the Leisure Class (1899)*, are highly symbolic; materials, cut, and

41   ornament are dictated only to a slight degree by considerations of warmth,

42   comfort, or practicability. The more we dress up in fine clothes, the more we

43   restrict our freedom of action. But by means of delicate embroideries, easily

44   soiled fabrics, starched shirts, high heels, long and pointed fingernails, and

45   other such sacrifices of comfort, the wealthy classes manage to symbolize,

46   among other things, the fact that they don't have to work for a living. On the

47 other hand, the no-so-wealthy, by imitating these symbols of wealth, sym-
48 bolize their conviction that, even if they do work for a living, they are just as
49 good as anybody else.
50   With the changes in American life since Veblen's time, many changes
51 have taken place in our ways of symbolizing social status. There have been
52 major changes in the fashion world, and flamboyant styles and striking
53 colors are now popular, inspired in part by the hippies, pop art, and new
54 sexual codes.
55   In Veblen's time a deeply tanned skin was indicative of a life spent in
56 farming and other outdoor labor, and women in those days went to a great
57 deal of trouble shielding themselves from the sun with parasols, wide hats,
58 and long sleeves. Today, however, a pale skin is indicative of confinement
59 in offices and factories, while a deeply tanned skin suggests a life of
60 leisure—of trips to Florida, Sun Valley, and Hawaii. Hence, a sun-
61 blackened skin, once considered ugly because it symbolized work, is now
62 considered beautiful because it symbolizes leisure. And pallid people in
63 New York, Chicago, and Toronto who cannot afford midwinter trips to the
64 West Indies find comfort in browning themselves with drugstore tanning
65 solutions.
66   Food, too, is highly symbolic. Religious dietary regulations, such as
67 those of the Catholics, Jews, and Mohammedans, are observed in order to
68 symbolize adherence to one's religion. Specific foods are used to symbolize
69 specific festivals and observances in almost every country—for example,
70 cherry pie on George Washington's birthday and haggis on Burns' Nicht.
71 And eating together has been a highly symbolic act throughout all of man's
72 known history: "companion" means one with whom you share your bread.
73 We select our furniture to serve as visible symbols of our taste, wealth,
74 and social position. We often choose our residences on the basis of a feeling
75 that it "looks well" to have a "good address." We trade in perfectly good
76 cars for later models, not always to get better transportation, but to give
77 evidence to the community that we can afford it.
78   Such complicated and apparently unnecessary behavior leads
79 philosophers, both amateur and professional, to ask over and over again,
80 "Why can't human beings live simply and naturally?" Often the complexity
81 of human life makes us look enviously at the relative simplicity of lives such

82   as those that dogs and cats lead. But the symbolic process, which makes
83   possible the absurdities of human conduct, also makes possible language
84   and therefore all the human achievements dependent on language. The fact
85   that more things can go wrong with motorcars than with wheelbarrows is no
86   reason for going back to wheelbarrows. Similarly, the fact that the symbolic
87   process makes complicated follies possible is no reason for wanting to return
88   to a cat-and-dog existence. A better solution is to understand the symbolic
89   process, so that instead of being its victims we become, to some degree at
90   least, its masters.*

---

*From *Language in Thought and Action,* Third Edition, by S. I. Hayakawa. Reprinted with permission by Harcourt Brace Jovanovich, Inc.

Practice Drills for Week 6

As soon as you have completed Chapters Twenty-five through Thirty and have spent at least six days doing the fourth set of practice drills, you should be ready to move ahead. Having spent six days doing the last six chapters, spend today just doing this set of practice drills, and tomorrow begin again to do a chapter each day prior to doing the practice drills.

The first drill is a type of study-reading drill which you can apply to your text-books if you are a student. If you are not a student, it is still a good drill: select anything that you would read which has information you must learn or would like to know. You might not want to study it as carefully as a student who had to pass a test on the subject, so when deciding your purpose for the reading take this into consideration. When you are breaking up the material, take larger sections, even whole chapters. Purpose always determines your approach and style of reading.

The most difficult part of the study-reading drill is to accurately set your purpose. Too many students feel they should learn "everything"; of course they don't really want to spend that much time. If you can determine your purpose in advance and learn the simple techniques of how to study-read each section, soon you will know how to learn when reading and be able to do it much better and faster than before. But the practice of the techniques takes time and initially it may seem slower than before; with patience and practice it is much more efficient.

Materials You Will Need for This Week's Drills

1. *A timing device.*
2. *Pen or pencil.*
3. *Paper.* Preferably unlined 8 1/2 × 11 inches.
4. *Textbook or nonfiction book* you wish to study or learn something from.
5. *Four to six books,* nonfiction and fiction.

DRILL NO. 18

Materials: Textbook or nonfiction book
           Pencil and paper
           Timing device
Estimated Time: 30 minutes

Purpose: Learn techniques for high responsibility reading, i.e., study, reports

Objective: Select a selection for study that should be able to be studied in thirty minutes and so on according to the new techniques.

DO THIS DRILL ONCE PER PRACTICE SESSION

Diagram:

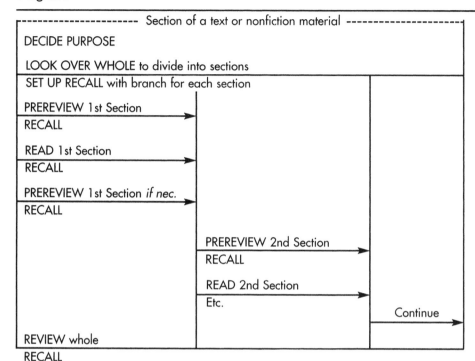

Explanation:

1. Select a section of a text or chapter of a book of nonfiction which you should be able to complete in 30 minutes.

   Decide what your purpose will be for reading it: how much should you be able to recall when you are done? Material from each paragraph? Just from each sub-heading? Just the main ideas from the whole section or chapter?

   Look over the section chosen to read to see how you will divide it according to your purpose: into paragraphs, pages, sections, or the whole chapter?

   Set up a recall pattern which reflects what you have decided to learn or get out of the material in advance: a "branch" or line for everything you will get. (Remember, this can be adjusted as you get into the material.)

2. For each section, whether it is a paragraph or a whole chapter:

   Preview just to find what it's about or the main point.

   Recall without looking back at the material.

   Read the same section to understand it as carefully *as your purpose demands.* Add to your recall. Then ask yourself if you've been able to recall as much as you feel you should in terms of your purpose. IF NOT THEN:

Re-read the same section.

Add to your recall. *When you are able to recall as much as you should, go on to the next section and repeat these steps till you have covered every section or* until your 30 minutes' practice time is nearly up.

3.   Review the whole quickly. Attempt to see how all of the parts that you've read carefully fit together to form the whole.
Add to your recall pattern if you wish.

DRILL NO. 19

Materials: Assorted books   Purpose: High speed visual practice
                   Pencil and paper
                   Timing device   Objective: Following the story line while
Estimated Time: 15 minutes   maintaining required rates

THIS DRILL MAY BE REPEATED

Diagram:

```
------------------------ Chapter or section of about 15 pages -----------------------
| DUSTING hand movement                               3 seconds/page |
|-------------------------------------------------------------------|
| RECALL anything on a diagonal recall pattern                      |
|                                                                   |
| CRISS-CROSSING hand movement                        6 seconds/page |
|-------------------------------------------------------------------|
| RECALL                                                            |
|                                                                   |
| SLASHING or PARAGRAPHING hand movement             10 seconds/page |
|-------------------------------------------------------------------|
| RECALL                                                            |
|                                                                   |
| DUSTING hand movement                             1-2 seconds/page |
|-------------------------------------------------------------------|
| RECALL                                                            |
|                                                                   |
| COMPUTE & RECORD slashing or paragraphing rate                    |
```

Explanation:

1.   Select a chapter or section of a chapter approximately fifteen pages long.

2.   Using the dusting hand movement, "dust" down each page spending no more than three seconds per page (count to yourself if you wish).
Set up a diagonal recall pattern and write down anything you can remember.

3.   Using the criss-crossing hand movement, repeat the entire section spending no more than six seconds per page (about three complete hand movements per page).
Add to your recall.

4. Using the slashing or paragraphing hand movement, repeat the entire section spending no more than ten seconds per page (about five complete hand movements per page).

READING PURPOSE: Attempt to connect the story line as you go.

Add to your recall.

5. Using the dusting hand movement, repeat the entire section spending no more than two seconds per page, preferably only one.
Add to your Recall.

6. Compute your practice reading rate in step 4; record it on your progress profile. Find the total number of words in the entire section, then divide that by the number of minutes taken to do the slashing or paragraphing through the material.

CAUTION: Make certain to maintain a practice reading rate in step 4 over 1,800 WPM.

See chart on page 269.

DRILL NO. 20

Materials: Assorted books
           Paper and pencil
           Timing device
Estimated Time: 12 minutes

Purpose: Practice rapid reading techniques and adjustment of techniques to form and purpose
Objective: Some comprehension with visual reading

THIS DRILL MAY BE REPEATED

Diagram:

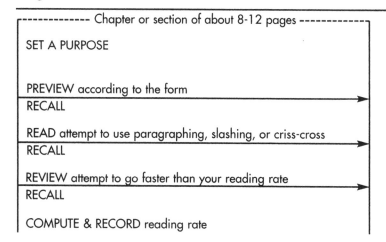

┌------------- Chapter or section of about 8-12 pages -------------┐
SET A PURPOSE

PREVIEW according to the form   →
RECALL

READ attempt to use paragraphing, slashing, or criss-cross   →
RECALL

REVIEW attempt to go faster than your reading rate   →
RECALL

COMPUTE & RECORD reading rate

Explanation:

1. Select a chapter or section of a chapter of about eight to twelve pages. Each day use a different type book, either fiction, nonfiction, or biography.
2. Preview the entire section according to its form: if (1) nonfiction, skim the beginnings and endings of section(s) to find what it's about; if (2) fiction or (3) biography, scan the entire section and find characters, setting and time that the story takes place. Begin a diagonal recall pattern.
3. Read the entire section, hand movement of your choice. Try to use paragraphing, slashing or criss-crossing, and underlining from time to time if necessary.

READING PURPOSE: Just barely follow the story or line of thought.

   Add to your recall pattern.
4. Review the entire section, attempting to go faster than your reading rate. Add to your recall pattern.
5. Compute your reading rate in step 3 and record it on your progress profile.

DRILL NO. 21

Materials: Books listed in Chapter One
  Timing device
Estimated Time: 15 minutes

Purpose: Practice reading at five times your initial reading rate

Objective: Maintain a reading rate of five times your initial rate with some comprehension

---

THIS DRILL MAY BE REPEATED

Diagram:

   Find initial reading rate and round down to nearest tenth
   Set up five sections ten times the amount

PRACTICE READ 3M

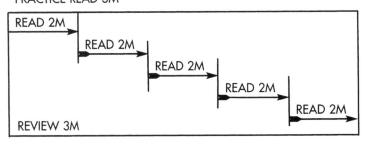

COMPUTE & RECORD any rate

Explanation:

1. Take your initial reading rate from Chapter Two. Round this amount down to the nearest tenth.

    Multiply this result by ten.

    Set up five sections of words approximately equal to the final amount.

    Mark the end of each section with a paper clip or small strip of paper sticking out from the page.

2. Using your hand as a pacer, practice read the entire amount of material in three minutes.

3. Using your hand as a pacer, attempt to read the first section in two minutes. You may use any hand movement you choose.

READING PURPOSE: Attempt to follow the story line. Make the mark even at the loss of comprehension.

4. Continue, reading each part in two minutes or less.
5. Review the whole in three minutes or less.
6. Compute the reading rate of any section and record it on your progress profile.

31

DEVELOP HIGH SPEED WITH THESE SPECIAL DRILLS

With all of the emphasis on speed, some students rebel, and insist on learning speed reading more gradually. It certainly sounds reasonable to speed up a little bit, wait till your comprehension catches up, then speed up some more. It sounds good, but it rarely works. People and methods which don't push you rarely get results worth wasting precious practice time. I have found that the best results are attained by pushing you as far as you care to be pushed, and then *a lot* further.

IT HELPS TO BE RELAXED

Your success in increasing your reading rate will be determined to a large degree by your ability to relax and maintain the suggested practice rates, even when they seem completely outlandish. Until he or she has learned the skill, it's often hard for the student to appreciate the techniques an instructor is using. In a classroom it often takes just about everything I've got to get some reluctant students to practice at high enough rates. I hope that you've got what it takes to get yourself up there.

Remember that you can't intellectualize this skill. Just because you understand *how* it works doesn't mean that you can do it. And it doesn't make it any easier to learn it. Let me give you two examples.

Before I went to work for Reading Dynamics, I was teaching rapid reading in an adult education course in a suburb of Pittsburgh. A young woman who was training to become a nurse was doing very well. She practiced diligently, *expected* to do well, cheerfully came to class pleased with any progress she had made. Sometimes there was no progress, a plateau had been reached, but she practiced on. When I handed in the results of the course midway through the term, the head of adult education came to see me. She was a very bright woman with a Ph.D., and was an excellent administrator. She was certain that this student couldn't be reading as fast as she was (several thousand words a minute) because the administrator knew that the student wasn't "bright" enough. I had to assure her that it was no mistake, that the student was one of those lucky people whose positive attitude and diligence pay off handsomely for them.

Another student I remember was working on a Ph.D. at a university in Pittsburgh. About six weeks through an eight-week course he was in my office in tears. He was not doing well and he was terrified that he would "flunk." He assured me that he was a straight "A" student, implying that this should guarantee his doing well in rapid reading. But he didn't want to hear me tell him that he just had to relax, practice with a positive attitude, and not attempt to *figure it out* or intellectualize it in some other way. Some very bright people have been away from learning *skills* so long that they no longer know how to learn them. Sometimes they are surprised to find out that they have to work as hard as the next fellow, something many are no longer used to doing. This student did make it through the course, but only with both of us working very, very hard.

RESULTS VARY WITH VARIOUS TEACHERS

When I first became National Director of Education for Evelyn Wood Reading Dynamics, it amazed me to find such different results from various institutes around the United States, Canada, and Europe—everywhere we were teaching. In my tours throughout our schools, working with the teachers and examining the school records, I found the answers. In some instances, in my opinion, the teachers were not very proficient with the skills, and some hardly seemed to believe in what they were teaching. Naturally they didn't get very good results. In fact, the results of the various institutes would invariably reflect the skills of the teachers. It was always satisfying to me to find that the best results and the best teachers were always under the personal direction of Evelyn Wood at the institute in Salt Lake City.

The teachers who are most comfortable with their own skills and who can obtain the highest reading rates from their students are always the ones who push them the most. Here are some drills which can help you achieve much higher rates, if you'll push yourself and keep up with them. Making the "mark" in a drill is always just a matter of (1) relaxing, (2) moving your hand and turning the pages quickly enough, (3) attempting to find *some* information no matter how fast you are going. The only reason you cannot go fast enough is if you (1) cannot turn the pages fast enough, or (2) refuse to just "look" at the print on the page in the allotted time, which might be only a second per page, and attempt to "read."

Since just about everybody can turn the pages fast enough with a little practice, and also can move his hand down the page quickly enough, then the only reason that you cannot make the "mark" is that *you* don't want to.

IS THE GLASS HALF EMPTY OR HALF FULL?

When I first started teaching for Evelyn Wood Reading Dynamics, I was told a story about Evelyn Wood. I've never asked her if it was true, but even if it isn't it certainly has become true for me from my experience. The story has it that at a certain point in the course Evelyn would ask a student how he or she was faring at the 2,000 words per minute, which they had been asked to practice. By his answer, she could quite accurately predict not only how well he would do but also how difficult her job in teaching him would be.

If the student answered that it was pretty frustrating to be going so fast, because he or she got so little at that rate, then he would have to work hard and the results might be slightly under average. But if the answer was something to the effect of "I'm amazed at how much information I can get going at that rate," then it would be easy teaching and the student would achieve above average results. What impressed me the most, and was true from my own experience, was that both of these students were probably "getting" the same amount of information at this point.

Today, when teaching rapid reading I place a lot more emphasis on comprehension techniques, study techniques, and recall techniques. This is because I have learned a lot more about them in recent years. When I learned rapid reading, the emphasis was primarily on high speed. Right from the beginning we were pushed and pushed and pushed. Those who couldn't keep up fell rapidly behind. Although I wouldn't go back to those teaching techniques today, I believe that a lot of the high speed work has much merit. I think you'll enjoy doing some special high speed drills in this chapter. Remember to stay cool, don't worry about what you're not getting, and see what you can get. I'll start off with the fastest drill of all.

EXERCISE NO. 43

Materials: *Basic list of books*

1. Select a novel or biography or book of nonfiction, preferably not too difficult and not too long (about 120 to 150 pages is preferable).

    Look over the back cover, inside the dust cover (if any), table of contents, and anywhere else besides the main body of the book for any clues to what the material will be about.

2. "Flash" the entire book by simply looking at each page for approximately one second. No hand movement is necessary, as turning the pages will act as your pacing device.

    Check how many pages are in the book and attempt to go through the entire book in that number of seconds.

3. On a piece of paper, begin a recall pattern. Make the recall pattern for the whole book; put down obvious main organization features of the book if any are apparent.

    Recall any general information about the book, also any "guesses" you might have from having perused the pages this fast.

4.   Using *one* slashing or criss-crossing hand movement per page, go through the entire book at a rate of approximately two seconds per page.

5.   Add to your recall pattern anything more that seemed to emerge from the book.

6.   Using *two* slashing or criss-crossing hand movements per page, go through the entire book at a rate of approximately four seconds per page.

7.   Add to your recall pattern anything more that you can.
     Optional: Begin from the beginning of the book and read as fast as you can, using any hand movement, and then compute your reading rate for one minute. Record this rate on your progress profile.

Sometimes it's hard to imagine what value these high speed drills have. You gain the most from them when they are done frequently and for decent practice periods (30 to 60 minutes). They will help to develop your highest range, and for this reason it's best to do them in easy materials. The value of developing your high range is simple. It will also help to bring your lowest range up. Thus high speed work even in easy books will also help to bring up the rate of your low speed work in difficult materials. This is because it helps to make you quicker at the simple recognition of groups of words.

EXERCISE NO. 44

Materials: *An easy book*

1.   Read for one minute, using any hand movement, mark where you stop with an "X."
     Optional: Compute your reading rate.

2.   Make a mark one page farther ahead of the point you read to in Step No. l.
     Practice read to the new mark, *in thirty seconds,* using any hand movement.

3.   Make a mark three pages farther ahead of the point you read to in Step No. l.
     Practice read to the new mark, *in thirty seconds,* using any hand movement.

4.   Make a mark six pages farther ahead of the point you read to in Step No. l.
     Practice read to the new mark, *in thirty seconds,* using any hand movement.

5.   Make a mark ten pages farther ahead of the point you read to in Step No. l.
     Practice read to the new mark, *in thirty seconds,* using any hand movement.

6.   Go back to the "X" mark, the point you read to in Step No. l.
     Read for one minute, using any hand movement, from this point.
     Mark where you stop with a "Y."
     Compute your reading rate. Record this rate on your progress profile.

7.   Optional: Repeat the drill, recalling whatever you can after each practice reading.

It's good from time to time to spend an hour just practicing at high speeds. Of course if you find it frustrating and very difficult, if not impossible to make the mark, then stay with the lower speed drills. But be certain to keep practicing at a speed which will benefit you.

PRACTICE AT THREE TIMES YOUR READING RATE

A general rule of thumb to practice is that if you wish to read at a certain rate, then you should be practicing at about three times that speed. For instance, if you wanted to be able to read 1,200 words per minute in novels and light material, you should plan to spend a fair amount of time practicing between 3,000 and 4,000 words per minute. Then you can begin to appreciate the value of the high speed drills. If you desire to read really fast, then fast practice is called for.

Of course you must, in a sense, work up to high speed practice. Before high speed practice is of value, you must be able to read well in a high linear reading range. For example, if you have difficulty getting good comprehension at 200 words per minute, you are not yet prepared to be practicing at the high visual rates. You should be able to get good comprehension at linear rates of around 600 words per minute before working in the extremely high ranges.

TURN TO PAGE 220 FOR THE PRACTICE DRILLS TO COMPLETE TODAY'S WORK.

32

READ YOUR NEWSPAPER INSTANTANEOUSLY

Your daily newspaper has an overriding purpose, to communicate *new* information and opinions pertinent to events that have happened very recently. Unfortunately, I have known many persons who feel obligated to go through the newspaper as though they were preparing for a test, often saving parts of it (to stack up on others from previous days) for whenever they find enough time to read it. Now is the time to learn how to deal with your newspaper in *as much time as you have for it,* or wish for it.

PRACTICE YOUR NEW TECHNIQUES WHERE IT'S EASY

Your newspaper is wonderful material for practicing your rapid reading techniques. There are several reasons for this. First of all, the width of the columns makes for easier, faster reading. When you have a relatively narrow column of print (four inches is ideal), you are able to see the maximum amount of words *which relate to one another.* The worst line of print to read is a line stretched clear across a page of standard 8-1/2 by 11-inch paper. Words above and below those at one side of the page may have little relationship to the words in the middle. Thus the additional words that you are seeing hardly help you at all. If the words were printed in too narrow a column, it would have the same negative effect. A study was made by one of the nation's leading newspapers to find the most effective width of a line of print. It was found to be four inches. And this is helpful both to the linear reader and to the rapid reader. That is also why paperback books tend to be easier to read. Their column width tends to be narrower than the average hard cover book.

FAMILIARITY BREEDS FASTER READING

The second reason the newspaper is easy to read and excellent for practicing your new reading techniques is due to your background knowledge. The principle was presented before and is particularly apt here:

> *The more prior knowledge the reader has of the subject of a passage of words, the faster it may be read.*

Many newspaper articles are largely *updating* information with which you are already familiar. As you follow a story from day to day, you build a lot of background knowledge. Even if the story is new, it often has a familiar theme: a political scandal, a fire, a fiftieth wedding anniversary. You only need find out the new names, locations, and details.

The third reason that the newspaper is easily read is the simplicity of its form. Much of the newspaper is composed of feature stories (recognizable by their by-line). These, and editorials, use the basic nonfiction format of writing, with a well-structured beginning and ending. This makes it easy to read efficiently. But this is not the only form of writing found in a newspaper. You also have to deal with columnists and news articles.

Columnists may give you some trouble. Many of them use an essay style, similar to a nonfiction format. But some, usually the gossip columnists, often write in short, choppy paragraphs which are whole unto themselves. These are called "items." It's difficult to read these quickly because they are so short and the thought changes so abruptly.

NEWS ARTICLES HAVE THE EASIEST FORM OF ALL

The most basic form used in the newspaper is the news article. These are the stories that usually appear on the front page and the first pages of the various sections. These stories carry the *news*, meaning that it will be out of date tomorrow. A feature story is more like a magazine article. It too may be timely, but it could usually wait a day or two, perhaps even a week.

The basic form of a news story is well known to all journalism students. It's like an inverted pyramid because the most important information is at the top, and everything that follows is of lesser importance. The reason for this is that it is a surer way of grabbing reader attention. Also, in case there is a late-breaking story of greater importance, it is always possible to cut *any* news article from the bottom up. In fact it may be cut at any point as long as it ends with a sentence, and the cut space is then used for another story. Some newspapers also take advantage of this to put in late advertisements.

Knowing this information, if you have only limited time, you can safely read just the beginning paragraphs of a news article and get the gist of the story. In fact, a few years ago a well-known newspaper made a dramatic presentation of how much news you get from television as opposed to what you could read in their newspaper. Only the top few paragraphs of each story were used in the television presentation.

Be careful in comparing the form of the news article with a feature story or editorial which uses the nonfiction form of beginning, development, and conclusion. These forms are almost direct opposites. In a news article, you are completely safe reading just the opening paragraphs or the beginning. In the nonfiction form, the endings are as important, sometimes more so, than the beginnings. Your attention to the form becomes very important, although only a second or two is necessary to find out what it is.

A NEW WAY TO READ THE NEWSPAPER

In order to read the newspaper in an efficient manner, it is necessary to have an overall approach to it. You will probably want to read the headlines of the front page first, or the sports page. It's hard to resist that because the newspaper is written to attract your attention in just that way. So look over the front page.

If your newspaper has a daily summary, as does the *New York Times* and the *Wall Street Journal,* this is where you should turn next. The editors do a splendid job of editing and previewing for you, so take full advantage of it. Read through the whole summary and find out what is important for you to read, in whatever amount of time you have. Then read it. If you are very pressed for time, simply preview it.

If your newspaper does not have a daily summary, it is up to you to make one yourself. Go through the entire paper very quickly. Read the headlines and first sentences if necessary to determine what they are about and if they're worth reading. With a pen make an "X" on the articles that you will read; then read them in the following manner.

The best system is going down one column after another, reading articles of interest only. Do not bother to turn the pages to find the rest of a story that is continued. You will have read the most important part already and if you wish you can read the rest of it later. That may seem a bit disjointed at first, and perhaps will take some getting used to, but it is much more efficient. What will undoubtedly amaze you is how good your memory is. If you are reading a story which is continued on another page, even though you break the continuity by reading other stories to complete the page and also read other pages before your story resumes, *if it is worth reading and remembering you will remember what you need to.* And with very little practice, perhaps for a week, you will get used to reading this way and become pleased with the time it saves you.

NARROW COLUMN HAND MOVEMENTS

Most newspaper columns are fairly narrow, usually slightly under the ideal width of four inches. For narrow columns it is easiest to use a one-finger hand movement. Two which especially lend themselves to narrow columns appear in Figure 23. Practice using both of them and see which you like the best.

Now that you understand the basic organization pattern of news articles, it is important to use this information. In this next exercise apply the new techniques you have learned, also use the new hand movements. Of course when you are previewing the first two or three paragraphs of a news article you may use either underlining or the zigzagging hand movements.

FIGURE 23. NARROW COLUMN HAND MOVEMENTS

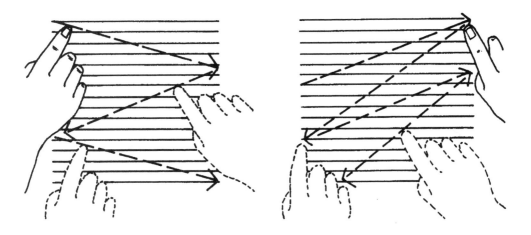

EXERCISE NO. 45

Materials: *Newspaper that you haven't read*
Pencil and pen, or two pens with different colored ink
Paper
Timing device

1. Select any news article to read. Make certain it is not a feature story (a feature story could be printed on several days as well as today, a news article is news only today).

   Using underlining or zig-zagging, preview the article by reading the first two or three paragraphs only. Time yourself.

2. Begin a recall pattern writing what the article is about.

   Journalists try to give you the "who, what, where, when, and why or how" right away. You can structure your recall pattern similarly.

   Record your preview time on your progress profile.

3. Read the *whole* news article, or as much as appears on the page.

   Time yourself.

4. Add to your recall pattern using a different colored ink.

   Record your reading time.

5. Repeat Steps No. 1 through 4 above with three more articles.

When you finish, compare the amount of information you found from previewing the article with what you got from reading the whole article. Be certain to take into consideration the different amounts of time spent.

Did you notice that after the first few paragraphs the information became less vital? Did you notice that more and more extraneous background "filler" was used toward the end of the article?

In terms of your reading purpose, how much of these news articles is of interest to you? Should you continue reading after a preview? Should you speed up your rate following the preview? When should you slow down? All of these questions should be a natural part of your reading a newspaper. Learning what not to read, when to speed up and when to slow down are all important aspects of becoming an efficient reader.

TURN TO PAGE 220 FOR THE PRACTICE DRILLS TO COMPLETE TODAY'S WORK.

33

DON'T WASTE YOUR TIME READING THE MAIL

For many people, just getting through their daily mail comprises the bulk of the reading they must face. Some executives spend as much as four hours or more a day reading. A study by the Harvard Business School showed that on the average the further up the ladder an executive moves, the more reading he faces.

The daily mail—including letters, newspapers, journals, reports and now printed e-mail—poses a great challenge because much of it is composed of short items; short pieces are usually the hardest ones to read quickly. You must be very careful to guard against the maximum danger, thinking that just because the material is short you can read it as quickly without your new techniques. True, if you have only one letter to read, whether or not you use your hand will hardly matter. But if you have ten letters, or any volume of mail worth mentioning, then it definitely does pay to use all of your rapid reading techniques. Saving 30 seconds here, a minute there, soon adds up, and much faster than you would imagine.

Time is one of the few things that we cannot replace. We all have the same amount of it each day and how we use it has a lot to do with how successful we are with our lives in whatever terms we define success. In order to work at your maximum efficiency, you must use many different techniques, only one of which is your newly increased reading rate.

THE FIRST RULE: HANDLE EVERYTHING ONLY ONCE

The greatest time saver is to handle a piece of paper only one time. When you first read a letter, jot your decision right on it. If you don't handle your own correspondence, your executive assistant can then answer the letter as per your instructions; or if you write your own letters on your PC, you will know immediately what to write. Don't make the mistake of reading your mail, then calling your assistant in and rereading the same mail in order to dictate your decisions and answers. Make the decision the first time, jot down the answer *on the letter.*

EVALUATE A LETTER'S IMPORTANCE RIGHT AWAY

In your own mind, or on the letter itself, immediately assign each letter a value of (1) top priority, (2) important, or (3) can wait. If a letter is a (1) and must be answered immediately and is of the utmost importance, jot your answer or decision down as soon as you read it and have it ready for your secretary. Any (2) letter should be important enough that an answer is also penned immediately *or* you can immediately route it to someone else who is capable of answering it. A (3) letter can be put off, and if you want to put it off, do so. You'll probably find that when it waits long enough you don't have to do anything with it at all except throw it out or file it. These are the letters to save for when you get "more time."

Some letters automatically fall into certain categories. A purchase order should be a (1), whereas a thank-you letter would be a (3), and most sales pitches are (3). A request for information might be a (2), and most reports are also (2s) and should immediately be read quickly through. Get into the habit of categorizing and assigning values as soon as you go through the mail, and immediately dealing with each item so that you don't have to handle it again.

Be certain to always use your hand when reading letters. They're short, but if you have many to read the seconds saved will soon add up. Always be on the lookout for numbers such as significant dates, costs, or other figures which may be of importance. They often lead you to important parts of the letter. Be quick to recognize standard parts of letters, general introductory comments and stock closing paragraphs, and cut right through them.

EXERCISE NO. 46

Materials: *Timing device set for twenty seconds and forty seconds*
Pencil and paper

1. On a piece of paper, list from "1" to "6." Going through the following "letters" one at a time, first preview the letter in twenty seconds. Try to identify what kind of letter it is—a report, sales pitch, thank you, or whatever.

2. After previewing the first letter, jot down what kind it is. If you can, assign the letter a value of (1), (2), or (3).

If you can already answer the letter after the preview, jot down your answer or decision of what to do with it on your paper.

3. If you need to read the first letter, allow up to forty seconds. After reading, jot down your answer or decision.

4. Continue Steps 1 through 3 on the rest of the letters.

KARBON KOPIERS
1234 Duluth Boulevard
Iowa City, Hawaii
(786) 123-4567

Mr. Thomas
Maurice Deer Company
4545 Charlotte Avenue
Tuscaloosa, Kentucky

Dear Tommy:

It was marvelous meeting up with you again on our trip back to the States. I'm just sorry that Jane and I didn't know you were visiting the Islands so that we could have had a big welcome for you.

As we were discussing on the plane, Karbon Kopiers could undoubtedly save you money with your extensive duplicating work. The prices you are now paying for your Standard Duplicating Equipment could probably be cut by a third, maybe even more. We can do this because of a unique new system, only recently marketed, which allows you to use any type of paper and also results in a lower manufacturing cost.

If you want our man to get in touch with you, just let me know. The new machine is such a success that we have a backlog of orders. However, we always keep a few aside for our special friends and customers. If you are interested, I will make certain that our representative in your territory understands the situation.

Tell Irene that we will be sending her the ginger perfume shortly and a few jars of macadamia nuts for you! Again, I hope we meet up either here or on the mainland in the coming year. Give my best regards to the rest of the family.

Sincerely yours,

Roland David

Roland David
President

RD:pc

LUMINESCENCE, INC. 340
Shadyside Boulevard
Cupertino, California

Dear Customer,

There are more ways than one to lick the high cost of living. And for retailers like you, one of the most effective ways is to order in volume wherever possible in order to take advantage of quantity discounts.

Let me just analyze how this could have worked for you last year. Our records show that during the year just ended you purchased 710 dozen assorted bulbs. Broken down, we show that this total was made up of 105 dozen 40-watt bulbs, 300 dozen 60-watt bulbs, and 305 dozen 100-watt bulbs. And since you never ordered more than 10 dozen of any of them at a single time, we had to process about 40 individual orders to serve you. In every case, you bought at the highest possible price, since discounts start to apply at the 25-dozen level.

In batches of 25 dozen for each order, you could have cut your total purchase costs for the year by $625. Just imagine—$625 to take home with you as additional profits! And if you had ordered 50-dozen lots, you could have latched on to another $500 in profits.

If it's a question of terms, please remember that we're always ready and willing to co-operate with customers whose credit with us is satisfactory. Yours most certainly is. So why not let me send one of our salesmen in to see you next week to help you set up a system for this year which will help you earn the biggest possible discounts?

I hope to hear from you soon.

Cordially,

R. Bronson

R. Bronson
Vice-President, Sales

UNION UNIVERSITY
Pikesville, California
OFFICE OF THE CHANCELLOR

March 1997

Mr. Ronald Fouts
3487 Biscayne Street
Oxford, Mississippi

Dear Ron:

Almost five years ago, the University launched one of the most ambitious fundraising efforts in the history of private higher education, the $300 million Campaign for Union.

Today, with the support of over 45,000 alumni and friends, we have reached **95%** of that Campaign goal. I speak not just for myself, but also for Campaign Co-Chairman Richard R. Godden, the Trustees, and a host of volunteers in saying that we are all tremendously gratified with the progress to date.

I realize that you have been a loyal supporter of Union through your gifts to the Annual Fund, and I thank you for that support. What I am asking of you now is no more than we have asked of every other friend of Union, alumni and non-alumni alike. That is, that you make one special gift to the Campaign—an investment in the University's future, over and above your annual gifts. The target date for complete Campaign success is late this spring.

A successful campaign goes far to ensure a number of things vital to a university: high quality education provided by a distinguished faculty; scholarship support for top-flight students, many of whom contribute from their own earnings to pay the high cost of a Union education; the provision of academic buildings such as expanded library facilities and modern laboratories, updating computer equipment and software; and, by no means least, additions to the endowment which is the veritable cornerstone of a private university's independence. It means, in short, a commitment to excellence.

I ask you to make that commitment now and, in so doing, to join all others who have already made it. With so much already achieved, with Union so close to its Campaign goal, won't you please support the Campaign to the best of your capacity so that you can join thousands of others at April's end in saying "We did it!" and thus join with increased pride in singing "Hail, Union. Hail!"

Sincerely yours,

J. B. Bernson

J. B. Bernson
Chancellor

BANK OF COLUMBUS
65 East Fifth Street
Columbus, Maryland

James O'Conner
Vice President

Mr. Chin Ho
870 Borne Street
Columbus, Maryland

Dear Mr. Ho:

Do you travel, entertain friends and occasionally snap up unexpected bargains? Would a cushion of ready cash provide you financial flexibility? If so, we have an unusual service a discerning person like you will appreciate . . . a $2,000 to $5,000 Cash reserve, coupled with a special Bank of Columbus/American Express Gold Bank Card.

With the special Gold Card, you have charge account privileges at thousands of establishments the world over, plus convenience and unparalleled buying power. No matter where business or pleasure may take you—hotels, airports, restaurants and shops—the Gold Card opens doors and identifies you as a preferred customer of our bank.

As soon as you're approved and your account is established, your Cash Reserve with us (minimum $2,000) is your money to use as you choose when you need extra funds FAST. It's that simple! There's no red tape, bank visits or questions asked!

Our unusual service has been specially designed to give you the comfort of knowing you'll always have funds available when and where needed. The enclosed brochure contains more details and includes an application for your use. We think the uniqueness, security and convenience offered will add valuable benefits to your own financial plan. Accept our invitation. Apply today!

Sincerely,

Jim O'Conner

Jim O'Conner

P.S. When we set up your new account, you'll get a special FREE gift . . . see the enclosed brochure.

Charles Dwyer, President
Benton & Dwyer
3400 Rennsbury Boulevard
Pittsburgh, PA.

Dear Mr. Dwyer,

When I left your employ two months ago, I forgot to ask you for a letter of recommendation. Now, I am being considered for a job with a well-known law firm in San Francisco and I wonder if you'd be kind enough to give me such a letter. My prospective employer has asked for details about my responsibilities with Benton & Dwyer, so I'd appreciate it if you can give him some indication of the duties which were mine.

Will you send your letter of recommendation directly to Mr. Wadsworth Adams at Adams & Niece, 22 Park Place, San Francisco, California?

Thanks very much for your help.

Sincerely,

Christopher O'Brien

Christopher O'Brien

Mr. Arvin Ardmore
123 West Street
Peoria, Ill.

Dear Mr. Ardmore,

Two weeks ago, when we spent a day together examining the various parcels of land that were available in downtown Syracuse, I thought you were seriously interested in the tract on the corner of Tracy and Skidmore Avenues.

Now I find that, if we move quickly, it may be possible to close the deal for that parcel for about $24,000 less than the price I quoted. The reason for this is that the owners need to put themselves into a better cash position right away.

Naturally, at this new price, the property will appeal to many others and I believe it will move very, very rapidly. As a matter of fact, I have another interested party, but feel that you should have first refusal because your interest takes precedence.

However, I cannot remain inactive on this very long. The best I can do is to give you a five-day option, meaning that you must make up your mind by Friday, September 19. I'd suggest, therefore, that you get in touch with me right away. I'm sure that this spot would be ideal for the purpose you have in mind. There aren't many attractive properties in good locations for this kind of money, as you know.

Will you let me hear from you right away, Mr. Ardmore?

Cordially,

Guy D. Gold

Guy D. Gold

If you subscribe to magazines or professional journals, use the techniques described in Chapter Thirty-five. Be certain to keep a few at home and some at the office to "read" whenever you have an extra five or ten minutes. You'll be able to get through a lot of extra materials like this by using time that is often "lost." Most magazines and newsletters fall into the (2) or (3) category, and they should usually be dealt with within a day or two or not at all, so put them wherever they should be for availability when you have the extra minutes.

The same goes for e-mail. I don't recommend using your hand movements on the screen. But it does make sense to print out your e-mail messages and review them using the same techniques you would use for letters that came in the mail.

If you conscientiously set your purpose and evaluate materials immediately, try to deal with most mail only once, use your hand to guide your reading—you should find yourself cutting a lot of time which you usually spend reading your mail. Some executives have been able to cut their mail-reading time in half. If you have much to do, it certainly is not an unrealistic goal and one well worth a little practice to achieve.

TURN TO PAGE 220 FOR THE PRACTICE DRILLS TO COMPLETE TODAY'S WORK.

34

DEVELOP THE
BOOK-A-DAY HABIT

President Theodore Roosevelt was known for reading a book a day before breakfast. Years ago, I was told that former Senator William Proxmire from Wisconsin, one of Reading Dynamics' graduates, read a book a day during his lunch hour. If you can establish such a habit, even if it is a book a week, you will find this worthwhile. If you want to develop this valuable habit, let it begin as a practice drill. Sooner than you imagine, it will become true reading.

One of the most exciting moments when I was learning speed reading was the time we first went through a whole novel in a single session. In fact, we "read" through the novel in about 20 minutes. Of course this was, at the time, a practice reading, but it wasn't long before it became a reality.

Drilling through an entire novel can be a valuable experience, especially if it is done many times. It is easiest to do in short novels at first, working up to longer and more difficult ones. It is especially helpful because it can aid you in developing a lifetime habit of reading more books.

Alan Lakein writes, in his book *How To Get Control of Your Time and Your Life*, that anyone can get a great deal of reading done if he will take advantage of the *lost* ten and fifteen minutes spent waiting for buses, in taxicabs, or whatever. If you always have available a book you're planning to read, these short periods are invaluable for chopping away at mammoth goals such as reading the great books. You'd be amazed how a few minutes here and there add up.

Lakein also suggests many ways of learning to set priorities and eliminate unnecessary reading. Though he is no speed reading advocate (he writes that he enjoys reading aloud, with his wife), his excellent techniques are certainly a sound portion of any intelligent approach to accomplishing a lot of reading.

FIRST DECIDE WHAT YOU WANT TO READ

Most of us waste a great deal of our time reading material which is ultimately of no great significance to us, not valuable for our work nor of ultimate satisfaction personally.

Learning how to decide what you really want to read is a lesson in itself. At the beginning of the book, I asked you to make a list of the ten books you would most want to read if you had only a few months left to live. This is a good way to begin planning. If you can do this every six months, you will be amazed how quickly you will start getting more of the reading done that you have always intended to.

Your birthday is the best time to make up a six months' reading list, followed by a date six months later. These are the best times because they are easy dates to remember. Review what you'd most like to read, and make a list of six or more books. It's best to start small. Don't make a list that will overwhelm you. Once you've read the first group, you can make a new list.

Mortimer Adler, perhaps the American "dean" of critical reading, suggests in his book *How to Read a Book* a list of the great books of the world. If you are interested in pursuing such a venture as attempting to read a lot of fine works, you'll find that almost all of these great books are available in low-cost paperback editions. Once you have made a list, you are ready to begin accomplishing your reading task.

HOW TO GET MORE BOOKS READ

Just like practicing for this course, if you wish to get more reading done it will be necessary to establish reading as a habit. For the next two weeks begin setting aside daily or every-other-day time for reading. As I suggested in an earlier chapter, when trying to establish new habits it is best to begin them in the morning. Once they are firmly established, move them to another time slot in your day. So select a time, even if it is only ten minutes a day. Another approach, which can be an alternative or in addition to your regular daily reading time, is to always carry a book and make use of the small amounts of time that seem to be *given* to you: waiting for a friend, time in the bathroom, between appointments, waiting for something to download on your computer, or whenever.

A-BOOK-A-DAY APPROACH

If you want to get into the habit of reading a book a day, or a book in a single sitting, start by assembling the books you plan to use. Remember, in the beginning the time will tend to be a practice-reading session, but soon it will change into a reading time. At first you may not feel as though you've gotten much out of the books, and if you wish you may use the books again, but preferably wait for at least a month. The first books should be selected accordingly.

One of the best ways to begin is by assembling a series of books by the same author. Once you become used to an author's style, it becomes increasingly easy to read his books. Hemingway might be a good author, and some of his short novels would be good to start with. John Steinbeck has always been popular with rapid reading courses because many of his books, such as *The Pearl* and *Of Mice And Men*, lend themselves quite easily to being read in a short period of time. These books average about 120 pages, which is a good length to start with.

This is also a good time to re-read books that you've enjoyed in the past. A really fine book is never completed or finished, because as you mature you will have more experience and background to bring to a book. Because of this, you will discover that if you re-read a book many years later you will find new things in it. Therefore re-reading books at this time can be beneficial for your practice and also an interesting and rewarding exercise.

PATRICK BUCHANAN READS THREE BOOKS IN TWO FLIGHTS

Years ago, when I was teaching President Nixon's staff at the White House, my students had so much reading to do that there was no time for practice. But small matter: they were so desperate to improve their reading speeds that they applied all the techniques eagerly. They ended up, without much practice at all, well ahead of the average class. One of the best students was Patrick Buchanan, then a speechwriter to President Nixon and later a Presidential candidate himself. After only four lessons, and having missed a lesson due to a sudden emergency flight to Hawaii to greet the astronauts on the famed Apollo 13 flight, Pat was especially pleased with his progress. He reported that he had been able to complete three books during the flights. This was quite an accomplishment, especially taking into consideration that as one of the President's special aides he didn't have all of his flight time for reading.

THE FORM OF FICTION

I discussed the form of fiction in an earlier chapter, but it would be good to review it here. Structure and organization, apart from chapters (usually without titles) and large blank spaces between some paragraphs, are usually not obvious in fiction. Being a type of art, form is largely disguised and the author tries to draw you into his story. Becoming involved, of course, is one of the joys of reading a good book.

Previewing a novel is primarily to find the elements necessary for the story to take place. It is also the time for warming up. Since reading is a skill, just as no dancer or athlete would dream of giving a good performance without a warm-up, neither should you expect to read fast without some sort of preparation.

It is good to preview for at least fifty pages, going very quickly, preferably using the dusting hand movement at about three seconds per page. Try to find who the major characters are, where the story takes place, and when. Also note how difficult the language is, how much of the material is descriptive and how much is dialogue. You are then warming up as well as getting some idea of what's to come.

In reading fiction, the steady flow of the material usually allows for high rates *once you're into the story*. It is most important to slow down at the beginnings of sections to "hook into" the story. Once you're into it you'll find it quite easy to speed up. It's also easy to speed up over descriptive passages; sometimes narrative passages, describing the action, require slower speeds in order not to miss essential details. Dialogue often supports fairly fast reading speeds.

If you wish to analyze the story, the time to do this is in the review. Go over the material again, looking for structural elements. Become aware of how one or more characters are trying to do something or desire something; usually this gets complicated, but ultimately the problem is resolved. This is often the basis of "form" in fiction. You may also look out for the main *crises* in the book which will be the major "problems"; there are usually little "problems" in every section, chapter or parts of chapters; these are divided by white spaces between paragraphs, when everything comes to a head. Following the climax, the story winds up with a *denouement*.

Analyzing a story is usually done only by students and serious readers. If you wish to pursue this further, I urge you to obtain a copy of Mortimer Adler's *How to Read a Book* which explains in great detail how to approach all sorts of materials more thoroughly. Here is an example of reviewing and analyzing the short story on page 149.

A STRUCTURAL REVIEW OF "THE COP AND THE ANTHEM"

This short story is obviously about Soapy and it takes place in New York City probably around the turn of the century. After noting these elements which are needed for the story to happen, you should try to ascertain the basic situation: what is the main character trying to do? O. Henry makes this clear from the beginning: winter is approaching and Soapy wants to escape it.

In *reviewing* for the purpose of analyzing it, you should first find what Soapy wants to do to avoid winter and what the result is. His usual plan is to get himself arrested and spend the three winter months "on the Island" or in jail. He makes six attempts to do this, all of which are frustrated. These include (1) Soapy's inability to even get into the fancy restaurant to order the meal that he had no money to pay for, (2) Soapy's brazenly breaking a shop window and practically handing himself over to the policeman, yet still failing to get arrested, and so on. You might wish to go back and find the other four.

With all of these failures Soapy finds himself in front of a church and fond memories flood back which result in his deciding to solve the problem in a new way. He decides to try a new tack and look for a job. It is precisely at this moment, when he is standing in front of the church apparently doing nothing, that he is arrested for just that, which when done in Soapy's clothes becomes loitering. This short section ("What are you doin' here?") is the "jam" that complicates his new attempt—and it is also the climax of the story.

The wrapping up of a story, or denouement, is usually best kept short as there is rarely much new or unexpected. In this case, it is all in the final sentence: "Three months on the Island," said the Magistrate in the Police Court the next morning.

In finding the story's structure it becomes easier to remember it because you have "discovered" the author's organization and "plan." In the following exercise, the emphasis will be on getting more practice at higher rates.

EXERCISE NO. 47

Materials: *Basic list*

1. Set your timer or tape recorder for five-minute intervals. If using a tape recorder, put in one-minute warnings every minute (four minutes left, three minutes left, etc.).
2. "Flash" the book, just turning pages; go through the entire book at about one second per page. Relax and just "look" at the whole page, trying to find preview information as outlined above. Begin a recall pattern, putting down organization features of the book (if any), main characters, setting, and time.
3. Using the dusting hand movement, go through as much of the book as you can in five minutes, again looking for preview information. Try to spend no more than three seconds per page. See how many pages you should cover in five minutes and stick to that amount. Add anything you can to your recall pattern.
4. Divide the book into 7,500-word sections.
    Read each section in five minutes.
    Add to your recall pattern briefly, after each five-minute reading.
5. Review the entire book in five minutes.
    Add to your recall pattern.

NAMES CAN BE A PROBLEM

When you are reading a novel, after the initial preview try to ascertain if there are any major reading problems. The usual one is odd or unusual names. You'll encounter this frequently in foreign novels, especially Russian ones in which the names are not familiar to most of us. A book I have often used in my classes is George Orwell's classic, *Animal Farm*, and it presents an interesting problem. The major characters are animals. I've found that if a few minutes are taken to establish the "cast" of characters, the class does well on a subsequent test, but if this isn't done, the class as a whole fares poorly.

Developing the cast of characters gives the reader a certain structure with which to relate information. To do this, write down the names of the characters who appear most frequently when you are previewing the first fifty or so pages. Add to the list any names which begin to come up again. Place names may also be important, so look out for those too. After the preview, go over the names several times. If you've been able to establish relationships, this will be helpful as well, but often this can't be done until you get into the story.

WHY READ NOVELS?

Perhaps because there is no better way to learn about yourself than to read novels and experience so fully other people's insights and experiences. It is a place of great intimacy, for authors will reveal their innermost thoughts and impulses and feelings through the characters they create. No other way can you gain so much experience, albeit vicarious, so quickly. Many great individuals have gained a valuable portion of their education through reading good novels, and luckily many have also shared their unique gifts with us through the novel. It is a wonderful world of pleasures and delights, one which needs no explanation. Read a few good novels and you'll soon know for yourself. It is truly one of the great privileges which only human beings can know, but it is available to all of us equally. We have only to partake of it.

TURN TO PAGE 220 FOR THE PRACTICE DRILLS TO COMPLETE TODAY'S WORK.

35

KEEP UP WITH YOUR MAGAZINES AND INFORMATIONAL READING

Nonfiction writing in magazines, journals, webzines and books on general subjects offers a great opportunity to keep up in your field, gain new insights, and be stimulated by new ideas. Unfortunately for many of us the magazines and books-to-read pile up too quickly by the side of our beds at home or in our in-boxes at work. The amounts of materials that are left unread must be staggering, as well as resulting guilt feelings experienced by millions. Yet you, as a speed reader, can deal with these materials satisfactorily and keep up.

A speech therapist, Karen Reidel, after taking the course kept a pile of professional journals near her desk. In the few minutes between seeing clients she would preview an entire magazine. She found this quite sufficient to keep abreast of her field because though she hadn't read everything, she knew where information was when she needed it. Her colleagues soon discovered that she was a tremendous source of information. They were unable to keep up with the flow of information being published so they would come to her if they had any problems they couldn't solve and didn't know where to find out about them.

Just being familiar enough with where to go for more specific information is certainly a valid purpose in reading. People who believe they must or should know and remember everything are not only bound to be disappointed and frustrated, but also will be squandering valuable time. And usually this belief keeps them from getting most of their reading done; losing out all the way around.

USE WISELY WHATEVER TIME YOU HAVE

Too often the speed reader falls behind because he or she doesn't use time wisely. My friend had always made good use of her time, but by adding her speed reading skills she was able to keep up in an enviable way. She was previewing, looking for new ideas and helpful information. When there was an article of special interest, she would read it again more carefully.

This approach to magazines is a great time saver. When your magazines first come in, get through them right away. I make it a practice to go through my magazines when I pick up my mail, taking about five minutes apiece. First, look over the table of contents to see if there is anything of special significance. Second, preview the entire magazine, looking over *all* the articles. If you weren't interested in the magazine, you wouldn't have subscribed to it. If it was a gift or someone else's magazine, either cancel the subscription or don't bother with it. Chances are you'll find information that is of interest to you, even though you might not think so from some of the titles.

You'll be amazed how much you can get out of a magazine or professional journal in a very short period of time. Like the novel-reading drill in the last chapter, at first when you're going very fast through the magazine you may not think that you're getting very much. But you'll find, in conversations or in situations when you need the information, that you will remember important points and new items. And most important, *you'll know where to go to get more detailed information.*

Perhaps in the beginning you must trick yourself. Go through your magazines and journals very quickly, tell yourself it is just for the sake of your reading practice and that you'll come back and re-read them later, *when you have more time*. In fact, since you'll be *really* reading them later on, you can afford to go even a little bit faster. It will probably surprise you that soon you won't feel the need to go back and *really* read them, because you'll know that you've already done so.

STOP BEING COMPULSIVE!

Not so long ago a good friend of mine was taking my course and having a great deal of difficulty with the practicing. He found the practice reading extremely frustrating, so much so that after much deliberation and consultation he decided to give up that aspect of the course. He still came to class, worked diligently while there, and applied all of the principles to the enormous reading load he faces as the executive vice-president of a well-known foundation.

I was concerned that he was not getting as much from the course as I felt he should. When I asked him about this, he told me that he had indeed gained a good deal from the classes. Though he had only doubled his speed, for him the greatest accomplishment was in being able to *not* read certain things. This was the first time I was ever complimented for teaching someone not to read.

He told me that he had always felt compulsive about reading everything that was put before him, the *whole* Sunday *New York Times* for instance, and every report and letter that came across his desk, in addition to all books in his field, which are multitudinous. Now, having learned to define his reading purposes, he was able to *not* read many things, only preview other items, and have enough time to read carefully the most important materials.

One of the reasons I feel that his story is so important is that he is an extremely bright individual, a graduate of Harvard University, and successful in his field. Many students of rapid reading think that their problems are unique or that they are lacking in intelligence because they are compulsive or slow in their reading. But these problems exist at all levels. Solving the problems begins with being able to determine your reading purpose and selecting what to read accordingly, and ends with developing good reading skills.

WHEN YOU FIND YOU'RE SLOWING DOWN

A recent student of mine shared a valuable experience which I think can be helpful to you. Everyone from time to time has the problem of finding his rate slowing down as he reads a newspaper, magazine, or book. This student said that when he found this happening, he used a newly-discovered "trick." He would immediately turn to another article or another part of the book and do some fast practice reading for a minute or so. When he returned to what he had been reading, he found it much easier to maintain his fast rates.

You may find it valuable to learn this magazine drill as a way of reading all magazines and journals. Try it now on any magazine you regularly read which you haven't had a chance to get to yet.

EXERCISE NO. 48

Materials: *A magazine you read regularly*
A timing device

1. Read the front cover to see if any articles which may be of special interest to you are highlighted.
   Turn to the table of contents and read through it.
   Ask yourself these questions:
   Is there anything you *must* read?
   Is there anything you should read?
   What is there that you would like to read?
   Mark, on the table of contents, any articles falling into the first category with a (1), into the second category with a (2), and the third with a (3).

2. Allow yourself a total of 20 minutes to "read" the magazine.
   Go through the *entire* magazine using paragraphing, slashing, criss-crossing, or any of the high-speed hand movement, in ten minutes.
   When you come to any (1) articles, which is highly unlikely in most reading, go at a slower rate, previewing and reading them with care.

3. Return to the table of contents and revise your evaluations: perhaps some (2s) are of no more interest, perhaps you were incorrect about some (3s), perhaps there are more articles which may interest you, or perhaps less.
   In the ten minutes remaining re-read the (2) articles as thoroughly as time permits. If any time is left over, go back to the (3) articles.

This drill could be adjusted to a 30-minute time period or to a ten-minute time period, according to the size and difficulty and importance of your magazine. Whatever you do with it, the principles of the drill remain the same. The emphasis is on knowing your purpose and selecting what is most important to you. Most significant is *getting through the magazine.*

I have a rule of thumb about my clothes: whatever I haven't worn in the last two years is given to Goodwill or Salvation Army, automatically, even if I think I'll wear it some day. I go through everything once a year, giving every article a second chance. I've learned to do this with my reading as well. It's far better to go briefly through a magazine—five minutes can be enough time—than to let it become one of an ever-increasing pile. As in dealing with your mail, try to handle magazines as you receive them. One of the best habits to get into is trying to handle every piece of mail, or magazine, or nonfiction book only once. In the time you waste picking articles up again, putting them down, storing them, organizing them, and whatever, you could easily be handling almost everything you really have to deal with.

HANDLE NONFICTION BOOKS THE SAME WAY

There are many wonderful and interesting books of non-fiction continually appearing in our bookstores and newsstands. Many people are afraid to buy them because they know they'll just stack up and not get read. But you can often tackle these books in the same manner that you do your mail and journals: immediately.

Often, general books have a single thesis or main idea. They are generally filled with lots of anecdotes, first-person experiences, examples, and lots of material to "sell" you on their idea and induce you to buy the book. Knowing this, and also knowing how such nonfiction books are usually organized, makes it easy for the speed reader to "read" these books in very short periods of time.

TRY THE DRUGSTORE DRILL

A colleague of mine, John Chamberlain, who is a very creative teacher, gives his rapid reading class a special drill which I think is useful to have as a lifetime habit. He tells them to go to the local drugstore, newsstand or nearby chain bookstore which sells paperback books. They are to stay for half an hour and "read" two nonfiction books. The catch is they are not allowed to buy them. They have to read each book in about fifteen minutes. Standing up and being under the constant watchful eye of the owner helps to keep their reading speed up. It's a valuable drill and a worthwhile way of getting many books covered. I'll outline a way to do such a drill in the next exercise so you can try it the next time you have the opportunity.

EXERCISE NO. 49

Materials: *Miscellaneous nonfiction books*

1. Go to any store which sells paperback books and which will allow you to "browse" comfortably.
    Select a book on any general subject, nonfiction, which would be of interest to you. Try to find one about 120 to 200 pages.
    Allow a total of 15 minutes for the following steps:
2. Read the front and back covers and any blurbs inside the covers which might tell you something about the book—anything outside of the main body of material.
3. Look over the table of contents very carefully. Try to find out if there is an introduction or first chapter which tells you the main idea of the book. Beware of introductions designed just to sell the book.
    Try to find out if there is a summary chapter which will tie the main points of the book together.
    Look for other key chapters which will give you the nuts-and-bolts of the argument: the how to do it, techniques, or the ideas themselves. Try to determine which chapters will just be filler or unnecessary.
4. Preview carefully the beginning and ending of the book where the key information falls, avoiding the enthusiastic come-on-buy-the-book sections.
5. Preview and read the key chapters that you have selected to read, *OR* go through the entire book very quickly, dipping in and out of the chapters using a high-speed reading hand movement.

CAUTION: Be certain to get to the end of the book in the time allotted! Often the ending, as in all nonfiction, has some of the most important information. Avoid getting caught up in interesting but unnecessary details.

Perhaps the hardest thing to learn in rapid reading is to speed up and let go of information that you don't really need. It seems that most of us were trained to be compulsive readers, who read everything, which keeps us from reading what we really want to. These drills should help you overcome any compulsiveness you still harbor, and they are good ways of handling a lot of reading materials that you will always encounter.

TURN TO PAGE 220 FOR THE PRACTICE DRILLS TO COMPLETE TODAY'S WORK.

36

FIND OUT JUST HOW FAR YOU'VE COME

Although you've come to the conclusion of this course, you're actually just at the end of the beginning. You've accomplished a tremendous amount if you've done all of the exercises in the book, and you've undoubtedly increased your reading skills a great deal if you've followed the sections with the practice drills. The greatest challenge yet lies ahead of you, maintaining and even improving the gains you've already made.

Now you must begin to plan and practice to set lifetime habits so that you'll be certain to keep up your reading rate and continue to get as much reading done as you need to. The techniques are already in your hands, but now you must begin to apply them in slightly different ways. That's why there is still another section of practice drills to do.

This section of practice drills is necessary for two reasons. First, you probably still need more high-speed practice. These drills will provide that for you. Second, you need drills that are readily applicable to more of your daily reading situations. It is hoped these drills will also meet those needs. So in effect, these are the continuation drills, the drills to continue working with as long as you wish.

DEVISE A SIX-MONTH PLAN

It would be good to set a six-month plan now to ensure that you will establish the habits necessary to cement these new techniques. As has already been suggested, you should decide upon a regular reading time if that is possible. Perhaps a half hour three times a week, maybe more. If this is not feasible, plan to use every spare fifteen minutes and carry reading materials with you.

If you know *when* you will be reading, you next must plan *what* to read. So set up a list of books you wish to read. Or if you have more reading than you can keep up with anyway, plan what you will read, setting priorities as to what is most vital, and begin with the first six items.

Plan to do a few drills during the next six months. "Forced" reading drills such as the ones in the final section of practice drills are excellent. They will help you to get into the habit of reading a book or a large portion of one in a single sitting. At first this will be a practice reading session, but soon you will find it is really reading.

HOW THOMAS WOLFE BECAME A SPEED READER

When renowned author Thomas Wolfe was growing up, he discovered the pleasures of his local library as well as evolving the frustrating idea that he wanted to read every book in it. He set out to do just that, setting a goal of going through two books a day, regardless of what he got from them. Eventually, he became a very fast reader, using what are very necessary techniques to do so: very fast practice and continually setting goals to get more reading accomplished.

Now that speedreading has become a respectable skill and we know how to teach it so much more efficiently, hopefully this book and your good practicing will enable you to become a super reader with far less effort and frustration.

A FEW TIPS

Remember to always decide what your reading purpose is prior to reading anything. This is a vital habit to establish for becoming an efficient reader. Be ruthless in evaluating what is worth reading. Your valuable time is irreplaceable; don't squander it on material that ultimately won't either bring you pleasure or answer needs for you as a student or a business person. Knowing what not to read is often as important as knowing what to read.

Always use your hand as a pacer. It seems that many look for a way to avoid this. But all research has shown that when you take away the pacing device, the reading rate tends to fall. With this method, if you have done your practicing, research has shown that you will still maintain a solid improvement of a couple of hundred words per minute. I wouldn't try to beat the odds. I don't think it's worth it when using the hand is so easy.

Though you may not always want to use your hand, try to use it for *some* reading *every* day in order to maintain your skills. That's all it takes. If you're in public you may try using a pencil to be less obvious. But I encourage you to show off your skills. Others will tend to be envious and it will reinforce your good habits.

Also, if you stop using your hand, do not think that all is lost. Many of the techniques in this book, once learned, are never lost. A study showed that of graduates who stopped using their hands, as soon as they started to use them again their rates went back up—not as far up as they did for those who used their hands continually, but enough to be encouraging. In other words, once you have the skills, you may get rusty but you'll never lose them.

And don't forget that whenever you wish to remember something, do a written recall after the reading. This is so easy and effective. There are many courses we take which we remember nothing about within a few short years. If you remember only to use your hand when you want to read fast, and to recall when you wish to remember, I think you'll find your time and energies well spent.

Now do your final testing and you will be ready to begin your new practice drills.

Ending Reading Evaluation

Materials: *A pencil or pen*
A timing device
Your testing book. The same one you used in Chapter Two, but select a different section which you haven't read.

1. Select a section of your testing book that is about 40 pages long and that you have not read.
2. Read as far as you can in the material for three minutes. Use your timing device.
3. At the end of the three minutes, make a mark where you stopped reading, then close the book.
4. On a piece of paper, write everything you can remember from the reading without looking back at the reading selection. Number the items as you write.
You may take up to six minutes; use your timing device.
5. Compute your reading rate and record it on your progress profile.

Practice Drills for Continuing

Now that you have completed this book, you have arrived at a new beginning: you must make a conscientious effort to maintain the gains you've made and to progress further if you wish to. The next few months are crucial in establishing good reading habits and in making your new skills comfortable. The only way this can be done is through regular use.

If possible, continue practicing at least twenty minutes a day for the next six weeks, gradually changing over to a "Lifetime Reading Plan." As your habits develop, you can taper off practicing, but any time you feel your rate beginning to slip, simply do a drill and bring it back up again.

The drills which follow are ones which we would use in the final week of a classroom course. They will be useful to you to use either for a final week of hard practice, or to do twenty minutes a day for the next six weeks. Of course you may go back and use any other drills in the book which you found particularly useful.

Materials You Will Need for These Drills

1. *A timing device.*
2. *Pen or pencil.*
3. *Paper or the word processing program on your PC.*
4. *Assorted books, nonfiction, biographies, and fiction.*
5. *Your daily newspaper.*

DRILL NO. 22

Materials: Assorted books
            Pencil and paper
            Timing device
Estimated Time: 15 minutes

Purpose: To develop reading rate
Objective: Obtain minimal comprehension
                 at maximum rates

THIS DRILL MAY BE REPEATED

Diagram:

---------------------- Chapter or section of about 20 pages ----------------------	
DUSTING hand movement	2-3 seconds/page
RECALL	
READ Choice of hand movement	8-10 seconds/page
RECALL	
DUSTING hand movement	1-2 seconds/page
RECALL	
COMPUTE & RECORD reading rate	

Explanation:

1. Select a chapter or section of a chapter approximately 20 pages long. If you are having difficulty with comprehension, select an easy book.

2. Using the dusting hand movement, "dust" down each page spending no more than two or three seconds per page. Always choose the faster rate if you're trying to achieve high speeds.

   Set up a diagonal recall pattern and write down anything you can remember.

3. Using your choice of hand movement (except underlining), repeat the entire section spending no more than eight or ten seconds per page (four or five complete hand movements).

   Add to your recall.

   If comprehension is poor, repeat this step, preferably with a different hand movement.

4. Using the dusting hand movement, repeat the entire section spending no more than one to two seconds per page.

   Add to your recall.

5. Compute your practice reading rate in Step 3.

   Find the total number of words in the entire section, then divide that by the number of minutes taken to practice it.

CAUTION: Make certain to maintain a practice reading rate in step 3 over 2,000 WPM.

DRILL NO. 23

Materials: Novels or biographies
      Timing device
Estimated Time: 30-60 minutes

Purpose: To maintain a fast reading rate through an entire book
Objective: Maintain a predetermined rate with comprehension

THIS DRILL MAY BE REPEATED

Diagram:

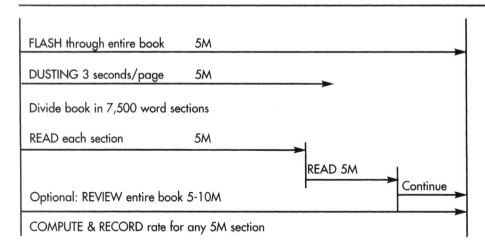

Explanation:

1. Select novels or biographies. If using novels, a series by the same author will be helpful. Arrange from shortest to longest or easiest to most difficult if it is possible to assess this before reading them.
   Plan to work through a book a day or a substantial portion of it.

2. Using the flashing technique, go through the entire book in five minutes.
   If there are any "problems," such as a large cast of characters, stop and develop a "cast list" so that you will be able to keep this straight as you are reading.

3. Using the dusting hand movement and moving at about three seconds per page, cover as much of the book as you can in five minutes.

4. Divide the book into 7,500-word sections.
   Read each section in five minutes. If using a tape recorder, note when each minute is up in order to help yourself maintain your pace.

5. Optional: Review the entire book in five to ten minutes. Use a new book each day for a week; then if you haven't gotten enough comprehension, you may re-use a book that you've practiced before.

6. Compute and record any five minute rate on your progress profile.

DRILL NO. 24

Materials: Daily newspaper
        Timing device
Estimated time: To be determined in drill

Purpose: Learn to read the newspaper
        more efficiently
Objective: Read more of the newspaper each
        day in the same amount of time.

THIS DRILL MAY BE REPEATED

1. Allow yourself a total of ten, 15, or 20 minutes to read the newspaper each day. Stick to that time for the whole week.
2. Begin timing yourself when you begin reading the paper. When your time is up, stop reading. Do not return to it later. Discipline yourself to handle the newspaper in a set amount of time.
3. Read the front page, then the news summary if there is one. If there is no news summary, rapidly go through the entire paper, checking which articles you will read. Allow no more than one minute.
4. Read the articles you have selected. Go through them rapidly, one column after another. If you get short on time, merely preview the articles and adjust your preview to their form (news article or nonfiction).
5. Record your time and the amount of the newspaper that you covered. Attempt to cover as much as you wish to read within the time period. Try to read more each day.

DRILL NO. 25

Materials: Nonfiction books of a general
        nature
        Timing device
Estimated Time: 30 minutes

Purpose: "Read" nonfiction books in
        shorter amount of time
Objective: Get satisfactory understanding
        of the book's main points

THIS DRILL MAY BE REPEATED

Diagram:

------------------ Chapter or section of about 100-200 pages ------------------	
LOOK OVER front and back covers, table of contentes	5M
PREVIEW beginning and ending or where main ideas are	10M
PREVIEW & READ key chapters OR	15M
READ dipping in and out of whole book	15M

Explanation:

1. Select a book or part of a book (100-200 pages) on any general subject which is of interest to you. If you are having any trouble with comprehension, use different books on the same subject during the week, starting with the easiest or most general.

2. Look over the front and back covers and everything else outside of the main body of material which might tell you something about the book, including the table of contents. Try to find if there are introductory and summary chapters and any other chapters having key information. Allow five minutes.

3. In ten minutes, preview carefully the beginning and ending of the book where the main ideas are presented.

4. Preview and read the key chapters that you have selected OR go through the entire book very quickly, dipping in and out of the chapters, in 15 minutes.

HOW TO MAINTAIN A CERTAIN PRACTICE READING RATE

1. *Find the average number of words per page for your book and go to the closest amount in the first column (If your number is in between, select a lower figure)*

2. *Move across the chart to the rate at which you wish to practice*

3. *Move down the column to find the number of seconds per page required to maintain your desired practice rate (Divide by two for the number of hand movements per page: each hand movement should be done in two seconds or less)*

WORDS PER PAGE	2	4	6	8	10	12	14	16
175	5,250	2,625	1,750	1,313	1,050	875	749	656
200	6,000	3,000	2,000	1,500	1,200	1,000	856	750
225	6,750	3,375	2,250	1,688	1,350	1,125	963	844
250	7,500	3,750	2,500	1,875	1,500	1,250	1,070	938
275	8,250	4,125	2,750	2,063	1,650	1,375	1,177	1,032
300	9,000	4,500	3,000	2,250	1,800	1,500	1,284	1,125
325	9,750	4,875	3,250	2,438	1,950	1,625	1,391	1,219
350	10,500	5,250	3,500	2,625	2,100	1,750	1,498	1,313
375	11,250	5,625	3,750	2,813	2,250	1,875	1,605	1,407
400	12,000	6,000	4,000	3,000	2,400	2,000	1,712	1,500
425	12,750	6,375	4,250	3,188	2,550	2,125	1,819	1,594
450	13,500	6,750	4,500	3,375	2,700	2,250	1,926	1,688

SECONDS PER PAGE

INDEX

PROGRESS PROFILE

NAME ___Don___ DATE COURSE BEGAN __3/10__

READING EVALUATION

Book(s) used: ___Sea of Glory - Nathaniel Philbrick___

WHEN TESTED	CHAPTER OF TEST BOOK	READING RATE (WPM)	RECALL (no. of items)
Beginning	2	148	18 Good
	1	233	5 Poor
Mid-Course			
Ending			

Book List:	Ex. No.	Rates (words per minute):		
	3	313	338	
1 _Lost to the West_ Lars Brownsworth	4	234	271	
2 _Altruistic Armadillos_	5			
3 _Meg: Primal Waters_	6			
4 _Meg: Hell's Aquarium_	11			
5 _The Hobbit_	12			
6 _The LOTR_	15			
7 _Teddy Biography_	17			
8 ___	27			
9 ___	36			
10 ___	43			
Topic: History, Fish Diving, Aquariums, animals	44			
	45	Prev. Rdg.	Prev. Rdg.	Prev. Rdg.

PROGRESS PROFILE

	Practice Drills	Item Recorded	1st day	2nd day	3rd day	4th day	5th day	6th day
Week 2	No. 1	WPM	203 264	264 291	308 346			
	No. 2	WPM	205 396	275 495	289 429			
	No. 3	WPM	407 356 393 462 484					
	No. 4	no. par.	15					
Week 3	No. 5	WPM						
	No. 6	WPM						
	No. 7	no. par.						
	No. 8	WPM						
Week 4	No. 9	no. par.						
	No. 10	WPM						
	No. 11	WPM						
	No. 12	WPM						
Week 5	No. 13	no. par.						
	No. 14	WPM						
	No. 15	WPM						
	No. 16	WPM						
	No. 17	WPM						
Week 6	No. 18	WPM						
	No. 19	WPM						
	No. 20	WPM						
	No. 21	WPM						
Cont. drills	No. 22	WPM						
	No. 23	WPM						
	No. 24	time						
	No. 25	WPM						

PROGRESS PROFILE

NAME _____ DATE COURSE BEGAN _____

READING EVALUATION

Book(s) used: _____

_____

WHEN TESTED	CHAPTER OF TEST BOOK	READING RATE (WPM)	RECALL (no. of items)
Beginning			
Mid-Course			
Ending			

Book List:	Ex. No.	Rates (words per minute):		
1 _____	3			
2 _____	4			
3 _____	5			
4 _____	6			
5 _____	11			
6 _____	12			
7 _____	15			
8 _____	17			
9 _____	27			
10 _____	36			
Topic: _____	43			
	44			
	45	Prev. Rdg.	Prev. Rdg.	Prev. Rdg.

PROGRESS PROFILE

	Practice Drills	Item Recorded	1st day	2nd day	3rd day	4th day	5th day	6th day
Week 2	No. 1	WPM						
	No. 2	WPM .						
	No. 3	WPM .						
	No. 4	no. par.						
Week 3	No. 5	WPM						
	No. 6	WPM						
	No. 7	no. par.						
	No. 8	WPM						
Week 4	No. 9	no. par.						
	No. 10	WPM						
	No. 11	WPM						
	No. 12	WPM						
Week 5	No. 13	no. par.						
	No. 14	WPM						
	No. 15	WPM						
	No. 16	WPM						
	No. 17	WPM						
Week 6	No. 18	WPM						
	No. 19	WPM						
	No. 20	WPM						
	No. 21	WPM						
Cont. drills	No. 22	WPM						
	No. 23	WPM						
	No. 24	time						
	No. 25	WPM						

PROGRESS PROFILE

NAME _____ DATE COURSE BEGAN _____

READING EVALUATION

Book(s) used: _____

_____

WHEN TESTED	CHAPTER OF TEST BOOK	READING RATE (WPM)	RECALL (no. of items)
Beginning			
Mid-Course			
Ending			

Book List:	Ex. No.	Rates (words per minute):		
1 _____	3			
2 _____	4			
3 _____	5			
4 _____	6			
5 _____	11			
6 _____	12			
7 _____	15			
8 _____	17			
9 _____	27			
10 _____	36			
Topic: _____	43			
	44			
	45	Prev. Rdg.	Prev. Rdg.	Prev. Rdg.

PROGRESS PROFILE

	Practice Drills	Item Recorded	1st day	2nd day	3rd day	4th day	5th day	6th day
Week 2	No. 1	WPM						
Week 2	No. 2	WPM						
Week 2	No. 3	WPM						
Week 2	No. 4	no. par.						
Week 3	No. 5	WPM						
Week 3	No. 6	WPM						
Week 3	No. 7	no. par.						
Week 3	No. 8	WPM						
Week 4	No. 9	no. par.						
Week 4	No. 10	WPM						
Week 4	No. 11	WPM						
Week 4	No. 12	WPM						
Week 5	No. 13	no. par.						
Week 5	No. 14	WPM						
Week 5	No. 15	WPM						
Week 5	No. 16	WPM						
Week 5	No. 17	WPM						
Week 6	No. 18	WPM						
Week 6	No. 19	WPM						
Week 6	No. 20	WPM						
Week 6	No. 21	WPM						
Cont. drills	No. 22	WPM						
Cont. drills	No. 23	WPM						
Cont. drills	No. 24	time						
Cont. drills	No. 25	WPM						

PROGRESS PROFILE

NAME _____ DATE COURSE BEGAN _____

READING EVALUATION

Book(s) used: _____

_____

WHEN TESTED	CHAPTER OF TEST BOOK	READING RATE (WPM)	RECALL (no. of items)
Beginning			
Mid-Course			
Ending			

Book List:		Ex. No.	Rates (words per minute):		
1 _____		3			
2 _____		4			
3 _____		5			
4 _____		6			
5 _____		11			
6 _____		12			
7 _____		15			
8 _____		17			
9 _____		27			
10 _____		36			
Topic: _____		43			
		44			
			Prev. Rdg.	Prev. Rdg.	Prev. Rdg.
		45			

PROGRESS PROFILE

	Practice Drills	Item Recorded	1st day	2nd day	3rd day	4th day	5th day	6th day
Week 2	No. 1	WPM						
	No. 2	WPM						
	No. 3	WPM						
	No. 4	no. par.						
Week 3	No. 5	WPM						
	No. 6	WPM						
	No. 7	no. par.						
	No. 8	WPM						
Week 4	No. 9	no. par.						
	No. 10	WPM						
	No. 11	WPM						
	No. 12	WPM						
Week 5	No. 13	no. par.						
	No. 14	WPM						
	No. 15	WPM						
	No. 16	WPM						
	No. 17	WPM						
Week 6	No. 18	WPM						
	No. 19	WPM						
	No. 20	WPM						
	No. 21	WPM						
Cont. drills	No. 22	WPM						
	No. 23	WPM						
	No. 24	time						
	No. 25	WPM						

PROGRESS PROFILE

NAME _____ DATE COURSE BEGAN _____

READING EVALUATION

Book(s) used: _____

_____

WHEN TESTED	CHAPTER OF TEST BOOK	READING RATE (WPM)	RECALL (no. of items)
Beginning			
Mid-Course			
Ending			

Book List:	Ex. No.	Rates (words per minute):		
1 _____	3			
2 _____	4			
3 _____	5			
4 _____	6			
5 _____	11			
6 _____	12			
7 _____	15			
8 _____	17			
9 _____	27			
10 _____	36			
Topic: _____	43			
	44			
	45	Prev. Rdg.	Prev. Rdg.	Prev. Rdg.

PROGRESS PROFILE

	Practice Drills	Item Recorded	1st day	2nd day	3rd day	4th day	5th day	6th day
Week 2	No. 1	WPM						
Week 2	No. 2	WPM						
Week 2	No. 3	WPM						
Week 2	No. 4	no. par.						
Week 3	No. 5	WPM						
Week 3	No. 6	WPM						
Week 3	No. 7	no. par.						
Week 3	No. 8	WPM						
Week 4	No. 9	no. par.						
Week 4	No. 10	WPM						
Week 4	No. 11	WPM						
Week 4	No. 12	WPM						
Week 5	No. 13	no. par.						
Week 5	No. 14	WPM						
Week 5	No. 15	WPM						
Week 5	No. 16	WPM						
Week 5	No. 17	WPM						
Week 6	No. 18	WPM						
Week 6	No. 19	WPM						
Week 6	No. 20	WPM						
Week 6	No. 21	WPM						
Cont. drills	No. 22	WPM						
Cont. drills	No. 23	WPM						
Cont. drills	No. 24	time						
Cont. drills	No. 25	WPM						

PROGRESS PROFILE

NAME _____ DATE COURSE BEGAN _____

READING EVALUATION

Book(s) used: _____

_____

WHEN TESTED	CHAPTER OF TEST BOOK	READING RATE (WPM)	RECALL (no. of items)
Beginning			
Mid-Course			
Ending			

Book List:	Ex. No.	Rates (words per minute):		
	3			
1 _____	4			
2 _____	5			
3 _____	6			
4 _____	11			
5 _____	12			
6 _____	15			
7 _____	17			
8 _____	27			
9 _____	36			
10 _____	43			
Topic: _____	44			
	45	Prev. Rdg.	Prev. Rdg.	Prev. Rdg.

PROGRESS PROFILE

	Practice Drills	Item Recorded	1st day	2nd day	3rd day	4th day	5th day	6th day
Week 2	No. 1	WPM						
	No. 2	WPM						
	No. 3	WPM						
	No. 4	no. par.						
Week 3	No. 5	WPM						
	No. 6	WPM						
	No. 7	no. par.						
	No. 8	WPM						
Week 4	No. 9	no. par.						
	No. 10	WPM						
	No. 11	WPM						
	No. 12	WPM						
Week 5	No. 13	no. par.						
	No. 14	WPM						
	No. 15	WPM						
	No. 16	WPM						
	No. 17	WPM						
Week 6	No. 18	WPM						
	No. 19	WPM						
	No. 20	WPM						
	No. 21	WPM						
Cont. drills	No. 22	WPM						
	No. 23	WPM						
	No. 24	time						
	No. 25	WPM						